W9-BKX-626

WITHDRAWN FROM
MACALESTER COLLEGE
LIBRARY

In the Company of Others

Studies in Social, Political, and Legal Philosophy
General Editor: James P. Sterba, University of Notre Dame

This series analyzes and evaluates critically the major political, social, and legal ideals, institutions, and practices of our time. The analysis may be historical or problem-centered; the evaluation may focus on theoretical underpinnings or practical implications. Among the recent titles in the series are:

In the Company of Others

Perspectives on Community, Family, and Culture

Edited by
Nancy E. Snow

Rowman & Littlefield Publishers, Inc.

ROWMAN & LITTLEFIELD PUBLISHERS, INC.

Published in the United States of America
by Rowman & Littlefield Publishers, Inc.
4720 Boston Way, Lanham, Maryland 20706

3 Henrietta Street
London, WC2E 8LU, England

Copyright © 1996 by Rowman & Littlefield Publishers, Inc.

All rights reserved. No part of this publication may be
reproduced, stored in a retrieval system, or transmitted
in any form or by any means, electronic, mechanical,
photocopying, recording, or otherwise, without the prior
permission of the publisher.

British Cataloging in Publication Information Available

Library of Congress Cataloging-in-Publication Data

In the company of others : perspectives on community, family, and
culture / edited by Nancy E. Snow.
p.   cm. — (Studies in social, political, and legal philosophy)
Includes bibliographical references and index.
1. Community—Philosophy. 2. Culture—Philosophy. 3. Family—
Philosophy. 4. Social structure. 5. Feminist theory. I. Snow,
Nancy E. II. Series.
B105.C46I5   1996 306'.01–dc20   95-43169   CIP

ISBN 0–8476–8144–0 (cloth : alk. paper)
ISBN 0–8476–8145–9 (pbk.: alk. paper)

Printed in the United States of America

The paper used in this publication meets the minimum requirements of
the American National Standard for Information Sciences—Permanence
of Paper for Printed Library Materials, ANSI Z39.48–1984.

For Pat Coffey

Contents

Acknowledgments

"Philosophers against the Family," by Christina Hoff Sommers, originally appeared in *Person to Person*, edited by George Graham and Hugh LaFollette (1989) and is reprinted by permission of Temple University Press and the author.

"Injustice in Families: Assault and Domination," by Sara Ruddick, originally appeared in *Justice and Care: Essential Papers*, edited by Virginia Held (1995) and is reprinted by permission of Westview Press and the author.

"On Care and Justice within the Family," by David B. Wong, originally appeared in *Contemporary Philosophy* vol. 15, no. 4 (1993) and is reprinted by permission of the author.

"Of Mothers and Families, Men and Sex: The Truth about Feminism," by Marilyn Friedman, is a revised version of material that originally appeared in *Political Correctness: For and Against*, by Marilyn Friedman and Jan Narveson (1995). It is reprinted by permission of Rowman & Littlefield and the author.

"Shaping Feminist Culture," by Virginia Held, originally appeared as chapter 5 in *Feminist Morality: Transforming Culture, Society, and Politics*, by Virginia Held (1994) and is reprinted by permission of the University of Chicago Press and the author.

Preface

Nancy E. Snow

To say that debates about community, family, and culture abound in the United States today is surely no exaggeration. We hear, for example, laments about the demise of community at the grass-roots level, especially in inner city neighborhoods. We witness attempts to polarize the idea of traditional family values and the values expressed in alternative families, such as gay and lesbian families. Feminism and multiculturalism have significantly affected both popular and academic culture in a wide variety of respects. Yet feminists are harangued in backlashes from the popular media, and debates over multiculturalism in curricula at all educational levels have been virulent. Concerns are voiced about the effects of popular culture, especially the mass media, on young people. The uncertainties of government funding of the arts alarm supporters of high culture of all political stripes in all corners of the country. Controversies continue to rage about new reproductive technologies and environmental versus economic interests.

Philosophers are not impervious to such debates. In this anthology a group of distinguished philosophers explores a range of overlapping and interweaving themes concerning community, family, and culture. In "Two Concepts of Community," Andrew Mason introduces the theme of community by addressing the foundational question, "What is a community?" His aim is to dispel some of the confusion surrounding the concept of 'community' by sorting through a variety of usages of the term. His analysis relies on the notion of an essentially contested concept. An example is the con-

cept of 'democracy'. Such a concept is appraisive in that it refers
to a complex valued achievement. The achievement is complex in
the sense that a number of elements constitute it. These elements
not only can be weighted differently but also can be interpreted
differently. Moreover, the accredited achievement can be modified
in light of changing circumstances. Thus, concepts can be essentially contested in several ways.

Mason identifies two ideal types of community: community in
the ordinary sense and community in the emancipatory sense. The
concept of the latter, he argues, is essentially contested, whereas
the concept of the former is not. Community in the ordinary sense,
he claims, is used at least implicitly in contemporary Anglo-American political philosophy, whereas community in the emancipatory
sense is familiar from the tradition of socialism. A community in
the ordinary sense is constituted by a group of people who share a
wide range of values, participate in a comprehensive way of life,
and strongly identify with the group, so much so that their identities might be partially constituted by their group membership.
Though a community in the emancipatory sense displays these features, it is further characterized by mutual concern among its members and an absence of systematic exploitation, oppression, or
injustice within the community. Mason in part justifies his identification of these two senses of community by exploring the different
roles played by each in language and social life. Though both senses are used evaluatively, the ordinary sense plays a largely explanatory role, whereas the emancipatory sense functions in a
predominantly critical way. Paying attention to these two senses of
'community', as well as the question of essential contestability,
Mason claims, helps to clarify one major source of misunderstanding about the nature of community.

Questions about the nature and value of community are explored
in a multicultural context by David B. Wong in "Community, Diversity, and Confucianism." He aims to show how Confucianism can
contribute to the contemporary debate between liberalism and communitarianism. Communitarians claim that liberalism, when called
on to explain why some members of society should make sacrifices
for the sake of others, cannot do so, since liberalism cannot appeal
to a strongly internalized sense of identification with other members of a community to justify altruistic sacrifices. Liberals worry
that the strong sense of community favored by communitarians undermines the conditions for the effective exercise of individual au-

tonomy and moral agency and provides inadequate distance from which to meaningfully criticize shared values, practices, and traditions.

Confucianism, Wong claims, has resources for answering these concerns. Two concepts found in the *Analects* of Confucius, *jen* and *li*, are the basis of his discussion. Roughly, *'jen'* refers to realized human capacities, a state of excellence or highest achievement. *'Li'* refers to traditional or customary norms governing conduct between people and, in the broadest sense, to civility, grace, graciousness, and respectful behavior. He argues that *jen* can be identified with some generalized innate tendencies that are present in human nature but that remain indeterminate as guides to action without further information. Such information takes the form of cultural templates, that is, blueprints, plans, or guidelines for acting. *Li* is a source of these cultural templates. An implication of this picture is that moral learning occurs through example, by observing *jen* and *li* on a daily basis and developing habits of perception, affection, and conduct. If moral learning occurs in this manner and not in some more abstract way, the family, or, more broadly, the primary group, becomes a crucial part of the process of moral learning and development. Thus community is an essential part of the process of moral development, but community in this sense must foster autonomous judgment, effective moral agency, and the capacity for a critical perspective on shared values, practices, and traditions because, as Wong points out, not only is creativity needed to preserve tradition while adapting it to changing circumstance, but the rules of *li* are themselves conflicting, ambiguous, and indeterminate; and thus in need of continuous interpretation. Here the Confucian notion of *yi*, which is the idea of appropriateness or fittingness in the context, is relevant, because the ability to judge what is fitting in the context helps individuals to act well when the rules of *li* are conflicting, ambiguous, or indeterminate. This ability, too, is learned in the context of community.

Wong's essay invites us to focus on a specific type of community, namely, on family. His identification of families as a primary locus of moral learning and development leads naturally to the questions pursued in the next three essays by Christina Hoff Sommers, Sara Ruddick, and Wong. Sommers asks, "What is a family? Is the traditional family disintegrating in contemporary Western society?" and Ruddick and Wong query, "By which moral norms and principles should relations within families be guided?"

In "Philosophers against the Family," Christina Hoff Sommers maintains that the traditional American family is in jeopardy and attributes its disintegration in part to views advanced by contemporary philosophers. Except for marriage, Sommers believes that the traditional family is constituted by biological relationships that are simply given. She ascribes the decline of the traditional family to two main sources: first, to feminists who launch a radical critique of traditional family relationships and, second, to moral philosophers who accept, either implicitly or overtly, a purely voluntaristic theory of moral obligation.

Feminists who advocate a radical critique of the traditional family reject that institution, Sommers claims, because it fails to live up to an assimilationist ideal, according to which differences between the sexes should be completely eradicated. According to this ideal, the eradication of disparities between the sexes entails the elimination of traditional gender roles, including those that presumably are based on biological differences between the sexes, such as childbearing and child rearing. Feminists who occupy Sommers's radical camp maintain that someday men will be able to and should perform even such functions as lactation and gestation. Sommers contends that this assimilationist ideal is obviously incompatible with the continuation of the traditional family; those who urge us to move toward it inevitably contribute to that institution's decline. In addition to disparaging feminist views on the traditional family, she further castigates feminists for criticizing femininity. These themes are taken up in part III by Marilyn Friedman in "Of Mothers and Families, Men and Sex: The Truth about Feminism."

Sommers also reproaches contemporary moral philosophers who, though not directly concerned with the family, in her view weaken the family through their analyses of related moral issues, such as abortion, infanticide, and the rights of children to divorce their parents. These philosophers weaken the family by assuming what Sommers calls the "volunteer theory of obligation," that is, the thesis that all moral obligations are voluntarily assumed. Adopting this theory of obligation leads philosophers to ignore the fact that there are, in Sommers's terms, "special duties," that is, duties not voluntarily assumed that devolve on specific individuals, such as duties of kinship. Taking seriously kinship duties, such as the duties of mother to child and of child to parent, provides for a different perspective on contemporary analyses of abortion, infanticide, and children's rights to divorce their parents, and highlights the negative effects such analyses can have on the traditional family.

Key to Sommers's approach is the notion that contemporary philosophical views affect the moral health and stability of families. This assumption is shared by Sara Ruddick and David B. Wong, who examine the justice and care perspectives as possible moral guidelines for family life. In "Injustice in Families: Assault and Domination," Ruddick urges that, just as feminists have sought to bring the care perspective more fully to bear on the public and the political, we should also move in the direction of making dominant theories of justice more applicable to families. She identifies one particular form of injustice within families—assault—explores its connections with domination, and suggests an ideal of justice for families: respect for embodied willfulness.

According to Ruddick, familial injustice occurs when a healthy adult inflicts physical pain on someone smaller or weaker. Several considerations, but especially connections between physical assault and domination, reveal family assault as a form of injustice. Domination is typically thought to be unjust. Assault, Ruddick argues, is not only an instrument of domination, but also a consequence of its failure. Dominators, who can care deeply for those they dominate, seek to control the conditions and outcomes of the actions of the dominated, frequently viewing the dominated as property. When assertions of willfulness by the dominated, seen by dominators as lack of compliance or obedience, lead to reassertions of control by dominators, the connections between domination and assault become especially clear. Ruddick suggests the principle of respect for embodied willfulness as an ideal of justice to inform and regulate nonassaultive familial relationships. Respect for embodied willfulness requires that family members abjure assault as an instrument of domination and renounce on principle projects of domination. Ruddick recognizes that forms of injustice other than assault and domination exist within families and thus that identifying a single type of injustice is unlikely to reveal the essence of family justice. Nevertheless, the principle of respect for embodied willfulness is clearly an important step toward a more comprehensive theory of justice within families.

In "On Care and Justice within the Family," David B. Wong identifies four distinct moral perspectives that ought to inform moral thinking about family life: the care perspective, communitarian justice, liberal justice, and a moral perspective that values cultural diversity. The interrelations among these perspectives, he argues, are complex. They overlap, inform each other, interweave, reinforce, and, at times, conflict. Though none provides a fully comprehensive and exhaustive moral approach to life within families, each adds something of value to moral thinking about families and can guide action within families, and none, he warns, should be omitted.

The first five contributions to this volume are marked by either an implicit or an explicit sensitivity to the effects of culture and of cultural diversity on communities and families. No matter what the primary group, be it family or a community of another type, ignoring the pervasive effects of culture on the group and on its individual members would be grossly naive. Culture itself, however, is not immune to philosophical scrutiny. The next five essays, by Virginia Held, Marilyn Friedman, Rosemarie Tong, Karen J. Warren, and A. Pablo Iannone, furnish critical and constructive analyses of contemporary culture. The first four proceed from feminist perspectives; Iannone's is from a multicultural vantage point.

"Shaping Feminist Culture," by Virginia Held, offers a sweeping feminist critique of contemporary culture in the United States, as well as positive suggestions for creating a truly feminist culture. Culture has the power of shaping consciousness. Consequently, controllers of culture have extensive power over our thoughts and feelings. Held contends that philosophers in the liberal tradition have ignored both the control of culture by economic forces and interests and the resulting restriction of effective expression to those with economic power and gender and racial advantage. The commercial control of culture is morally objectionable for additional reasons. For example, the mass media and advertising have reinforced racial and gender stereotypes, glorified and eroticized violence and domination, presented women's bodies as disposable commodities, and distorted social reality. Studies have shown that excessive television viewing can have harmful effects on children and adolescents. Program content, driven by economic forces, is increasingly violent and brutal, and economic censorship limits discussion of controversial issues. Held argues for a feminist transformation that would liberate culture from serving the values of commerce and allow it to promote instead the values of delight, well-being, aesthetic worth, and heightened awareness, and she suggests practical strategies for achieving such a change.

Feminist ideas for transforming culture and society have not been met always with open arms. Antifeminist backlashes have been widely publicized, especially in popular media, but also in academic publications. With an extended array of arguments Marilyn Friedman takes on the backlash, aiming in "Of Mothers and Families, Men and Sex: The Truth about Feminism" to destroy distortions of feminist views about motherhood, families, men, and sex. She engages, among others, the views of Christina Sommers. Her targets are the claims that feminists are contemptuous of full-time homemakers and mothers and that they are hostile toward family life. This, she argues, is false. Feminists do not reject homemaking or motherhood or family life but do challenge the *male domination* of traditional family life. At its worst, male domination involves physical abuse and male tyranny over family life; at its mildest, it is benevolent paternalism. Either way, the subordination and vulnerability it creates for women threaten women's self-determination and moral integrity, as well as their material well-being and that of their children.

Friedman continues her piece by extensively addressing the charges that feminists hate men and sex. Among many points, she reminds us that focusing on men misconstrues the point of feminism, which is to empower women. Agreeing with Held, she realizes that our culture is saturated with media images of male sexual domination and female sexual submission that not only demean women, but also manipulate the sexual desires of both women and men. She urges that we no longer tolerate portrayals that eroticize male domination and female submission, thereby influencing women to shape the expression of their sexuality to please men, regardless of the cost to themselves. Finally, she observes that feminist cautions about safe sex are not sex phobic but sheer common sense, given the social and health problems currently associated with sex, such as overpopulation, teen pregnancy, and sexually transmitted diseases.

Female sexuality and reproductive rights and technologies have been ongoing feminist themes and areas where feminism has significantly impacted philosophical thought, public policy, and social practice. In "Procreative Liberty: Beyond Liberal, Radical, and Cultural Feminist Assessments," Rosemarie Tong asks whether feminists can advance current debates about new reproductive technologies—in particular about surrogate, or what she calls "gestational," motherhood. She believes they can but argues that, taken individually, no single liberal, radical, and cultural feminist approach to gestational motherhood serves women's best interests. A mediated

feminist approach is needed, she claims, that will allow us to identify the combination of competing feminist solutions that will best
undermine patterns of male domination and female subordination.

This approach incorporates Sarah Lucia Hoagland's ontology.
Hoagland replaces the concept of autonomy with that of 'autokoenomy,' which comes from the Greek words for self (*auto*) and
community (*koinonia*). The autokoenomous woman, according to
Tong, knows that she is a self in relation to other selves, though
neither inferior nor superior to them. Moral value emerges from
connections made between autokoenomous women. This ontology
should be coupled with a positional epistemology, according to
which the perspective of each person is situated and partial and the
whole truth can be reached only by conversations with others. En-
dorsing these perspectives leads Tong to recommend an adoption
approach to gestational motherhood, according to which the gestational mother would be allowed to control the course of her pregnancy, receive reimbursement, and change her mind about
relinquishing the child. Some feminists might be unhappy with giving the gestational mother the parental edge, but after weighing pros
and cons Tong argues that, given the traditional undervaluing of the
gestational connection, privileging the gestational mother is appropriate.

Environmentalism has become a part of our global culture. Here,
too, feminism has made an impact, largely through the work of
Karen J. Warren, who contributes "Longing for Home: An Ecofeminist Philosophical Perspective." Despite the differences among
ecofeminists, all agree that important connections exist between
ways in which women and other subdominant groups are treated
and ways in which the nonhuman natural environment is treated.
As a theory of ecojustice, ecofeminism uses sex/gender analysis to
reveal the connections among all forms of domination. Central to
this project is an understanding of oppressive conceptual frameworks, several key features of which Warren explains. As an ecofeminist philosopher, she has, she says, become interested in the concept
of home and in the work that has been done on it in the context of
societies that have traditionally devalued both women and home.
She believes that important insights are to be gained from ecofeminism about what a home is or should be and that they can tell us
why, in prefeminist societies disfigured by patriarchy, colonialism,
racism, and classism, it might not be possible to be or to feel at
home. In such a context, she claims, the 'longing for home' might

be the best we can do. Women and nature are, of course, integral to any adequate ecofeminist analysis of 'home' and the 'longing for home'.

A different sense of 'longing for home' is explored in the concluding essay of the anthology. In "Cross-Cultural Ecologies: The Expatriate Experience, the Multiculturalism Issue, and Philosophy," A. Pablo Iannone argues for two theses and formulates two hypotheses. First, he identifies four salient features of the expatriate experience: (1) ambiguity about one's evoked or hoped-for homeland; (2) fluidity with respect to the expatriate's interactions with and adaptations to his or her foreign environment; (3) heightened awareness of local conventions; and (4) increased reliance on convention-settling processes. Second, he argues that, because these characteristics are analogous to some features of philosophy, examining the expatriate experience can provide new directions for philosophical contributions to the multiculturalism issue.

In the course of arguing for these theses, he formulates and gives reasons for two hypotheses. The first is that the salient features of the expatriate experience can help us to understand and deal with the cross-cultural conflicts and cultural fragmentation at the heart of the multiculturalism issue. The second is that these features can help by revealing the concerns typically involved in the multiculturalism issue and by identifying the convention-settling processes used to resolve multicultural disputes.

To sum up: the essays comprising *In the Company of Others: Perspectives on Community, Family, and Culture* explore a wide-ranging array of themes. Foundational questions about the meaning of 'community' are broached by Mason; the nature and value of community and family are further examined in a multicultural context by Wong. Sommers pursues concerns about the disintegration of the traditional family in contemporary Western society, whereas Ruddick and Wong open another area of inquiry into families by asking which moral norms should inform and regulate family life. The volume finishes with a series of essays that examine and criticize culture itself. Held's critique of contemporary commercial culture, Friedman's defense of feminism against a multipronged backlash, Tong's study of gestational motherhood, and Warren's ecofeminist analysis of 'home' and of the 'longing for home' articulate positions on respects in which contemporary culture fails to meet feminist standards for a just, caring society and make suggestions for effecting feminist transformations of culture. Finally, Iannone's unique contribution reminds us that both contemporary culture and academic philosophy in the United States have much to learn from other cultures, including the often-overlooked but vitally important experience of expatriates. As with many of the themes developed in previous essays in this volume, Iannone's exploration of the expatriate experience calls attention to the fact that being in the company of others, though frequently rewarding, is often difficult.

The essays included here represent outstanding and creative contributions to three ever-growing areas of philosophical interest. They also serve as invitations to others to join ongoing discussions of community, family, and culture.

A final introductory word: many people deserve thanks for their help with this project. Foremost among them are Jim Sterba, the general editor of Rowman & Littlefield's "Studies in Social, Political, and Legal Philosophy" series, Jennifer Ruark, the philosophy editor at Rowman & Littlefield, and Julie Kuzneski, the production editor at Rowman & Littlefield. They patiently and generously suffered through my many questions and mistakes and were incredibly supportive. I would also like to thank the contributors for their unflagging support, especially during the book's early stages. I owe David Wong and R. Paul Churchill special debts of gratitude. Mark Munns supplied diligent research assistance, and John D. Jones and Tracey Hassinger provided technical assistance. I gratefully acknowledge financial support from Reverend John L. Treloar, S.J., chair of the philosophy department, and from Reverend Thaddeus Burch, S.J., dean of the graduate school, both at Marquette University. Maria Carl, Patrick Coffey, Katie Elliott, Margaret Frittitta, Adam Grabowski, Francis Greene, Sandy Henke, and Siobhan Moroney provided personal support and encouragement. My thanks to all.

Part I

Community

1

Two Concepts
of Community

Andrew Mason

Talk of community is highly fashionable. People refer to various kinds of community: the international community, which supposedly has been made possible by a new world order emerging at the end of the Cold War; national communities, which politicians often promise to rebuild in the face of increasing crime and lawlessness; and the local or neighborhood communities, which are sometimes said to be threatened by gentrification or redevelopment. Some also speak of the business community's reaction to a rise in interest rates or the gay community's response to the defeat of proposed legislation that would have equalized the age of consent for heterosexuals and homosexuals. The diversity in ordinary usage is reflected in academic discourse. Philosophers, for instance, write about linguistic communities, moral communities, political communities, ethnic communities, or cultural communities, and some think of polities, families, tribes, or nations as communities. In political philosophy in particular, the concept of community has experienced something of a renaissance. The 1980s witnessed a series of criticisms of liberalism that came to be referred to as communitarian.

It is not just the variety of putative kinds of community that is bewildering, however, or even the variety of social groups described as communities. There are also vigorous disputes over what counts as a community. Some argue that communities have to be face to face, while others allow that they may unite those who do not know each other. Some maintain that members of a community must inhabit the same locale, while others allow that they may be dispersed

geographically. Some argue that communities must involve relationships of a certain moral quality, for example, where exploitation is
absent, while others allow that feelings of solidarity may be sufficient, even if these feelings rest on illusions or misconceptions about
the moral character of the relationship.

The sheer variety of ordinary and theoretical usages, and the
disputes that occur within them, can give rise to the worry that
'community' has no descriptive meaning and is used by people simply to commend to others the social arrangements they think desirable, with the consequence that there are no properties common to
those things that are labeled communities, except perhaps the property of evincing the speaker's approval. More cynically, it might be
thought that the term 'community' is often applied to a group in
order to distract attention away from the deep division within it and
thereby serves the interests of its dominant class. I shall try to answer some of these worries, though not by supplying necessary and
sufficient conditions for the proper use of 'community', since I am
skeptical about the value of attempting to do so. The main purpose
of the paper is to clarify: to make sense of the variety of usages of
the term 'community' and to remove some of the confusions that
surround them. (Unlike concepts such as 'justice,' 'freedom,' and
'equality,' the notion of community has not received the analytical
attention it deserves.[1]) In particular, I shall suggest that we need to
distinguish between two different concepts of community that play
different roles in ordinary usage (and that are distinguished partly
in terms of these roles) but that have descriptive content.

Is Community an Essentially Contested Concept?

One proposal that might seem to promise an account of why the
term 'community' is used so widely, and why disputes over its proper use occur and persist, is the idea that it denotes an essentially
contested concept.[2] What is an essentially contested concept? W. B.
Gallie introduced the notion by saying that it is a concept whose
nature it is to be open to endless dispute, and he listed a number of
criteria that need to be satisfied by a concept in order for it to be
essentially contested.[3] An essentially contested concept is appraisive:
it accredits a valued achievement. This accredited achievement is
complex, that is, made up of a number of different elements. These
elements can reasonably be weighted differently, and disputes arise

over the proper application of the concept when people do so. Those who give a particular weight to the elements acknowledge that others weight them differently. Furthermore, the accredited achievement admits of unpredictable modification in the light of changing circumstances.

As examples of essentially contested concepts, Gallie gives the concepts of democracy, social justice, work of art, and a Christian life. Consider his reasons for classifying the concept of democracy as essentially contested: it accredits a valued achievement since democracy is widely regarded as a valuable form of government. This achievement is internally complex, Gallie claims, because it makes reference to three elements: the power of the people to choose and remove governments, equality of opportunity to attain positions of political leadership and responsibility, and active participation of citizens in political life at all levels. Contestants can, and do, weight these elements differently. Furthermore, the concept of democracy is open in character because "democratic targets will be raised or lowered as circumstances alter."[4]

Gallie might have added (as subsequent writers have) that concepts are essentially contestable not just because people can reasonably attach different weights to the elements that make up the achievements they accredit, but also because these elements may reasonably be interpreted differently. For example, Gallie's analysis of the concept of democracy invites the thought that what counts as having the power to choose and remove governments, what counts as equality of opportunity to attain political positions, and what constitutes active participation in political life are all matters of reasonable dispute. So one essentially contested concept is related to a group of other concepts whose proper uses are themselves contested.[5]

Is community an essentially contested concept, that is, a concept of which there are a number of reasonable conceptions, with the matter of political dispute being which of them is the best? If so, can this at least partially account for the extensive use made of the concept and for the disputes over the nature of community? This suggestion has some plausibility. The concept of community often seems to be used to represent a valued achievement. That achievement is complex because it involves a number of different elements: for example, shared values, participation in a shared way of life, and identification with the group as a whole. People interpret these elements differently or weight the presence or absence of them differently and hence disagree over what counts as a community. Although this explanation may seem as though it has some power, I do not think that it captures the way in which the term 'community' functions in ordinary usage. My point is made best by considering a worry that Gallie expressed about his initial criterion for marking off essentially contested concepts: that they may fail to distinguish genuine essentially contested concepts from terms that conceal two different concepts, and hence are radically ambiguous, disputes over which are simply the result of confusing these concepts.[6]

Gallie argues that we can distinguish essentially contested concepts from ambiguous terms by employing a number of further criteria, the most important of which are that an essentially contested concept must be derived from an original exemplar whose authority is recognized by all the contestants and that continuous competition between rival users of the concept must make probable or plausible the claim that the original exemplar's achievement has been sustained or developed in an optimum fashion.[7] Can a plausible case be made for saying that the concept of community is derived from an original exemplar in this way? Raymond Plant, Harry Lesser, and Peter Taylor-Gooby suggest that although there is no single exemplar that inspires the contestants, there are different exemplars to which they appeal.[8] For example, some hark back to the Greek *polis* as the paradigm of community and others to the feudal village, and some look to a future vision, but this would not satisfy Gallie that the concept is essentially contested as opposed to radically confused, for it would leave open the possibility that those who appealed to different exemplars simply had different concepts of community.[9]

Perhaps the problem lies in Gallie's conditions for distinguishing essentially contested concepts from ambiguous terms. Perhaps these are too restrictive and there need be only an area of agreement on what counts as a community, or on what fails to count as a community, in order to justify the claim that people share the same underlying concept. I think Gallie's conditions are too restrictive, but I doubt whether it is possible to show that the term 'community' is univocal on any plausible set of more permissive conditions. It is employed to express two different concepts of community, and confusion is created by failing to distinguish them. Only one of these concepts is essentially contested—or, at least, this is what I shall argue.

An Ambiguity in the Notion of Community

How do we distinguish one social and political concept from another? What would justify the claim that there are two different concepts of community at work? One plausible answer is that there are two different concepts of community if two different definitions of it can be given, but it would not be easy to show this, because, like many terms, 'community' is hard to define. If Wittgenstein is correct, we should not suppose in advance that every concept can be specified by some set of necessary and sufficient conditions that determine its proper application on every occasion. I would not wish to rule out the possibility that 'community' could be given different analyses of this sort; however, I do not think that we need to provide definitions of the different concepts it involves in order to show that it is ambiguous. It is enough to construct 'ideal types' and to show that these ideal types play different roles in our language and social life.[10]

In both of the concepts of community that I shall distinguish, a community differs from what I shall call a mere society or association. Let me stipulate that a mere association consists of people who interact with one another primarily on a contractual basis in order to further their own self-regarding interests.[11] According to the first ideal type, a community has a different character, because it is constituted by a group of people who share a wide range of values and an encompassing or comprehensive way of life and identify strongly with the group, perhaps to the extent that their very identities are partially constituted by their attachment to it. (I mean 'a way of life' to be understood broadly here, so that it covers a set of rule-governed practices, though they must be at least loosely woven together. These would include fairly specific activities such as greeting friends or grieving the loss of a loved one, as well as more general activities such as playing a sport or engaging in scientific research.) This concept of a community seems to be present in a considerable amount of recent Anglo-American political philosophy.[12] I shall refer to it as the ordinary concept or ordinary sense of community.

The description I have given of the ideal type of community in the ordinary sense does not specify necessary conditions for being such a community. A group of people may constitute a community even if they share only some of the same values and if the way of life in which they participate is not all-encompassing, for example.

Community comes in degrees, and the ordinary concept of community is inherently vague: its application requires a judgment about whether members of a group share enough values, whether they participate in a way of life that is sufficiently encompassing, and whether they identify sufficiently strongly with the group. For this reason not much is to be gained by trying to specify precisely the degree of shared values or the extent of a shared way of life that needs to be present in order for a group of people to count as a community in the ordinary sense.

According to the second ideal type, a community is not just a group of people who share a wide range of values and an encompassing way of life and identify strongly with the group. The individual members also must be mutually concerned and there must be no major systematic exploitation, oppression, or injustice.[13] I shall refer to this as the emancipatory concept or emancipatory sense of community. It is to be found particularly in the socialist tradition. John Baker, for example, gives expression to it when he writes that "there can be no genuine sense of community between degrader and degraded or exploiter and exploited—these relationships mock the very idea of community."[14] Again, the description I have given of this ideal type of community does not provide the necessary conditions because it allows that people may constitute a community in the emancipatory sense even if, for example, they do not share a wide range of values.

The notion of mutual concern that is central to the emancipatory concept of community can function in different ways. In some variants of the emancipatory concept, each member of a community must be concerned for the others simply because they are all members of the same community. This concern may take the form of each member recognizing and fulfilling special obligations and responsibilities to promote the well-being of other members, where these obligations and responsibilities are regarded as deriving solely from the nature of their relationships to one another. According to other variants that have more cosmopolitan leanings, one member of a community must be concerned for the others because they are human beings or sentient creatures whom the member happens to be in a special position to help, not essentially because they are members of the same community. If this concern were understood in terms of each member recognizing and fulfilling special obligations and responsibilities, then those obligations and responsibilities would have to be regarded as in some way derived from general obligations to all human beings.[15]

The notion of concern is itself vague but can be given some clarification. Concern is incompatible with indifference but does not demand the kind of self-sacrifice in which an individual is prepared always to subordinate her interests to those of others. Someone may have concern for others but nevertheless give priority to her own self-regarding interests—concern admits of degree—but a person who has concern for others must give their interests genuine weight in her deliberations, rather than merely determine how her own self-regarding ends could be achieved best. It is difficult to say much more of a general nature about the notion of concern, because in specific cases what counts as concern will depend on the nature of the relationship involved. Consider, for example, the (noncommunal) relationship between doctor and patient.[16] Whether a doctor is genuinely concerned for her patients depends on (among other things) the attention she gives them, the care with which she considers different possible courses of action, and her willingness to give time when needed. In professional roles such as these, concern can exist in the absence of any particular feelings. A concerned doctor need not even particularly like her patients. What it is to have and express concern for a friend will be different from this: it may require sympathetic identification, experiencing another's feelings as if they were one's own. Likewise, what counts as concern in a communal relationship will depend on the nature of the community, including factors such as its size and what binds it together. For example, mutual concern at the level of the nation-state might require an intolerance of inequality except when it is licensed by something similar to John Rawls's difference principle: one person would be unwilling to be better off than others unless this somehow led to the others being made better off as a result.

How the Two Concepts Are Distinguished

Both the ordinary and emancipatory concepts of community are employed in ordinary discourse and in theoretical contexts, even though they are rarely distinguished.[17] A group of people might count as a community in the ordinary sense but not the emancipatory sense. They might share values, have common goals (which they conceive not simply as goals each person has, but as goals of the group), and even acknowledge some special obligations to one another, for example, to participate in public life or promote the common good as they conceive it, without being mutually concerned and while systematically exploiting one another. Imagine, for example, that a group that includes men and women shares sexist values and participates in an encompassing way of life in which the former exploit the latter (though they might not describe their behavior in these terms). Each strongly identifies with the group, and each acknowledges special obligations to the others to contribute in gender-specific ways to the good of the group as they conceive it (e.g., women acknowledge a special obligation to other members of the group to take care of their own children and look after the home, whereas men acknowledge a special obligation to work outside the home and participate in public affairs). Examples of this sort are certainly conceivable and are perhaps not hard to find in practice. They would count as communities in the ordinary sense but not in the emancipatory.

It might be thought that when community is defined in terms of solidarity, we have an unambiguous version of the emancipatory concept, but that is not so. Indeed, the notion of solidarity sometimes facilitates a confusion between the two ideal types of community that I have distinguished. If solidarity is regarded as a form of commitment that requires mutual concern and the absence of major systematic exploitation, oppression, and injustice, then an account of community in terms of solidarity will be a variant of the emancipatory concept. If, however, solidarity is defined merely as a sense of belonging together or as identification with a group, then an account of community that incorporates it may be simply a variant of the ordinary concept.

Solidarity might be defined also in terms of the recognition of special responsibilities or special obligations. Whether a notion of community that incorporated solidarity would express the ordinary or the emancipatory concept would depend in part on the content of these obligations or responsibilities. If these obligations were special obligations to foster the well-being of one's fellows, then an account of community that incorporated them would be at least a partial representation of the emancipatory concept, but if they were merely special obligations to participate in public life or pursue the good of the group as its members conceive it, then such an account might well be consistent with the ordinary concept. Consider in this light Derek Phillips's account of community. He distills from the work of Michael Sandel, Charles Taylor, Alasdair MacIntyre, and Robert Bellah and his co-authors Richard Madsen, William M. Sullivan, Ann Swidler, and Steven M. Tipton, the following definition: "A community is a group of people who live in a common territory, have a common history and shared values, participate in various activities, and have a high degree of solidarity."[18] Phillips goes on to define solidarity in terms of a sense of belonging together and social interdependence, where these are taken to imply a recognition of special obligations and responsibilities, but he fails to distinguish between different types of special obligation and, as a result, he in effect attributes the emancipatory concept to all these writers, whereas it is not always clear which concept of community their accounts are expressing.[19]

The two concepts of community that I have distinguished are perhaps best contrasted in terms of the roles they play in our language and social life, and it is these different roles that provide part of the justification for claiming that two different concepts are being used. The ordinary concept often plays an explanatory role. Since it centrally involves the idea of identification, one of its main roles is in explaining people's allegiances and hence their behavior. When we classify a group of people as a community, we do so at least partly because the individual members identify with the group. A correct understanding of people's identifications is clearly of great importance in explaining their behavior and their general orientation to the world; in particular, it helps us to understand phenomena such as alienation, social cohesion, and social conflict. Tariq Modood, for example, argues that one reason why social theorists in Britain were taken by surprise by the Moslem reaction to Salman Rushdie's *The Satanic Verses* was because they failed to recognize the enormous importance of religious commitment to many Asians living there. According to Modood, some theorists mistakenly thought that because the wider society identified Moslems as blacks, it was this category that would need to be employed to explain their behavior.[20] There is, arguably, a Moslem community in Britain, but no black community that includes Asians, and we have to appeal to membership in the Moslem community to explain the importance of religious commitments to Moslems living in Britain.

The ordinary concept of community also has an important role to play in evaluative contexts: a sense of belonging and social cohesion are valuable (in general) for various reasons, so normative questions about when and how communities should be given special protection, about the kind of jurisdiction a community should have over its members, and about whether community is something to be pursued at the level of the state, inevitably appear on the political agenda and are fertile ground for political philosophers,[21] but they are not involved in the very identification of a group as a community.

The emancipatory concept of community plays largely a critical role: it is used primarily in order to either condemn social and political arrangements or praise them. Some social relationships are described as communal in order to praise them, whereas others are described as lacking in community in order to condemn them and to hold up an alternative model as a vision of something better. William Morris, for example, criticizes capitalism and argues that a truly communal life requires the elimination of the capitalist.

> . . . the capitalist or modern slave-owner has been forced by his very success . . . to organize his slaves, the wage-earners, into a co-operation for production so well arranged that it requires little but his own elimination to make it a foundation for communal life. . . .[22]

The communal life is one that involves brotherhood and cooperation rather than "selfish greed and ceaseless competition."[23] Marx also employs a version of the emancipatory concept of community to criticize relations under capitalism (and earlier forms of social and economic organization) and to sketch an alternative vision.

> The illusory community, in which individuals have up till now combined, always took on an independent existence in relation to them, and was at the same time, since it was the combination of one class over against another, not only a completely illusory community, but a new fetter as well. In the real community the individuals obtain their freedom in and through their association.[24]

Marx argues that only communist society is a true community and that only in a true community is personal freedom possible for all.

Only the emancipatory concept of community is genuinely essentially contested, although the ordinary concept does meet a number of the criteria for being essentially contested. The ordinary concept accredits a valued achievement. It is internally complex because it makes reference to a number of different elements: shared values, an encompassing way of life, and identification with the group. It is open to different interpretations, because these elements might reasonably be weighted differently by different people. It is not, however, essentially contested, because the very identification of community in the ordinary sense is not a site of political controversy. People disagree about whether communities in this sense should be given special protection, whether they should be allowed to coerce their individual members to conform to traditions, and whether the practices they contain are desirable, but there are rarely serious disputes over whether some group of people constitutes a community in the ordinary sense: that is usually granted for the sake of argument.[25]

The emancipatory concept is genuinely essentially contested, however. The identification of community in the emancipatory sense is a site of political controversy because it involves the application of other moral notions—exploitation, oppression, and justice—each of which is open to a number of reasonable interpretations. For example, socialists such as Morris and Marx see the relationship between capitalist and worker as fundamentally exploitative and think that the abolition of private ownership of the means of production would end all exploitation. Some feminists, however, would disagree and argue that men might continue to exploit women even after capitalism had been transcended, because women might continue to perform unremunerated work for men in fulfilling their familial obligations.[26] Different theories of exploitation thereby generate different conceptions of the emancipatory concept of community.

Theorists sometimes employ both of the notions of community that I have distinguished. Marx is a clear example. He sometimes refers to feudal villages as though they were communities, apparently employing community in the ordinary sense, but on other occasions regards these villages as illusory communities, apparently employing the term in the emancipatory sense. In *The German Ideology*, he refers to "the previous substitutes for community" (particularly the state as conceived by the Hegelians) and "the illusory community."[27] Yet in other writings he also refers to villages in nineteenth-century India as communities. He deplores the loss of an ancient form of civilization under British colonialism while emphasizing the oppressiveness of these village communities.

> . . . we must not forget that these idyllic village communities, inoffensive though they may appear, had always been the solid foundation of

oriental despotism. . . . these little communities were contaminated by
distinctions of caste and by slavery. . . .[28]

There is nothing wrong with employing both senses of community,
but it would be confused to suppose that community in the emancipatory sense is more of a community or is a more authentic community than community in the ordinary sense.

The ambiguity in the idea of community also might make us
wonder whether it is common practice to trade on this ambiguity
by correctly describing a group as a community in the ordinary sense
but implicitly claiming for it the moral qualities of community in
the emancipatory sense when they are in reality lacking. 'Community' might then function in a way that is in some respects similar
to Ernest Gellner's imaginary concept of 'boble'. 'Bobility' is used
either to characterize people who display various virtues such as
courage or generosity or to characterize people who merely hold a
certain social position or office. Gellner proposes that:

> Bobility is a conceptual device by which the privileged class of the
> society in question acquires some of the prestige of certain virtues re-
> spected in that society, without the inconvenience of needing to prac-
> tice it, thanks to the fact that the same word is applied either to
> practitioners of those virtues or to occupiers of favoured positions.[29]

If 'community' does sometimes function in a similar way, it may
serve the ideological purpose of diverting attention away from the
relationships of exploitation that exist within a way of life.

I have argued that for many purposes it is important to distinguish between two different concepts of community: what I have
called the emancipatory concept, which is essentially contested and
largely plays a critical role, and what I have called the ordinary
concept, which, though it plays a role in evaluative contexts, is not
essentially contested. I have not attempted to resolve all the disputes that occur over the nature of community; I have tried merely
to diagnose one major source of confusion.[30]

Notes

1. Cf. Derek L. Phillips, *Looking Backward: A Critical Appraisal of Communitarian Thought* (Princeton, N.J.: Princeton University Press, 1993), 7.

2. Raymond Plant, Harry Lesser, and Peter Taylor-Gooby explore this idea and give it a qualified endorsement in their *Political Philosophy and Social Welfare* (London: Routledge and Kegan Paul, 1980), chap. 9.

3. See W. B. Gallie, "Essentially Contested Concepts," *Proceedings of the Aristotelian Society* 56 (1955–56): 167–98. Those sympathetic to the notion of an essentially contested concept have included William Connolly, *The Terms of Political Discourse*, 2d ed. (Oxford: Martin Robertson, 1983); Steven Lukes, *Power: A Radical View* (London: Macmillan, 1974); and Susan Hurley, *Natural Reasons: Persons and Polity* (Oxford: Oxford University Press, 1989).

4. Gallie, 186.

5. The notion of an essentially contested concept has been subject to a considerable amount of criticism. I have tried to answer some of it in my *Explaining Political Disagreement* (Cambridge: Cambridge University Press, 1993), chap. 2.

6. See Gallie, 175.

7. See Gallie, 180.

8. See Plant et al., 209.

9. Plant et al. seem to recognize this point when they say that "[t]his feature of community would make it perhaps more radically contested than any other central social and political concept" (p. 210) but do not in my view fully appreciate its implications.

10. Other writers, such as Stanley Benn and Joel Feinberg, have also been more concerned with community as an ideal type than with providing a definition of 'community' that might determine its proper use on every occasion. See Stanley Benn, *A Theory of Freedom* (Cambridge: Cambridge University Press, 1988), 214; and Joel Feinberg, *The Moral Limits of the Criminal Law: Volume 4: Harmless Wrongdoing* (New York: Oxford University Press, 1988), 102.

11. See Ferdinand Tonnies, *Community and Association*, trans. C. P. Loomis (London: Routledge and Kegan Paul, 1955).

12. See, for example, Feinberg, 101–5. Many political philosophers seem to presuppose this concept, though it is difficult to be sure because they often do not provide an account of what they mean by 'community'. See, for example, Robert Nozick, *Anarchy, State, and Utopia* (Oxford: Blackwell, 1974), especially 307ff; Marilyn Friedman, "Feminism and Modern Friendship: Dislocating the Community," *Ethics* 99 (1989): 275–90; Alasdair MacIntyre, *After Virtue: A Study in Moral Theory* (London: Duckworth, 1981), especially 204–5, 233.

13. It might be said that genuine mutual concern is incompatible with systematic exploitation, oppression, or injustice and hence that the existence of mutual concern would make unnecessary the requirement of no systematic exploitation and so on, but that is not obviously so. Could not masters and slaves be genuinely mutually concerned, even though the former oppressed and exploited the latter?

14. John Baker, *Arguing for Equality* (London: Verso, 1987), 35.

15. Cf. Robert E. Goodin, *Protecting the Vulnerable: A Reanalysis of Our Social Responsibilities* (Chicago: Chicago University Press, 1985).

16. Naomi Scheman makes the following points in more detail in "On Sympathy," *The Monist* 62 (1979): 322.

17. Nicola Lacey and Elizabeth Frazer make a related distinction between descriptive and ideological senses of community. See Nicola Lacey and Elizabeth Frazer, "Blind Alleys: Communitarianism," *Politics* 14 (1994): 76.

18. Phillips, 14.

19. Phillips, 16–17, 75–80, 115–21, 146–48. Phillips's failure to distinguish between different types of special obligation undermines part of his case for saying that the exemplars to which contemporary communitarians such as MacIntyre appeal are not genuine communities. It is not clear that MacIntyre, Taylor, or Bellah, et al., for example, regard special concern for the well-being of one's fellows (as opposed to the fulfillment of special obligations to promote the common good, conceived as the good of the group) as a requirement of community.

20. See Tariq Modood, *Not Easy Being British: Colour, Culture, and Citizenship* (London: Trentham, 1992), especially 54–55.

21. In this context, see especially Will Kymlicka, *Multicultural Citizenship: A Liberal Theory of Minority Rights* (Oxford: Clarendon Press, 1995).

22. A. L. Morton, ed. *The Political Writings of William Morris* (London: Lawrence and Wishart, 1979), 177.

23. Morton, 171. See Caroline McCulloch, "The Problem of Fellowship in Communitarian Theory: William Morris and Peter Kropotkin," *Political Studies* 32 (1984): 437–50, for a fuller discussion of Morris's conception of community.

24. Karl Marx and Friedrich Engels, "The German Ideology," *Collected Works* vol. 5 (London: Lawrence and Wishart, 1976): 78. *The German Ideology* was written in 1845–46, but not published until later.

25. There are some disagreements of this sort: for example, people do sometimes disagree over whether there is a gay community in the ordinary sense, but these disputes are not widespread.

26. See Christine Delphy and Diane Leonard, *Familiar Exploitation* (Cambridge: Polity, 1992).

27. Marx and Engels, 78.

28. Karl Marx and Friedrich Engels, *Selected Works*, vol. 1 (Moscow: Foreign Languages Publishing House, 1962), 350–51. (The passage is taken from an article on British rule in India in the *New York Daily Tribune*, 25 June 1853.)

29. Bryan Wilson, ed., *Rationality* (Oxford: Blackwell, 1970), 41–42.

30. I would like to thank Roger Crisp, Brad Hooker, Rick Momeyer, David Novitz, and Nancy Snow for their comments on an earlier draft.

2

Community, Diversity, and Confucianism

David B. Wong

Some of us find an irony in the dissolution of communism as a credible alternative to Western capitalist democracy. Declarations of victory by our political leaders ring hollow when we confront within our society a lack of will to address the ways in which we fall far short of our ideals. What is dispiriting about our situation, for example, is not just the persistence of a class mostly located in the urban cores that is disproportionately poor, uneducated, raised in families and communities lacking the resources to provide a stable and nurturing environment, and beset with drugs and crime. The problem is not just demoralized and deteriorating urban schools. It is the lack of concerted will to address these ills. It is the fact that if enough Americans wished it, state legislatures and Congress would at least try to address these issues through policies that might or might not work but that at least could be tried. It is also the fact that many of these signs of social decomposition and decay are reflected throughout the larger society, regardless of race and class.[1]

This growing sense of unease with ourselves is, I suspect, partly responsible for the strong interest in the communitarian attack on liberalism in contemporary Anglo-American ethical theory. The kind of liberalism that is the object of attack consists of three claims: first, that there is a significant plurality of conceptions of the good life that reasonable and informed people accept; second, that principles of right action and of justice should be neutral toward such conceptions of the good life insofar as the justification of such principles does not depend on accepting any one conception; and third,

17

that a necessary feature of a right and just social order is that it protect the freedom to choose among competing conceptions as long as they conform to principles of right and justice. Communitarianism comes in many different versions, but they all share the theme that the right and the good cannot be divorced in the way that liberalism requires, that a viable conception of the right must presuppose some conception of the good.

A communitarian argument is that liberalism, when it calls on people to make personal sacrifices for the sake of achieving a just society, cannot adequately explain why they should do so. Suppose, as many liberals believe, that achieving a just society requires significant redistribution of income and wealth. This means persuading those who are currently better off that the sacrifices required of them are acceptable. Communitarians argue, however, that liberal justifications of redistribution are inconclusive at best. In the end, the communitarians argue, the better off will be able to accept sacrifices only if they see their good as individuals as intertwined with the common good, and seeing this requires that they recognize that others participate in the constitution of their identities and their achievements.

Michael Sandel, for example, has argued that when this mode of self-understanding becomes widespread within a group, its members regard each other less as others and more as participants in a common identity, "be it family or community or class or people or nation." A consequence of such a self understanding is that:

> when "my" assets or life prospects are enlisted in the service of a common endeavor, I am likely to experience this less as a case of being used for others' ends and more as a way of contributing to the purposes of a community I regard as my own. The justification of my sacrifice, if it can be called a sacrifice, is not the abstract assurance that unknown others will gain more than I will lose, but the rather more compelling notion that by my efforts I contribute to the realization of a way of life in which I take pride and with which my identity is bound.[2]

I suspect a good deal of the power of such arguments derives from the sense of unease that many of us have about our willingness as Americans to address ourselves seriously to the nation's ills. The communitarian argument is a diagnosis of what is wrong and of what the cure must be. On the other side, liberals raise questions about that cure: whether identification with community allows for enough critical distance on its moral failings, whether emphasizing the role that others play in constituting our identities results in depriving us of any true *agency* of any significantly active part in constituting ourselves, and, finally, whether we in this heterogeneous, pluralistic society really are prepared to give up a political philosophy that prohibits the state from enforcing any particular conception of the good.

We could go in a number of different directions in carrying this debate further. The direction I want to take in this paper is to ask what implications a plausible theory of moral development would have for the communitarian and liberal views. What would such a theory say about the necessary conditions for cultivating moral commitments that are strong enough to motivate individuals to accept significant sacrifices? Must there be identity-constituting communities? Would such communities leave enough room for critical reflection on their traditions and for individual agency in the formation of identities? To what extent does promoting such communities undermine the values of protecting diversity and the freedom to choose among competing conceptions of the good?[3]

Communitarians such as Michael Sandel, Alasdair MacIntyre, and Michael Walzer have addressed all or some of these questions from within the Western tradition.[4] An alternative method of investigation is to explore other traditions that emphasize the importance of identity-constituting communities and that connect them with the conditions for cultivating strong moral commitment. Confucianism is such a tradition, and I will attempt to sketch a picture of the Confucian approach to the issues raised here.

There are many ways to present an interpretation of the Confucian approach, as well as many interpretations. Let me present my interpretation by explaining how I understand the complex relation between two central Confucian concepts: that of *jen* and *li*.

In the *Analects* of Confucius, *jen* refers most of the time to the highest ethical ideal that encompasses all individual desirable qualities. Some qualities most frequently associated with *jen* are an emotional sensitivity and concern for the well-being of others, filial piety, respect for elders, and the ability to endure adverse circumstances. *Jen* connotes realized human capacities, a state of highest achievement, to be admired by and be a source of inspiration for the community. At one point Confucius identifies *jen* with the particular virtue of loving persons, perhaps implying that such love is central to all manifestations of comprehensive human excellence. *Li* originally referred to the rites of sacrifice to spirits and ancestors conducted by rulers. The word later broadened in meaning to refer to norms governing ceremonious behavior in social and political contexts such as the reception of envoys. Still later, the meaning broadened more to include all traditional and customary norms governing conduct between people, especially as the occupants of interrelated social positions. *Li* in the broadest sense embraces civility, graciousness, grace, and respectful behavior.

The importance placed on *li* is one of the most distinctive elements of Confucius's *Analects*. In a number of places in that work, Confucius is said to have remarked on the intimate connection between *jen* and *li*. When asked about *jen* (in 12:1), Confucius said, "To return to the observance of *li* through overcoming the self constitutes *jen*."[5] He describes (in 1:2) filial piety as the basis of *jen* in the sense that it is an essential starting point for cultivating *jen*, and filial piety is explained in another place (2:5) in terms of the observance of *li*. These passages could lead to a reading of Confucius as an extreme traditionalist who advocated an uncritical acceptance of customary norms and conventions. On such a reading, Confucius believed that *li* wholly constitutes *jen*. To be *jen* is nothing more nor less than to observe the customary norms and conventions of one's society. Kwong-loi Shun calls this the "definitionalist" interpretation of the relation between *jen* and *li*.[6]

Another possible interpretation is that *li* is a means to cultivating and expressing *jen* but does not define *jen*. On this "instrumentalist" interpretation,[7] *jen* is usually construed as a configuration of character traits that is intelligible independently of the general observance of *li*. For example, the instrumentalist interpretation construes the custom of observing a three-year mourning period on the death of a parent as a means of expressing and sustaining one's reverence for the deceased parent. For someone who falls short of having such love, observance of such *li* may have the effect of instilling it. Acting in a certain way, in other words, may cultivate the feeling appropriate to that action. On the instrumentalist interpretation, the ideal of *jen* provides a perspective from which one can justify the acceptance or revision of a rule of *li*. One can evaluate a rule as a better or worse way of expressing and cultivating an independently definable *jen*. On the definitionalist interpretation, *jen* cannot provide such a critical perspective on *li*, since it is wholly constituted by the observance of *li*.

A textual passage that seems to support the instrumentalist interpretation, in fact, is a passage in which Confucius advocates the retention of a rule of *li* and departure from another rule. In 9:3, Confucius says,

> A ceremonial cap of linen is what is prescribed by *li*. Today black silk is used instead. This is more frugal and I follow the majority. To prostrate oneself before ascending the steps is what is prescribed by *li*. Today one does so after having ascended them. This is casual and, though going against the majority, I follow the practice of doing so before ascending.[8]

Confucius is discussing two cases of conflict between contemporary common practice and older rules of the tradition governing the conduct of rituals in ancestral temples. His position in the first case favors frugality over the older rule, on the assumption that the original purpose of the ceremony is unaffected by saving on the cap material, but the common practice in the second case is unacceptable precisely because it alters the meaning of the ceremony. It shows disrespect for the prince, who presides over the ceremony, to bow only after ascending the steps to the upper hall. The implication of this passage is that the spirit appropriate to *jen*, of love and respect, is not wholly constituted by but rather provides a basis for evaluating rules of *li*.

Clearly, neither the instrumentalist nor the definitionalist interpretations is entirely satisfactory. The definitionalist interpretation runs counter not only to the passage I just discussed, but to ones in which Confucius suggests that the superiority of the culture of his home state of Lu, the Chou culture, rests partly on its having built on the cultures of the previous two dynasties. Yet the instrumentalist version conflicts with those passages that strongly suggest that *jen* is at least partly, if not wholly, constituted by *li*. We need an interpretation that is more complex and subtle than either of these alternatives.

One way of seeing how a third alternative is possible is to presuppose a philosophical anthropology that admits a significant degree of plasticity in human nature. This anthropology need not deny that we have innate tendencies, but in Clifford Geertz's words, such tendencies would be extremely general, diffuse, and variable and in need of guidance by "cultural templates."[9] His "templates" are plans, recipes, rules, instructions, or programs for governing behavior. They became necessary during the course of the several million that years it took for the genus *Homo* to make the transition to a cultural mode of life—organized hunting and gathering practices, a family organization, and reliance on significant symbols in language, art, myth, and ritual for orientation, communication, and self-control. The central nervous system of the species evolved during this transition. As culture developed incrementally, a selective advantage was given to those individuals who were able to exchange the advantages of the regularity and precision of detailed genetic control over conduct for the greater advantages of generalized innate propensities that were far more flexible and adaptable.

Generalized innate tendencies are compatible with a broad range of actions. We cannot rely on our genetic programs even to determine how to go about eating or express our sexuality, to mention two drives that seem to be among the closest to being genetically controlled. To supply the additional information to act, we rely heavily on cultural templates. Otherwise, our plastic, flexible, and incomplete natures would not be effective bases for action. That is why Geertz calls us incomplete animals who complete ourselves through culture.[10]

Of course, Confucius had no theory of evolution, but the conception of human beings as self-completing through cultural templates fits nicely with his emphasis on the necessity of *li* for realizing one's humanity. *Li* is certainly one of the primary sources of cultural templates. Now consider Confucius's remark that *jen* is loving persons and put that together with his remark that submitting to *li* is *jen*. On the instrumentalist interpretation of *jen* this aspect of *jen* would be an internal emotional state that could also be expressed and cultivated by the Chou *li* but that could be expressed and cultivated by another *li*, though perhaps not as well. The philosophical anthropology here attributed to Confucius implies, however, that *jen* is not a determinate condition of character that can be defined independently of any particular set of *li*. This anthropology implies that *jen* is not reducible to but is completed by some particular set of *li*. It implies that loving people is something we come to have and to understand as love through our culture and particularly through *li*, which specifies what it is to love one's children, one's parents, and one's elders, for instance.

The philosophical anthropology here attributed to Confucius is, then, support for the idea that *jen* is partially constituted by *li*, but what I have said also implies that there is a component of *jen* that is already given by our incomplete natures. If submitting to *li* helps to shape our natures, there is still something there to be shaped, so it is not as if *jen* is exhausted by any particular *li*. Confucius does not explicitly express views about what innate components there are in human nature that are given shape by *li*, but throughout the *Analects* he clearly does presuppose that human beings who are not completely corrupted are capable of responding to the call to live a noble life.

What might underlie such a capability was taken up explicitly by his successors Meng-tzu and Hsun Tzu. Meng-tzu, of course, is famous for his belief that our natures contain the seeds of goodness. He believed, for example, in the primitive compassionate response to the distress of others, illustrated by his example of the spontaneous, unreflective response of an adult to seeing a child fall into a well (*Meng-tzu* 2A:6). In accordance with Confucian philosophical anthropology, Meng-tzu emphasizes that this innate response is only a font, or beginning, of virtue, to be completed through learning and through nurturance by others.[11]

At this point, however, one major element is missing from the complex relation between *jen* and *li*. So far, individuals appear as the passive objects of shaping through *li* and other cultural templates. Some interpretations leave it at that. Herbert Fingarette, who deserves a great deal of credit for the contemporary renewal of Western philosophical interest in Confucius, characterizes the Confucian individual as "raw material" to be shaped by *li*, lacking an autonomous center of choice.[12] As productive as Fingarette's interpretation has been in stimulating interest in Confucius, this aspect of it contributes to a reading of him as a moral "other" to the West, exemplifying values antithetical to Western ones that celebrate individual agency and autonomy. This interpretation leaves out all elements in Confucian philosophy that emphasize the inwardness of moral development, the necessity of *self*-cultivation—elements that Tu Wei-ming has effectively emphasized in his writing.[13]

Individuals, in the Confucian philosophy, are subjects who exercise judgment and make choices. This is in part because *li* can be conflicting and ambiguous, and if human nature is indeterminate, so is *li*. Striving toward *jen* cannot simply be submitting to *li*, because we must perform the kind of interpretative activity that allows us to make more coherent and more determinate sense of the *li* we have inherited. Relevant here is another crucial Confucian notion: that of *yi*. This usually is translated as rightness or righteousness, but a more informative translation would relate it to the idea of fittingness or appropriateness to the context. The ability to judge what is right for the context enables individuals to act well when the rules of *li* are indeterminate, conflicting, and ambiguous. This ability is also necessary because the circumstances to which rules must be applied are continually changing and evolving. The effective exercise of individual judgment in response to fresh circumstances calls for a degree of creativity. The kind of problem for which creativity is needed is often one of preserving tradition while adapting it to suit new circumstances.[14]

To summarize: the instrumentalist interpretation of the relation between *jen* and *li* is inadequate because the concrete, action-guiding meaning of *jen* is drawn from the customs, norms, and conventions that our culture has given us—because *jen* as a set of inner states and dispositions is incomplete and too often inchoate without the *li* that serves to focus and direct them. Conversely, the definitionalist interpretation is incorrect because it ignores those impulses that are shaped by *li* but do not originate from *li*, and it ignores the way in which individuals must exercise critical judgment and creativity when the rules of *li* are conflicting and indeterminate or do not cover the circumstances in which one must act. The resulting picture is of a complex interaction between individuals and their inherited traditions. That which is inherited does shape them, but because the rules of *li* are conflicting, indeterminate, ambiguous, and in need of being continuously interpreted and adapted to new circumstances, individuals have the opportunity not only to exercise judgment, but also to influence the content of *li* itself. The agency of the individual can now be seen to assume a crucial role in the picture of moral development unfolding from Confucian philosophical anthropology.

Further, the individual agency provided by Confucianism includes the possibility of meaningful criticism of *li*. Such criticism is illustrated by Maxine Hong Kingston's story "White Tigers" in her *Woman Warrior*.[15] The story retells the traditional ballad of a young woman who takes the place of her aged father when he is called into the army. In the course of that retelling, Kingston juxtaposes the valor and resourcefulness of the woman warrior with the subordinate place allotted to women in the traditional culture. Some have heatedly criticized her alleged distortion of the traditional ballad. The result, her critics say, is the portrayal of a misogynist culture that plays into the Western stereotype of the Chinese as the moral other.[16]

While it is clear to me that Kingston is changing the ballad in various ways to make her points, it is also clear that she is directly confronting one of the gravest failings of the tradition in its treatment of women, and while the story may be used by those who have an interest in maintaining the stereotype of the Chinese as the moral other, it may also be read as a protest directed to all within the tradition—the protest that women have not been allowed to contribute to the community in ways in which they are fully capable of contributing. The story gains its power from its juxtaposition of the woman warrior's satisfaction in demonstrating her "perfect filiality,"[17] on the one hand, and on the other hand the contemporary narrator's inability to win from her family appreciation for any of her worldly achievements. The protest of the story, in other words, may be read as an appeal to the core values in the tradition of community and filiality and the demand that women be given a full opportunity to realize those values.

We have, then, a picture of moral development in which our characters become more determinate through the guidance of *li* and in which *li* is subject to critical reflection. When we critically reflect on *li*, we reflect on that which shapes our characters in the fullest sense—not only beliefs in a narrowly cognitive sense, but habits of feeling, behavior, and perception. To explain why this implication of the Confucian picture is an especially important one, let me use Michael Oakeshott's distinction between two forms of the moral life.

Under the first of these forms, the moral life is an unreflective "habit of affection and behavior."[18] The daily situations of normal life do not present us with problems calling for reflection on alternative courses of action and decision according to some rule or ideal. We instead unreflectively follow a tradition of conduct in which we have been brought up. We do not learn rules or precepts by heart and subsequently practice them, but acquire habits by living with people who habitually behave in a certain way. We learn them as we learn our native language. What is learned, of course, *may* be formulated in rules or precepts, but we typically do not learn them through rules and precepts. The education by means of which we acquire habits of affection and behavior is "carried on, in practice and observation, without pause in every moment of our waking life, and perhaps even in our dreams."[19] This education is not compulsory, says Oakeshott, but inevitable, because "it is impossible to engage in any activity whatever without contributing" to it.[20] The second form of moral life, by contrast, treats the daily situations of

moral life as presenting problems to be solved through application
of ideals and rules adopted on reflection. Moral education under
this form requires intellectual training in the "detection and appreciation" of moral ideals, training in their "intellectual management"
and in their application to concrete situations.[21]

In the end, Oakeshott judges these two forms to be ideal extremes of the moral life, although neither one of which is, by
itself, a likely form. It is the combination of these two, he says,
that is the more promising. Giving primary emphasis to the latter
form results in a certain hollowness that has come to pervade modern life.

> Lacking habits of moral behavior, we have fallen back upon moral opin-
> ions as a substitute; but, as we all know, when we reflect upon what
> we are doing we too often conclude that it is wrong. Like lonely men
> who, to gain reassurance, exaggerate the talents of their few friends,
> we exaggerate the significance of our moral ideals to fill in the hol-
> lowness of our moral life.[22]

Confucianism attempts to balance habit and reflection. In its emphasis on education through observation and interaction with persons who serve as models and in its refusal to give comprehensive
principles from which the correct action in any given context can
be deduced, it indicates the importance that it places on habits of
affection and behavior in its picture of moral development. These
habits cannot be deduced from general principles or values. Rather,
they constitute the concrete determination of what principles or
values mean in practice. They include perceptual habits that determine what features of situations constitute salient reasons for acting as well as habits of feeling and behaving in response to the
daily situations of life. These are all aspects of moral commitment
that are not well subsumed under some purely cognitive model of
believing in the right things.

Conversely, the notions of *jen* and *yi*, for the reasons discussed
earlier, have the critical edge associated with ideals pursued reflec-
tively. The Confucian notion of *li* represents the attempt to make
habit reflective and not to leave it behind in the pursuit of abstract
ideals. *Li*, after all, consists of formulated rules, the product of reflection on what we have observed and absorbed through living with
others. The complex relation between *jen* and *li* reflects the thought
that unreflective habit can be made reflective and responsive to
moral ideals, that the individual moral agent can extract coherent

themes from the mass of tradition that informs our habits and then
return to the tradition and correct it.

I said that understanding the Confucian emphasis on the reflective shaping of character habits is important because I believe that
the Anglo-American philosophical tradition has lost sight of that aspect of moral commitment. The Kohlbergian model of moral development illustrates our focus on the reflective pursuit of ideals.[23] That
model, primarily based on what we would say about hypothetical
moral problems and dilemmas, illustrates our neglect of what we
feel, perceive, and do in our daily lives. As a result, we have neglected the kind of education that Oakeshott rightly characterizes
as inevitable and as taking place every waking moment of our lives.
Confucianism is optimistic about our ability to shape or reshape
habits with the help of moral exemplars and *li*. Emulating exemplars and following *li* are part of one complex process. Following
li is not a simple matter of deducing instances from generalizations.
In Confucianism, application of general rules depends on the exercise of judgment that is sensitive to the salient and particular features of the situation at hand. These features indicate which rules
are relevant and suggest specific modes of action by which the relevant rules may be obeyed. This kind of judgment is shown by and
learned from persons who already have it.

The continual emphasis on learning from exemplars, even when
the learning is of rules, is one reason for the most striking and most
frequently noted feature of the Confucian picture of moral development: its emphasis on the family as the first and foremost community in which we develop our moral commitments. Through
regular, face-to-face interaction within the family individuals learn
through having others model for them the expression of *jen* through
the following of *li*. The exercise of individual judgment in interpreting *li*, choosing among conflicting *li*, and in judging what is *yi*
must be shown to a significant extent on particular occasions and
cannot be deduced from some general principle. It is within the
family that one learns to understand the viewpoints of others and
to integrate them into one's identity, so that the others' well-being
becomes intertwined with one's own. It is within the family that one
learns to trust others enough so that one may receive correction and
advice from them.

One way of putting the rationale for the Confucian emphasis on
family is that only a group capable of fostering this kind of trust,
only a group capable of entering into the identities of its members

this deeply, could nurture the excellences of moral character; once we recognize such excellences as involving not only the reflective commitment to ideals but habits gained through living with others, habits that help to complete our incomplete natures and flesh out our ideals, this rationale seems powerful.[24]

This picture of moral development resonates with the notion of the primary group developed by the American sociologist Charles Horton Cooley. Cooley emphasized the importance of interactive process between group and individual in the formation of individual human nature and the development of norms and ends. He called primary those groups most influential in the process, such as family, household group, and the old-fashioned neighborhood. Such groups facilitate insight into the moods and states of mind of others and tend to result in a "certain fusion of individualities in a common whole, so that one's very self, for many purposes at least, is the common life and purpose of the group."[25] Let me use the phrase "primary group" in attempting to generalize and to abstract from the Confucian tradition what we can learn about moral development. The term is appropriate because it covers not just the family, but all small groups that enter the identities of individuals and are crucial in the development of their norms and values. It also avoids the suggestion that the family, in order to play a crucial role in moral development, must be structured as it is in traditional Chinese culture or, indeed, as it is in traditional American culture.

The emphasis on the crucial role of primary groups in moral development suggests a necessary direction for future investigation into the issues of moral development raised here. If small primary groups in which face-to-face interaction and teaching take place are the groups that first command our loyalties, we need to study the ways in which such loyalties can expand to much larger social structures. The Confucian model of moral development starts with small primary groups and then conceives the individual's concern to radiate outward, eventually to embrace all. In other words, small primary groups have an essential mediating function in the formation of commitments with a much larger scope of concern. There is, in fact, some sociological evidence that small primary groups do perform such a mediating function. For example, Edward Shils describes some classic studies showing the importance of primary group loyalty for military morale. What emerged from these studies was the relative unimportance of direct identification with the total symbols of the military organization as a whole, of the state, or of the political cause in the name of which a war is fought, as contrasted with the feelings of strength and security in the military primary group and of loyalty to one's immediate comrades. The soldier's motivation to fight is not derived from his perceiving and striving toward any strategic or political goals; it is a function of his need to protect his primary group and to conform with its expectations. The military machine thus obtains its inner cohesion . . . through a system of overlapping primary groups. The effective transmission and execution of commands along the formal line of authority can be successful only when it coincides with this system of informal groups.[26]

In reflecting on this and other studies of the function of primary groups in larger social structures, Shils maintains that

individuals who are members of larger social structures make their decisions and concert their actions within those structures, not by the direct focus of attention on the central authority and the agents who bear the symbols of that authority, but rather by identification with some individual with whom they have primary-group relationships and who serves to transmit to them ideas from and concerning the larger structure.[27]

In conceiving just how it is that the moral concerns and commitments fostered in primary groups could give rise to larger concerns and commitments, we also must inquire into the possible role of associations that are intermediate between primary groups and large-scale societies—intermediate in terms of size and intimacy of interaction. Such associations may serve as channels of communication from the smallest primary groups to the largest structures containing them.

William de Bary recently has identified two reasons for the failure of Confucianism to be more influential than it has been in its native country: (1) an inability to realize its ideal of education for all people, which would infuse a unified national consciousness, and (2) a failure to mobilize the people as a politically active body, capable of supporting that body's initiatives and proposed reforms. The second failure, suggests de Bary, was linked to the lack of an infrastructure of politically effective associations that could serve as channels of communication and influence between the family and local forms of community, on the one hand, and the ruling elite, on the other.[28]

Strikingly, a major and justifiable concern of many political theorists in this country is the disappearance or eroding authority of precisely such an intermediate infrastructure. If we take the Confucian model of moral development seriously, we will share this concern. Two very different traditions have converged on the problem of fostering mediating structures that could broaden and channel outward the commitments formed in primary groups. Perhaps this indicates that we have a finger on an important source of our problems.

Let us now consider again the issues that communitarians raised about liberalism. The picture of moral development drawn from Confucianism implies that identity-constituting communities are among the necessary conditions for cultivating strong commitments to moral ideals. I have tried to show how the picture unfolds plausibly from a possible philosophical anthropology and a full-blooded conception of what moral commitment is. I have tried to show that the picture provides for both critical reflection on the traditions of one's community and for individual agency in the formation of identity. If the picture is right, we must compromise liberal neutrality toward conceptions of the good, because promoting community means promoting some conceptions of the good over others. It means favoring those conceptions that accord a high value to community itself. Moreover, promoting and sustaining particular communities would seem to favor the conceptions of the good that these communities embody and that serve as part of their unifying basis.

What, however, about the question of whether we are prepared to compromise liberal neutrality in a heterogeneous, pluralistic society? The question could be put a bit differently. Our concern for community is one reason for the renewed relevance Confucianism has for us, but another reason is our concern for diversity. The renewal of interest in Confucianism draws strength from the growth of multiculturalism as an ideal—the ideal of respect for other cultures and of understanding how these cultures are sources of satisfaction and sustenance for their bearers. Multiculturalism, in turn, derives from a positive valuation of diversity itself. Such a positive valuation can stem from the belief that there is no single configuration of all the values that human beings rightly prize that is suitable for all and that fully realizes all the kinds of human excellence these values represent. Liberalism protects diversity insofar as it enjoins the state to be neutral toward differing conceptions of the good. To that extent, at least, liberalism and multiculturalism converge. The values of community and diversity come into tension with each other when we try to promote community across groups with distinct cultures and shared values. This tension gives rise to the current worry that multiculturalism results in an ethnic balkanization that erodes the authority of common democratic institutions.

I believe that there is an inevitable degree of tension between the concerns for community and for diversity. Yet there are ways to make this tension a creative and not a destructive one. A crucial question here is whether identity-constituting communities must necessarily cohere around a uniform set of shared values. The assumption that they must seems to underlie much communitarian thought, but we should recognize that some degree of diversity of fundamental belief will always appear in the most unified of human communities.[29] As Alasdair MacIntyre has observed, viable moral traditions are ongoing dialogues and debates over the nature of their core values and the relative priorities among them.[30] I go further in claiming that there are often standoffs in these debates, where opposing sides seem to be equally reasonable in holding their positions. This is true because of the diversity in the range of important human values. Any enduring tradition, I believe, will embrace at least some values such as liberty, equality, community, and diversity itself that are in tension with each other. The specific meaning and priority given to each value relative to others will distinguish traditions from one another, but even within a tradition, the meanings and relative priorities are disputable and disputed.

Disagreement can be a sign of the health and vitality of a tradition, especially if the parties to it are still able and desire to regard their opponents as members of the same tradition. I suspect that no tradition could be flexible enough to survive for any appreciable period of time unless it allowed significant latitude in what counted as sharing the same values at bottom and believing the same things on the important matters. In the task of containing conflict between members of a community, there is a need for such latitude and, indeed, a use in letting general values remain general and in some respects vague and indeterminate. If we were clear and specific on what our values were, we would have to be too clear and too specific on the ways in which we are opposed to each other.

In thinking about the tension between community and diversity, then, we must keep in mind that a community need not be based on total agreement on a conception of the good, but that it can be based on a number of different ties: a shared history, including a shared history of debate and disagreement, or some shared ends important enough to keep people together despite other ends that are not shared. This is not to say that communities can exist in the face of unlimited disagreement on the most fundamental values. It is important to find common ground, and most of this paper is an attempt to do so with respect to the Confucian tradition and liberalism. I have been suggesting that liberalism may have to concede the importance of community to realize its own ends. Liberalism need not give to community the sort of primacy it enjoys in the Confucian tradition, but there may have to be significant overlap between the two traditions on the importance of community.

Nevertheless, the sort of community that should be valued in a pluralistic society is one that can persist in the face of deep disagreements between its members. A conception of this sort of community arises from the Confucian tradition. Consider Antonio Cua's interpretation of the Confucian virtue of *jen*. This virtue, he says, involves an attitude toward human conflicts as subjects of arbitration rather than adjudication. Arbitration is an attempted resolution of disputes oriented toward the reconciliation of the contending parties.[31] According to Cua, the arbitrator is "concerned with repairing the rupture of human relationship rather than with deciding the rights or wrongs of the parties," and, accordingly, attempts to shape "the expectations of the contending parties along the line of mutual concern, to get them to appreciate one another as interacting members in a community."[32] Under Confucianism, says Cua, an appeal to objective principles that specify rights and wrongs is likely to alienate people from one another, instead of encouraging them to maintain or develop relationships. I depart from Cua in that I find the value of adjudication to be in Confucianism; I agree with him, however, that arbitration is also present as a value.

Arbitration should be present. Living with others in productive ways, despite our moral differences with them, is itself morally valuable. Cooperation in the face of differences can be a particularly strong form of respect for persons, and being able to show this kind of respect is a sign of moral maturity. The willingness to live with others despite moral differences promotes cooperation on the moral ends that are shared. To return to the problem of the tension between community and diversity, the suggestion is that we must promote community, but of the sort that can accommodate differences both within itself and with other communities.[33]

I want to suggest again that the Confucian emphasis on *li* may be relevant. This suggestion might seem surprising. To advocate the use of *li* would seem to amount to promoting the shared set of values that rules for appropriate behavior embody. Yet consider the aspect of *li* that could be rendered by the English term 'civility'. This term connotes a kind of respect and regard accorded to others that can survive the existence of serious disagreement with them. Civility enables constructive discussion and cooperation in the face of disagreement. Civility has fared poorly in our society, resulting in a public discourse that is increasingly mean spirited and pathologically divisive.[34]

In terms of the philosophical anthropology sketched earlier, *li* has a transformative, directing function. It reinforces certain impulses and desires and makes them more determinate and action guiding. It serves to instill habits that form the marrow and bone of our interactions with others. It also has a specifying function: spelling out in concrete terms what it is to properly express respect toward others. If we keep these general functions in mind, we can see a use for *li* in a democratic, pluralistic society.

One application of this idea is relevant to the debate over newly emerging norms on university and college campuses concerning politically correct language. Such norms prohibit not only explicitly racist, sexist, or homophobic language but also language and symbols that evoke painful, offending, and humiliating memories of the history, both past and current, of oppression and persecution. The debate over these norms involves difficult issues about the legitimate constraints on speech, but arguments against these norms often construe them as nothing more than attempts to enforce the left-wing political orthodoxy of certain professors. Such arguments reflect an alarming lack of awareness of what is lost when free speech is taken as an absolute, eliminating sanctions of any kind against those unheedful of the ways their words can offend or wound. What is lost is exactly the civility that promotes and sustains communities that can accommodate serious disagreements.

So far I have talked about the democratic *li* that may govern the habits of speech, but how we govern the way we talk with each other also shapes the way we think about what others have to say to us. It is now a commonplace in elementary and high schools to espouse the values of critical thinking, dissent, and independence of thought. If these values are to be effectively realized, however, they must be embodied in concrete norms by which teachers create a favorable climate for students to express themselves, to disagree with their teachers and others, and to make meaningful and intelligent choices in determining what and how they learn. Students further need to be given ways of expressing and of symbolizing how there can be community with those who are in deep disagreement with them. It also strikes me that we educators have done a poor job in thinking about what it might concretely mean for students to truly listen, not only to us, but to each other in discussion. We need to think, for example, about whom we praise and for what, about our *li* in these matters and whether we ought not to revise it. Do we tend to reserve our highest praise for virtuoso performances in which students are able to effectively destroy the positions of others or for interactions that manifest the attitude that others may have some basis for their beliefs and a willingness to revise one's own positions in the light of a deeper understanding of that basis? These habits of listening and responding to others, encouraged by *li*, would have to be at the very center of an ongoing community capable of accommodating differences.

To conclude, it perhaps should not be surprising that I, an educator, should find it most natural to give examples of the possibilities and problems for community in education, but such an emphasis on educational communities is not just personal or parochial. Schools, colleges, and universities have at least the potential to enter into the identities of their members, yet their mission is to direct the moral concerns of their members beyond their own boundaries. We who are members of such communities have the good fortune to be charged with something important to do, but so far we have not thought well enough about how to do it.

Notes

1. As Jennifer Hochschild has observed, "Fewer Americans of all races and classes are holding jobs, getting or staying married when they have children, abstaining from illegal drugs." See "The Politics of the Estranged Poor," *Ethics* 101 (1991): 568.

2. Michael Sandel, *Liberalism and the Limits of Justice* (Cambridge: Cambridge University Press, 1982), 143.

3. Sometimes communitarians neglect these questions of moral psychology in favor of giving metaphysical arguments against liberalism, to the effect that it presupposes some gravely erroneous metaphysical conception of the self, an atomistic self shorn of all social characteristics and ties. I believe, though shall not argue for it here, that such accusations are difficult to

sustain against sophisticated and metaphysically noncommittal theories of liberalism such as that of John Rawls. See his *A Theory of Justice* (Cambridge: Harvard University Press, 1971). For a discussion of this issue, see Wong, "Flourishing and Finding One's Identity in Community," in Peter A. French, Theodore E. Uehling, Jr., and Howard K. Wettstein, eds., *Ethical Theory: Character and Virtue* (Notre Dame, Ind.: University of Notre Dame Press, 1988), 324–41.

4. For MacIntyre, see his *After Virtue* (Notre Dame, Ind.: University of Notre Dame Press, 1984) and *Whose Justice? Which Rationality?* (Notre Dame, Ind.: University of Notre Dame Press, 1988); for Walzer, see *Interpretation and Social Criticism* (Cambridge: Harvard University Press, 1987).

5. Translation based on D. C. Lau, *The Analects* (Harmondsworth, Middlesex, England: Penguin, 1979), 112.

6. Shun, Kwong-loi, *"Jen and Li in the Analects,"* presently in manuscript form.

7. This term is from Shun, *"Jen and Li in the Analects."*

8. Translation taken from Lau, 96.

9. Clifford Geertz, "Ideology as a Cultural System," in *The Interpretation of Cultures* (New York: Basic Books, 1973), 217–18.

10. Geertz, "The Impact of the Concept of Culture on the Concept of Man," in *The Interpretation of Cultures*, 49–51.

11. For a discussion of how the Confucian philosophical anthropology operates in Meng-tzu's theory of reasons for action, see my "Is There a Distinction between Reason and Emotion in Mencius [Meng-tzu]?" and a reply to a commentary by Craig Ihara, *Philosophy East & West* 41 (1991): 31–44, 55–58.

12. Herbert Fingarette, *Confucius: The Secular as Sacred* (New York: Harper, 1972).

13. See, for example, his *Humanity and Self-Cultivation: Essays in Confucian Thought* (Berkeley: Asian Humanities Press, 1979), especially chapters 1 and 2.

14. Indeed, a recent interpretation of *yi* likens Confucius's philosophy to the French existentialism of Jean-Paul Sartre and to American pragmatism. David Hall and Roger Ames interpret *yi* as implying a creative act whereby the exemplary person confers a personal meaning on *li* in application to his or her present and unique circumstances. Their interpretation of the creative act makes it less a matter of *judging* what is appropriate to circumstance and self, and more a matter of *deciding*. See *Thinking through Confucius* (Albany: State University of New York Press, 1987), 78–79. While I think Hall and Ames overemphasize the purely volitional element in their interpretation of *yi*, they do fasten on a genuine element of Confucian philosophy that allows a considerable degree of novelty to enter into the application of *li*.

15. Maxine Hong Kingston, *The Woman Warrior: Memoirs of a Girlhood among Ghosts* (New York: Alfred A. Knopf, 1976).

16. See, for example, Frank Chin, "Come All Ye Asian American Writers of the Real and the Fake," in Jeffery Paul Chan, Frank Chin, Lawson Fusao

Inada, and Shawn Wong, eds., *The Big Aiiieeeee!* (New York: Penguin, 1991), 1–93.

17. Chan, et al., 45.

18. Michael Oakeshott, "The Tower of Babel," in Stanley G. Clarke and Evan Simpson, eds., *Anti-Theory in Ethics and Moral Conservatism* (Albany, New York: State University of New York Press, 1989), 187.

19. Oakeshott, 188.

20. Oakeshott, 187–88.

21. Oakeshott, 192.

22. Oakeshott, 198.

23. Lawrence Kohlberg, *The Philosophy of Moral Development* (San Francisco: Harper and Row, 1981).

24. See the previously cited "On Flourishing and Finding One's Identity in Community" and also "Universalism versus Love with Distinctions: An Ancient Debate Revived," *Journal of Chinese Philosophy* 16 (1989): 252–72, for further discussion of the reasons why such moral growth must typically begin in the family.

25. Charles Cooley, Robert C. Angell, and Lowell J. Carr, *Introductory Sociology* (New York: 1933), 55–56, quoted in the introduction by Charles P. Loomis and John C. McKinney to Ferdinand Tonnies, *Community and Society (Gemeinschaft und Gesellschaft)* (New Brunswick, N.J.: Transaction, 1988), 14–15.

26. Edward Shils, "The Study of the Primary Group," in Daniel Lerner and Harold D. Lasswell, eds., *The Policy Sciences: Recent Developments in Scope and Method* (Stanford: Stanford University Press, 1951), 64.

27. Shils, 67.

28. See William de Bary, *The Trouble with Confucianism* (Cambridge: Harvard University Press, 1991), 96–97; 101–3.

29. See my "Coping with Moral Conflict and Ambiguity," *Ethics* (July 1992): 763–84, for the argument that fundamental moral disagreement is more pervasive and more a regular feature of life in communities that we normally count as moral communities sharing the same beliefs.

30. See Alasdair MacIntyre, *After Virtue* (Notre Dame, Ind.: University of Notre Dame Press, 1984), and *Whose Justice? Which Rationality?* (Notre Dame, Ind.: University of Notre Dame Press, 1988).

31. Thomas Seung has pointed out to me that the word 'arbitration' may be a misleading label for the sort of process Cua has in mind, since it usually implies the intervention of a third party. Perhaps 'negotiation' is a better term that allows for a reconciliation that can be effected by the contending parties themselves.

32. "The Status of Principles in Confucian Ethics," *Journal of Chinese Philosophy* 16 (1989): 281.

33. An extended discussion of the moral value of accommodation, its rationale, and its application is in my "Coping with Moral Conflict and Ambiguity."

34. De Bary notes that Confucianism is now revived as a subject of socio-logical study or as a moral philosophy. There are supporters for two of the three values that Confucius identifies with the noble person in the *Analects*: *jen* and letters (or scholarship), but de Bary notes, rites seem to have no advocates in the modern world. While this may indicate something about the viability of Confucianism, de Bary concludes, it may also tell us something about what is most lacking in the modern world: social forms and institu-tions supportive of both civility and civilization. See *The Trouble with Con-fucianism*, 45.

Part II

Family

3

Philosophers against the Family

Christina Hoff Sommers

Much of what commonly counts as personal morality is measured by how well we behave within family relationships. We live our moral lives as son or daughter to this mother and that father, as brother or sister to this sister or that brother, as father or mother, grandfather or granddaughter to this boy or that girl or that man or woman. These relationships and the moral duties they define were once popular topics of moral casuistry; but when we turn to the literature of recent moral philosophy, we find little discussion of what it means to be a good son or daughter, a good mother or father, a good husband or wife, a good brother or sister.

Modern ethical theory concentrates on more general topics. Perhaps the majority of us who involve ourselves with ethics accept some version of Kantianism or utilitarianism, yet these mainstream doctrines are better designed for telling us about what we should do as persons in general than about our special duties as parents or children or siblings. We believe, perhaps, that such universal theories can account fully for the morality of special relations. In any case, modern ethics is singularly silent on the bread-and-butter issues of personal morality in everyday life. However, silence is only part of the problem. With the exception of marriage itself, family relationships are a biological given. The contemporary philosopher is, on the whole, actively unsympathetic to the idea that we have any duties defined by relationships into which we have not entered voluntarily. We do not, after all, choose our parents or siblings, and even if we do choose to have children, this is not the same as choos-

41

ing, say, our friends. Because the special relationships that constitute the family as a social arrangement are, in this sense, not voluntarily assumed, many moralists feel bound in principle to dismiss
them altogether. The practical result is that philosophers are found
among those who are contributing to an ongoing disintegration of
the traditional family. In what follows I shall expose some of the
philosophical roots of the current hostility to family morality. My
view that the ethical theses underlying this hostility are bad philosophy will be made evident throughout the discussion.

The Moral Vantage

Social criticism is a heady pastime to which philosophers are pro-
fessionally addicted. One approach, Aristotelian in method and tem-
perament, is antiradical, though it may be liberal, and approaches
the task of needed reform with a prima facie respect for the norms
of established morality. It is conservationist and cautious in its recommendations for change. It is, therefore, not given to such proposals as abolishing the family or abolishing private property and,
indeed, does not look kindly on such proposals from other philosophers. The antiradicals I am concerned about are not those who
would be called Burkean. I shall call them liberal, but this use of
"liberal" is somewhat perverse since, in my stipulative use of the
term, a liberal is a philosopher who advocates social reform but
always in a conservative spirit. My liberals share with Aristotle the
conviction that the traditional arrangements have great moral weight
and that common opinion is a primary source of moral truth. A good
modern example is Henry Sidgwick with his constant appeal to
common sense, but philosophers such as John Stuart Mill, William
James, and Bertrand Russell also can be cited. On the other hand,
because no radical can be called a liberal in my sense, many so-
called liberals could be excluded perversely. Thus when John Rawls
toys with the possibility of abolishing the family because kinship
bias is a force inimical to equality of opportunity, he is no liberal.

The more exciting genre of social criticism is not liberal-Aristo-
telian but radical and Platonist in spirit. Its vantage is external or
even supernal to the social institutions it has placed under moral
scrutiny. Plato was as aware as anyone could be that what he called
the cave was social reality. One reason for calling it a cave was to
emphasize the need as he saw it for an external objective perspective on established morality. Another consideration in calling it a

cave was his conviction that common opinion was benighted and that reform could not be accomplished except by substantial consciousness raising and enlightened social engineering. Plato's supernal vantage made it possible for him to look on social reality in somewhat the way the Army Corps of Engineers looks on a river that must have its course changed and its waywardness tamed. In our own day much social criticism of a Marxist variety has taken this radical approach to social change, and, of course, much contemporary feminist philosophy is radical.

Some philosophers are easily classifiable as radical or liberal. John Locke is clearly a liberal, Leon Trotsky is clearly a radical. I remarked a moment ago that there is a radical strain in Rawls, but it is a strain only: Rawls's attitude to social reality is not finally condescending. On the other hand, much contemporary social criticism is radical in temper. In particular, I shall suggest that the prevailing attitude toward the family is radical and not liberal, and the inability of mainstream ethical theory to come to grips with the special obligations that family members bear to one another contributes to the current disregard of the commonsense morality of the family cave. We find, indeed, that family obligations are criticized and discounted precisely because they do not fit the standard theories of obligation. If I am right, contemporary ethics is at a loss when it comes to dealing with parochial morality; but few have acknowledged this as a defect to be repaired. Instead the common reaction has been: if the family does not fit my model of autonomy, rights, or obligations, then so much the worse for the family.

To illustrate this, I cite without comment four recent views on some aspects of family morality.

1. Michael Slote[1] maintains that any child capable of supporting itself is "morally free to opt out of the family situation." To those who say that the child should be expected to help his needy parents for a year or two out of reciprocity or fair play, Slote responds:

> The duty of fair play presumably exists only where past benefits are voluntarily accepted . . . and we can hardly suppose that a child has voluntarily accepted his role in family . . . life.[2]

2. Virginia Held[3] wants traditional family roles to be abolished and she recommends that husbands and wives think of themselves as roommates of the same sex in assigning household and parental

tasks. (She calls this the "Roommate Test.") To the objection that such a restructuring might injure family life, she replies that similar objections were made when factory workers demanded overtime pay.

3. The late Jane English[4] defended the view that adult children owe their parents no more than they owe their good friends. "[A]fter friendship ends, the duties of friendship end." John Simmons[5] and Jeffrey Blustein[6] also look with suspicion on the idea that there is a debt of gratitude to the parents for what, in any case, they were duty bound to do.

4. Where Slote argues for the older child's right to leave, Howard Cohen[7] argues for granting that right to young children who still need parental care. He proposes that every child be assigned a "trusted advisor" or agent. If the child wants to leave his parents, his agent will be charged with finding alternative caretakers for him.

The philosophers I have cited are not atypical in their dismissive attitude to commonsense morality or in their readiness to replace the parochial norms of the family cave with practices that would better approximate the ideals of human rights and equality. A theory of rights and obligations that applies generally to moral agents is, in this way, applied to the family with the predictable results that the family system of special relations and noncontractual special obligations is judged to be grossly unfair to its members.

Feminism and the Family

I have said that the morality of the family has been relatively neglected. The glaring exception to this is, of course, the feminist movement. Although the movement is complex, I am confined primarily to its moral philosophers, of whom the most influential is Simone de Beauvoir. For de Beauvoir, a social arrangement that does not allow all its participants full autonomy is to be condemned. De Beauvoir criticizes the family as an unacceptable arrangement since, for women, marriage and childbearing are essentially incompatible with their subjectivity and freedom.

> The tragedy of marriage is not that it fails to assure woman the promised happiness . . . but that it mutilates her; it dooms her to repetition

and routine. . . . At twenty or thereabouts mistress of a home, bound permanently to a man, a child in her arms, she stands with her life virtually finished forever.[8]

For de Beauvoir the tragedy goes deeper than marriage. The loss of subjectivity is unavoidable as long as human reproduction requires the woman's womb. De Beauvoir starkly describes the pregnant woman who ought to be a "free individual" as a "stockpile of colloids, an incubator, an egg."[9] As recently as 1977 she compared childbearing and nurturing to slavery.[10]

It would be a mistake to say that de Beauvoir's criticism of the family is outside the mainstream of Anglo-American philosophy. Her criterion of moral adequacy may be formulated in continental existentialist terms, but its central contention is generally accepted: who would deny that an arrangement that systematically thwarts the freedom and autonomy of the individual is *eo ipso* defective? What is perhaps a bit odd to Anglo-American ears is that de Beauvoir makes such scant appeal to ideals of fairness and equality. For her, it is the loss of autonomy that is decisive.

De Beauvoir is more pessimistic than most feminists she has influenced about the prospects for technological and social solutions, but implicit in her critique is the ideal of a society in which sexual differences are minimal or nonexistent. This ideal is shared by many contemporary feminist philosophers. The views of Richard Wasserstrom, Ann Ferguson, Carol Gould, and Alison Jaggar are representative.

Wasserstrom's approach to social criticism is Platonist in its hypothetical use of a good society. The ideal society is nonsexist and "assimilationist."[11] Social reality is scrutinized for its approximation to this ideal and criticism is directed against all existing norms. Take the custom of having sexually segregated bathrooms: whether this is right or wrong "depends on what the good society would look like in respect to sexual differentiation." The key question in evaluating any law or arrangement in which sex difference figures is: "What would the good or just society make of (it)?"[12]

Thus the supernal light shines on the cave, revealing its moral defects. There, in the ideal society, gender in the choice of lover or spouse would be of no more significance than eye color. There the family would consist of adults but not necessarily of different sexes and not necessarily in pairs. There we find equality ensured by a kind of affirmative action that compensates for disabilities. If women are somewhat weaker than men, or if they are subject to lunar disabilities, then this must be compensated for. (Wasserstrom compares women to persons with congenital defects for whom the good society makes special arrangements.) Such male-dominated sports as wrestling and football will be eliminated, and marriage, as we know it, will not exist. "Bisexuality, not heterosexuality or homosexuality, would be the typical intimate, sexual relationship in the ideal society that was assimilationist in respect to sex."[13]

Other feminist philosophers are equally confident about the need for sweeping change. Ann Ferguson wants a "radical reorganization of child rearing." She recommends communal living and a deemphasis on biological parenting. In the ideal society "[l]ove relationships and the sexual relationships developing out of them would be based on the individual meshing-together of androgynous human beings."[14] Carol Gould argues for androgyny and for abolishing legal marriage. She favors single parenting, coparenting, and communal parenting. The only arrangement she opposes emphatically is the traditional one where the mother provides primary care for the children.[15] Alison Jaggar, arguing for a "socialist feminism," wants a society that is both classless and genderless. She looks to the day of a possible transformation of such biological functions as insemination, lactation, and gestation "so that one woman could inseminate another . . . and . . . fertilized ova could be transplanted into women's or even men's bodies." This idea is partly illustrated in a science fiction story that Jaggar praises in which "neither sex bears children but both sexes through hormone treatments suckle them. . . ."[16] To those of us who find this bizarre, Jaggar replies that this betrays the depth of our prejudice in favor of the "natural" family.

Though they differ in detail, the radical feminists hold to a common social ideal that is broadly assimilationist in character and inimical to the traditional family. Sometimes it seems as if the radical feminist simply takes the classical Marxist eschatology of the *Communist Manifesto* and substitutes "gender" for "class." Indeed, the feminist and the old-fashioned Marxist do have much in common. Both see their caves as politically divided into two warring factions: one oppressing, the other oppressed. Both see the need of raising the consciousness of the oppressed group to its predicament and to the possibility of removing its shackles. Both look forward to the day of a classless or genderless society. Both deny the value and naturalness of tradition. Both believe that people and the institutions they inhabit are as malleable as clay, and both groups are zealots, paying little attention to the tragic personal costs to be paid for the revolution they wish to bring about. The feminists tell us little about that side of things. To begin with, how will the benighted myriads in the cave who do not wish to "mesh together" with other androgynous beings be reeducated? How are children to be brought up in the genderless society? Plato took great pains to explain his methods; would the new methods be as thoroughgoing? Unless these questions can be given plausible answers, the supernal attack on the family must always be irresponsible. The appeal to the just society justifies nothing until it can be shown that the radical proposals do not have monstrous consequences. That has not been shown. Indeed, given the perennially dubious state of the social sciences, it is precisely what cannot be shown.

Any social arrangement that falls short of the assimilationist ideal is labeled sexist. It should be noted that this characteristically feminist use of the term sexist differs significantly from its popular or literal sense. Literally, and popularly, sexism connotes unfair discrimination, but in its extended philosophical use it connotes discrimination, period. Wasserstrom and many feminists trade on the popular pejorative connotations of sexism when they invite us to be antisexist. Most liberals are antisexist in the popular sense, but to be antisexist in the technical, radical philosophical sense is not merely to be opposed to discrimination against women; it is to be for what Wasserstrom calls the assimilationist ideal. The antisexist philosopher opposes any social policy that is nonandrogynous, objecting, for example, to legislation that allows for maternity leave. As Alison Jaggar remarks: "We do not, after all, elevate 'prostate leave' into a special right of men."[17] From being liberally opposed to sexism, one may in this way be led insensibly to a radical critique of the family, a critique whose ideal is assimilationist and androgynous, because it is very clear that the realization of the androgynous ideal is incompatible with the survival of the family as we know it.

The neological extension of such labels as sexism, slavery, and prostitution is a feature of radical discourse. The liberal too sometimes calls for radical solutions to social problems. Some institutions are essentially unjust. To reform slavery or a totalitarian system of government is to eliminate it. Radicals trade on these extreme practices in characterizing other practices. They may, for example, characterize low wages as slave wages and the workers who are paid them as slave laborers. Taking these descriptions seriously may start one on the way to treating a free-labor market system as a slave system that, in simple justice, must be overthrown and replaced by an alternative system of production. The radical feminist typically explains that, existentially, women, being treated by men as sex objects, are especially prone to bad faith and false consciousness. Marxist feminists see them as part of an unawakened and oppressed economic class. Clearly, we cannot call on a deluded woman to cast off her bonds before we have made her aware of her bondage. So the first task of freeing the slave woman is dispelling the thrall of a false and deceptive consciousness. One must raise her consciousness to the reality of her situation. (Some feminists acknowledge that it may in fact be too late for many of the women who have fallen too far into the delusions of marriage and motherhood, but the educative process can save many from falling into the marriage and baby trap.)

In this sort of rhetorical climate nothing is what it seems. Prostitution is another term that has been subjected to a radical enlargement. Alison Jaggar believes that a feminist interpretation of the term prostitution is badly needed and asks for a "philosophical theory of prostitution." Observing that the average woman dresses for men, marries a man for protection, and so forth, she says: "For contemporary radical feminists, prostitution is the archetypal relationship of women to men."[18]

Of course, the housewife Jaggar has in mind might be offended at the suggestion that she is a prostitute, albeit less well paid and less aware of it than the professional street prostitute. To this the radical feminist reply is (quoting Jaggar):

> [I]ndividuals' intentions do not necessarily indicate the true nature of what is going on. Both men and women might be outraged at the description of their candlelit dinner as prostitution but the radical feminist argues this outrage is due simply to the participants' failure or refusal to perceive the social context in which their dinner date occurs.[19]

Apparently, this failure or refusal to perceive affects most women. Thus we may even suppose that the majority of women who have been treated to a candlelit dinner by a man prefer it to other dining alternatives they have experienced. To say that these preferences are misguided is a hard and condescending doctrine. It would seem that most feminist philosophers are not overly impressed with

Mill's principle that there can be no appeal from a majority verdict of those who have experienced two alternatives.

The dismissive feminist attitude to the widespread preferences of women takes its human toll. Most women, for example, prefer to have children and those who have them rarely regret having them. It is no more than sensible from a utilitarian standpoint to take note of such widespread preferences and to take it seriously in planning one's own life. A significant number of women, however, discount this general verdict as benighted, taking more seriously the idea that the reported joys of motherhood are exaggerated and fleeting, if not altogether illusory. These women tell themselves and others that having babies is a trap to be avoided, but for many women child-lessness has become a trap of its own, somewhat lonelier than the more conventional traps of marriage and babies. Some come to find their childlessness regrettable; this sort of regret is common to those who flout Mill's reasonable maxim by putting the verdict of ideol-ogy over the verdict of human experience.

Feminists against Femininity

It is a serious defect of American feminism that it concentrates its zeal on impugning femininity and feminine culture at the expense of the grass-roots fight against economic and social injustices to which women are subjected. As we have seen, the radical feminist attitude to the woman who enjoys her femininity is condescending or even contemptuous. Indeed, the contempt for femininity reminds one of misogynist biases in such philosophers as Kant, Rousseau, and Schopenhauer, who believed that femininity was charming but incompatible with full personhood and reasonableness. The femi-nists deny the charm, but they too accept the verdict that feminin-ity is weakness. It goes without saying that an essential connection between femininity and powerlessness has not been established by either party.

By denigrating conventional feminine roles and holding to an assimilationist ideal in social policy, the feminist movement has lost its natural constituency. The actual concerns, beliefs, and aspirations of the majority of women are not taken seriously except as illustra-tions of bad faith, false consciousness, and successful brainwash-ing. What women actually want is discounted and reinterpreted as to what they (have been led to) think they want (a man, children).

What most women enjoy (male gallantry, candlelit dinners, sexy clothes, makeup) is treated as an obscenity (prostitution).

As the British feminist, Janet Radcliffe Richards, says:

> Most women still dream about beauty, dress, weddings, dashing lovers, domesticity and babies . . . but if feminists seem (as they do) to want to eliminate nearly all of these things—beauty, sex conventions, families and all—for most people that simply means the removal of everything in life which is worth living for.[20]

Radical feminism creates a false dichotomy between sexism and assimilation, as if there were nothing in between. This view ignores completely the middle ground in which a woman can be free of oppression and nevertheless feminine in the sense abhorred by many feminists. Women are simply not waiting to be freed from the particular chains that the radical feminists are trying to sunder. The average woman enjoys her femininity. She wants a man, not a roommate. She wants children and the time to care for them. When she enters the work force, she wants fair opportunity and equal treatment. These are the goals that women actually have, and they are not easily attainable, but they will never be furthered by an elitist radical movement that views the actual aspirations of women as the product of a false consciousness. There is room for a liberal feminism that would work for reforms that would give women equal opportunity in the work place and in politics, but would leave unimpugned the basic institutions that women want and support, that is, marriage and motherhood. Such a feminism is already in operation in some European countries, but it has been obstructed here in the United States by the ideologues who now hold the seat of power in the feminist movement.[21]

In characterizing and criticizing American feminism, I have not taken into account the latest revisions and qualifications of a lively and variegated movement. There is a kind of Feminism of the Week that one cannot hope to keep abreast of short of divorcing all other concerns. The best one can do for present purposes is attend to central theses and arguments that bear on the feminist treatment of the family. Nevertheless, even for this limited purpose it would be wrong to omit discussion of an important turn taken by feminism in the past few years. I have in mind the recent literature on the theme that there is a specific female ethic that differs from the male ethic in being more concrete, less rule oriented, more empathic and caring, and more attentive to the demands of a particular context.[22]

The kind of feminism that accepts the idea that women differ from men in approaching ethical dilemmas and social problems from a care perspective is not oriented to androgyny as a positive ideal. Rather, it seeks to develop a special female ethic and to give it greater practical scope.

The stress on context might lead one to think that these feminists are more sympathetic to the family as the social arrangement that shapes the moral development of women since the family is the context for many of the moral dilemmas that women actually face. One sees as yet, however, no attention being paid to the fact that feminism itself is a force working against the preservation of the family. Psychologists such as Carol Gilligan and philosophers such as Lawrence Blum concentrate their attention on the moral quality of the caring relationships, yet these relationships themselves are not viewed in their concrete embedment in any formal social or institutional arrangement.

It should also be said that some feminists are moving away from the earlier hostility to motherhood.[23] Here, too, one sees the weakening of the positive assimilationist ideal in the acknowledgment of a primary gender role, but child rearing is not seen primarily within the context of the family, but as a special relationship between mother and daughter or (more awkwardly) between mother and son, a relationship that effectively excludes the male parent. The new celebration of motherhood remains largely hostile to traditional familial arrangements.

It is too early to say whether a new style of nonassimilationist feminism will lead to a mitigation of the feminist assault on the family or even on femininity. In any case, the recognition of a female ethic of care and responsibility is hardly inconsistent with a social ethic that values the family as a vital (perhaps indispensable) institution, and the recognition that women have their own moral style may well be followed by a more accepting attitude toward the kind of femininity that some feminists currently reject. One may even hope to see the holier-than-thou aspects of feminism fade into a relaxed recognition that both sexes have their distinctive graces and virtues. Such a feminism would not be radical but liberal.

The Indirect Attack

The philosophers I now discuss do not criticize the family directly; in some cases they do not even mention the family. Each one, however, holds a view that subverts, ignores, or denies the special moral relations that characterize the family and are responsible for its functioning. If they are right, family morality is a vacuous subject.

Judith Thomson maintains that an abortion may be permissible even if the fetus is deemed a person from the moment of conception,[24] because in that case being pregnant would be like having an adult surgically attached to one's body. It is arguable that if one finds oneself attached to another person, one has the right to free oneself even if such freedom is obtained at the price of the other person's death by, say, kidney failure. For purposes of this discussion, I refer to the fetus as a prenatal child. I myself do not think the fetus is a person from the moment of conception, nor does Thomson, but here we are interested in her argument for the proposition that abortion of a prenatal child/person should be permissible.

Many have been repelled by Thomson's comparison of pregnancy to arbitrary attachment. Thomson herself is well aware that the comparison may be bizarre. She says:

> It may be said that what is important is not merely the fact that the fetus is a person, but that it is a person for whom the woman has a special kind of responsibility issuing from the fact that she is its mother.[25]

To this Thomson replies: "Surely we do not have any such 'special responsibility' for a person unless we have assumed it explicitly or implicitly." If the mother does not try to prevent pregnancy, does not obtain an abortion, but instead gives birth to the child and takes it home with her, then, at least implicitly, she has assumed responsibility for it.

One might object that although pregnancy is a state into which many women do not enter voluntarily, it is nevertheless a state in which one has some responsibility to care for the prenatal child. Many pregnant women do feel such a prenatal responsibility and take measures to ensure the prenatal child's survival and future health, but here one must be grateful to Professor Thomson for her clarity. A mother who has not sought pregnancy deliberately bears no special responsibility to her prenatal child because she has neither implicitly nor explicitly taken on the responsibility of caring for it. For example, the act of taking the infant home from the hospital implies voluntary acceptance of such responsibility. By choosing to take it with her, the mother undertakes to care for the infant and no longer has the right to free herself of the burden of motherhood at the cost of the child's life.

The assumption, then, is that there are no noncontractual obligations or special duties defined by the kinship of mother to child. As for social expectations, none are legitimate in the morally binding sense unless they are underpinned by an implicit or explicit contract freely entered into. If this assumption is correct, sociological arrangements and norms have no moral force unless the moral agent who is bound by them voluntarily accepts them. I call this the volunteer theory of moral obligation. It is a thesis that is so widely accepted today that Thomson saw no need to argue for it.

Michael Tooley's arguments in defense of infanticide provide another solid example of how a contemporary philosopher sidetracks and ultimately subverts the special relations that bind the family.[26] Tooley holds that being sentient confers the prima facie right not to be treated cruelly and that possession of those characteristics that make one a person confers the additional right to life. Tooley then argues that infants lack these characteristics and so may be painlessly killed. In reaching this conclusion, Tooley's sole consideration is whether the infant intrinsically possesses the relevant right-to-life-making characteristic of personality—a consideration that abstracts from any right to care and protection that the infant's relation to its parents confers on it causally and institutionally. For Tooley, as for Thomson, the relations of family or motherhood are morally irrelevant, so it is perhaps not surprising that one finds nothing in the index under "family," "mother," or "father" in Tooley's book on abortion and infanticide.

Howard Cohen is concerned strictly with the rights of persons irrespective of the special relations they may bear to others.[27] Just as Thomson holds that the mother's right to the free unencumbered use of her body is not qualified by any special obligations to her child, so Cohen holds that the child's right to a no-fault divorce from its parents cannot be diminished because of the special relation it bears to them. Where Thomson is concerned with the overriding right of the mother, Cohen is concerned with the right of the child. Yet, including Tooley, all three philosophers agree that the right of a child is not less strong than the right of any adult. Indeed, Thomson compares the unborn child to a fully grown adult and Tooley holds that any person—be it child, adult, or sapient nonhuman—is equal in rights.

Our three philosophers are typical in holding that any moral requirement is either a general duty incumbent on everyone or else a specific obligation voluntarily assumed. Let us call a requirement a 'duty' if it devolves on the moral agents, whether or not they have voluntarily assumed it (it is, for example, a duty to refrain from murder), and let us call a requirement an 'obligation' only if it devolves on certain moral agents but not necessarily on all moral agents. (One is, for example, morally obligated to keep a promise.) According to our three philosophers, all duties are general in the sense of being requirements on all moral agents. Any moral requirement that is specific to a given moral agent must be grounded in his or her voluntary commitment. Thus there is no room for any special requirement on a moral agent that has not been assumed voluntarily by that agent. In other words, *there are no special duties*. This is what I call the volunteer theory of obligation. According to the voluntaristic thesis, all duties are general and only those who volunteer for them have any obligations toward them.

This thesis underlies Cohen's view that the child can divorce its parents, because it is unnecessary to consider whether the child has any special duties to the parents that could conflict with the exercise of its right to leave them. The same thesis underlies Thomson's view that the woman who had not sought pregnancy has no special responsibility to her unborn child and that any such responsibility that she may have later is assumed implicitly by her voluntary act of taking the infant home with her. This thesis also underlies Tooley's psychobiological method for answering the moral question of infanticide by determining the right-making characteristics of personhood: all we need to know about the neonate is whether or not it possesses the psychological characteristics of personhood. If it does, then it has a right to life. If it does not, then it is not a person and thus may be killed painlessly. It is unnecessary to consider the question of whether the child has a special relation to anyone who may have a special responsibility to see to the child's survival.

What I call the volunteer thesis is one that many contemporary Anglo-American philosophers hold confidently. It is easy to see that the thesis is contrary to what Sidgwick called Common Sense, because it means that there is no such thing as filial duty per se, no such thing as the special duty of mother to child, and generally no such thing as a morality of special family or kinship relations, all of which is contrary to what people think. Most people think that we do owe special debts to our parents even though we have not assumed voluntarily our obligations to them. Most people think that what we owe to our own children does not have its origin in any voluntary undertaking, explicit or implicit, that we have made to them. Many people also believe that we owe special consideration to our siblings even at times when we may not feel very friendly to them. If there are no special duties, however, then most of these prima facie requirements are misplaced and without moral force and should be looked on as archaic survivals to be ignored in assessing our moral obligations.

The idea that to be committed to an individual is to have made a voluntarily implicit or explicit commitment to that individual is generally fatal to family morality because it looks on the network of felt obligation and expectation that binds family members as a sociological phenomenon that is without presumptive moral force. The social critics who hold this view of family obligation usually are aware that promoting it in public policy must further the disintegration of the traditional family as an institution, but whether they deplore the disintegration or welcome it, they are bound in principle to abet it.

It may be that so many philosophers have accepted the voluntaristic dogma because of an uncritical use of the model of promises as the paradigm for obligations. If all obligations are like the obligation to keep a promise, then indeed they could not be incumbent on anyone who did not undertake to perform in a specified way. There is no reason, though, to take promises as paradigmatic of obligation. Indeed, the moral force of the norm of promise keeping must itself be grounded in a theory of obligations that moral philosophers have yet to work out.

A better defense of the special duties would require considerably more space than I can give it here.[28] I believe, however, that the defense of special duties is far more plausible than rival theories that reject special duties. My primary objective has been to raise the strong suspicion that the volunteer theory of obligation is a dogma that is very probably wrong and misconceived, a view that is certainly at odds with common opinion.

Once we reject the doctrine that a voluntary act by the person concerned is a necessary condition of special obligation, we are free to respect the commonsense views that attribute moral force to many obligations associated with kinship and other family relationships. We may then accept the family as an institution that defines many special duties but that is nevertheless imperfect in numerous respects. Nevertheless, we still face the choice of how, as social philosophers, we are to deal with these imperfections. That is, we have the choice of being liberal or conservative in our attitude toward reform.

Burkean conservatives would change little or nothing, believing that the historical development of an institution has its own wisdom. They oppose utopian social engineering, considering it altogether immoral in the profound sense of destroying the very foundations of the special duties; but Burkeans also oppose what Karl Popper called "piecemeal social engineering," which seeks to remedy unjust practices without destroying the institution that harbors them.[29] Burkeans believe, on empirical grounds, that reform is always dangerous: that it usually has unforeseen consequences worse than the original injustices sought to be eliminated. Thus, conservatives are much like environmental conservationists in their attitude toward an ecological system: their general advice is extreme caution or hands off.

Liberals are more optimistic about the consequences of reform. Like conservatives, they believe that the norms of any tradition or institution not essentially unjust have prima facie moral force. All of this means that we can rely on our commonsense beliefs that the system of expectations within the family is legitimate and should be respected. The liberal will acknowledge that a brother has the right to expect more help from a brother than from a stranger and not just because of what he has done for him lately. The case is the same for all traditional expectations that characterize family members. On the other hand, there may be practices within the family that are systematically discriminatory and unfair to certain members. Unlike conservatives, liberals are prepared to do some piecemeal social engineering to eliminate injustice in the family.

It should be said that the appeal to common sense or common opinion is not final, because common sense often delivers conflicting verdicts on behavior, but a commonsense verdict is strongly presumptive. For example, there is the common belief that biological mothers have a special responsibility to care for their children, even their unwanted children. One takes this as presumptive evidence of an objective moral responsibility on the part of the mother. Note that the verdict of common sense is not really a verdict at all. Rather, it is evidence of a moral consideration that must enter into the final verdict on what to do and how to behave. Thomson ignores common sense when she asserts that the mother of a child, born or unborn, has no special responsibility to it unless she has in some way voluntarily assumed responsibility for it. Now, to say that a pregnant woman may have a moral responsibility to her unborn child does not entail that abortion is impermissible, because there are other commonsense considerations that enter here and other responsibilities that the mother may have (to her other children, to herself) that may conflict and override the responsibility to the fetus, so common sense is often not decisive. One may say that a commonsense opinion is symptomatic of a prima facie duty or liberty, as the case may be. Yet it still remains for the casuist to determine the weight of the duty in relation to other moral considerations that also may have the support of common sense. Politically and morally, lack of respect for common sense fosters illiberalism and elitism. Here we have the radical temper that often advocates actions and policies wildly at odds with common opinion—from infanticide to male lactation, from no-fault divorce on demand for children to the roommate test for marital relationships.

The Broken Family

In this final section we look at certain of the social consequences of applying radical theory to family obligation. I have suggested that, insofar as moral philosophers have any influence on the course of social history, their influence has recently been in aid of institutional disintegration. I shall now give some indication of how the principled philosophical disrespect for common sense in the area of family morality has weakened the family and how this affects the happiness of its members. Although much of what I say here is fairly well known, it is useful to say it in the context of an essay critical of the radical way of approaching moral philosophy, because there are periods in history when the radical way has great influence, and it is worth seeing what happens when Plato succeeds in Syracuse.

The most dramatic evidence of the progressive weakening of the family is found in the statistics on divorce. Almost all divorce is painful and most divorce affects children. Although divorce does not end, but merely disrupts, the life of a child, the life it disrupts is uncontroversially the life of a person who can be wronged directly by the actions of a moral agent. One might therefore expect that philosophers who examine carefully the morality of abortion also would examine carefully the moral ground for divorce. Here, too, however, the contemporary reluctance of philosophers to deal with the special casuistry of family relations is evidenced. For example, there are more articles on euthanasia or on recombinant DNA research than on divorce.

Each year there are 1,250,000 divorces in the United States affecting more than one million children. The mother is granted custody in ninety percent of the cases, although legally it is no longer a matter of course. There is very persuasive evidence that children of divorced parents are affected seriously and adversely. Compared with children from intact families, they are referred more often to school psychologists, are more likely to have lower IQ and achievement test scores, are arrested more often, and need more remedial classes.[30] Moreover, these effects show little correlation to economic class. Children in the so-called latency period (between six and twelve) are the most seriously affected. In one study of children in this age group, one-half of the subjects showed evidence of a "consolidation into troubled and conflicted depressive behavior patterns." Their behavior patterns included "continuing depression and low self-esteem combined with frequent school and peer difficulties."[31]

One major cause for the difference between children from broken and intact families is the effective loss of the father. In the majority of cases the child has not seen the father within the past year. Only one child in six has seen his or her father in the past week; only sixteen percent have seen their fathers in the past month; fifteen percent see them once a year; and the remaining fifty-two percent have had no contact at all for the past year. Although fifty-seven percent of college-educated fathers see their children at least once a month, their weekly contact is the same as for all other groups (one in six).[32]

It would be difficult to demonstrate that the dismissive attitude of most contemporary moral philosophers to the moral force of kinship ties and conventional family roles has been a serious factor in contributing to the growth in the divorce rate, but that is only because it is so difficult in general to demonstrate how much bread is baked by the dissemination of philosophical ideas. It is surely fair to say that the emphasis on autonomy and equality, when combined with the philosophical denigration of family ties, may have helped to make divorce both easy and respectable, thereby facilitating the rapid change from fault-based to no-fault divorce. If contemporary moralists have not caused the tide of family disintegration, they are avidly riding it. On the other side, it is not difficult to demonstrate that there is very little in recent moral philosophy that could be cited as possibly contributing to stemming the tide.

In the past two decades there has been a celebrated resurgence of interest in applied or practical ethics. It would appear, however, that the new enthusiasm for getting down to normative cases does not extend to topics of personal morality defined by family relationships. Accordingly, the children who are being victimized by the breakdown of the family have not benefited from this. Indeed, we find far more concern about the effect of divorce on children from philosophers a generation or two ago, when divorce was relatively rare, than we find today. Thus, Bertrand Russell writes:

> [H]usband and wife, if they have any love for their children, will so regulate their conduct as to give their children the best chance of a happy and healthy development. This may involve, at times, very considerable self-repression. And it certainly requires that both should realize the superiority of the claims of children to the claims of their own romantic emotions.[33]

And while Russell is not opposed to divorce, he believes that children place great constraints on it: "[P]arents who divorce each other except for grave cause appear to me to be failing their parental duty."[34]

Discerning and sensitive observers of a generation ago did not need masses of statistics to alert them to the effects of divorce on children, nor did it take a professional philosopher (citing statistics gathered by a professional sociologist) to see that acting to dissolve a family must be evaluated morally primarily in terms of what such action means for the children.

Writing in the *London Daily Express* in 1930, Rebecca West says:

> The divorce of married people with children is nearly always an unspeakable calamity. It is only just being understood . . . how much a child depends for its healthy growth on the presence in the home of both its parents. . . . The point is that if a child is deprived of either its father or its mother it feels that it has been cheated out of a right.[35]

West describes the harmful effects of divorce on children as effects of "a radiating kind likely to travel down and down through the generations, such as few would care to have on their consciences."

I have quoted West in some fullness because her remarks contrast sharply with what one typically finds in contemporary college texts. In a book called *Living Issues in Ethics*, the authors discuss unhappy parents and the moral questions they face in contemplating divorce: "We believe that staying together for the sake of the children is worse than the feelings and adjustment of separation and divorce."[36] The authors give what they feel to be a decisive reason for this policy: "Remaining together in an irreconcilable relationship violates the norm of interpersonal love."[37]

One of the very few philosophers to discuss the question of divorce and its consequences for children is Jeffrey Blustein in his book *Parents and Children*. Blustein looks with equanimity on the priority of personal commitment to parental responsibility, pointing out that:

> [t]he traditional view . . . that the central duties of husband and wife are the . . . duties of parenthood is giving way to a conception of marriage as essentially involving a serious commitment between two individuals as individuals.[38]

Blustein also tells us (without telling us how he knows it) that children whose parents are unhappily married are worse off than if their parents were divorced: "Indeed it could be argued that precisely on account of the children the parents' unhappy marriage should be dissolved."[39] The suggestion that parents who are unhappy should get a divorce for the sake of the children is extremely contemporary.

To my knowledge, no reliable study has yet been made that compares children of divorced parents to children from intact families whose parents do not get along well together, so I have no way of knowing whether the claims of these authors are true. Moreover, because any such study would be compromised by certain arbitrary measures of parental incompatibility, one should probably place little reliance on them. It is, therefore, easy to see that contemporary philosophers are anxious to jump to conclusions that do not render implausible the interesting view that the overriding question in considering divorce is the compatibility of the parents and that marital ties should be dissolved when they threaten or thwart the personal fulfillment of one or both of the marital partners.

These philosophers set aside special duties and replace them with an emphasis on friendship, compatibility, and interpersonal love among family members, but, this has a disintegrative effect. That is to say, if what one owes to members of one's family is largely to be understood in terms of feelings of personal commitment, definite limits are placed on what one owes because as feelings change, so may one's commitments. The result is a structure of responsibility within the family that is permanently unstable.

I have, in this final section, illustrated the indifference of contemporary philosophers to the family by dwelling on their indifference to the children affected by divorce. Nevertheless, I hope that it is clear that nothing I have said is meant to convey that I oppose divorce. I do not. Neither Russell nor West nor any of the sane and compassionate liberal thinkers of the recent past opposed divorce. They simply did not play fast and loose with family mores, did not encourage divorce, and pointed out that moralists must insist that the system of family obligations is only partially severed by a divorce that cuts the marital tie. Morally, as well as legally, the obligations to the children remain as before. Legally, this is still recognized. In a moral climate, however, where the system of family obligation is given no more weight than can be justified in terms of popular theories of deontic volunteerism, the obligatory ties are too fragile to survive the personal estrangements that result from divorce. It is, therefore, to be expected that parents (especially fathers) will be off and away doing their own thing—and the law is largely helpless.

I have no special solutions to the tragedy of economic impoverishment and social deprivation that results from the weakening of family ties. I believe in the right of divorce and do not oppose even no-fault divorce. I do not know how to get back to the good old days when moral philosophers had the common sense to acknowledge the moral weight of special ties and the courage to condemn those who failed in them—the days when, in consequence, the climate of moral approval and disapproval was quite different from what it is today. I do not know how to make fathers ashamed of their neglect and inadvertent cruelty. What I do know is that moral philosophers should be paying far more attention to the social consequences of their views than they are. It is as concrete as taking care that what one says will not affect adversely the students whom one is addressing. If what students learn from us encourages social disintegration, then we are responsible for the effects that this may have on their lives and on the lives of their children. This then is a grave responsibility, even graver than the responsibility we take in being for or against something as serious as euthanasia or capital punishment—since most of our students will never face these questions in a practical way.

I believe, then, that responsible moral philosophers are liberal or conservative but not radical. They respect human relationships and traditions and the social environment in which they live as much as they respect the natural environment and its ecology. They respect the family. William James saw the rejection of radicalism as central to the pragmatist way of confronting moral questions.

> [E]xperience has proved that the laws and usages of the land are what yield the maximum of satisfaction. . . . The presumption in cases of conflict must always be in favor of the conventionally recognized good. The philosopher must be a conservative, and in the construction of his casuistic scale must put things most in accordance with the customs of the community on top.[40]

A moral philosophy that does not give proper weight to the customs and opinions of the community is presumptuous in its attitude and pernicious in its consequences. In an important sense it is not a moral philosophy at all, because it is humanly irrelevant.[41]

Notes

1. Michael Slote, "Obedience and Illusions," in Onora O'Neill and William Ruddick, eds., *Having Children* (New York: Oxford, 1979), 320.

2. Slote, 230.

3. Virginia Held, "The Obligations of Mothers and Fathers," in Joyce Trebilcot, ed., *Mothering Essays in Feminist Theory* (Totowa, N.J.: Rowman & Allanheld, 1983), 7–20.

4. Jane English, "What Do Grown Children Owe Their Parents?" in O'Neill and Ruddick, 351–56.

5. A. John Simmons, *Moral Principles and Political Obligation* (Princeton: Princeton University Press, 1979), 162.

6. Jeffrey Blustein, *Parents and Children: The Ethics of the Family* (New York: Oxford, 1982), 182.

7. Howard Cohen, *Equal Rights for Children* (Totowa, N.J.: Rowman & Littlefield, 1980), 66.

8. Simone de Beauvoir, *The Second Sex*, trans. H. M. Parshley (New York: Random House, 1952), 534.

9. De Beauvoir, 553.

10. De Beauvoir, "Talking to De Beauvoir," *Spare Rib* (March 1977), 2.

11. Richard Wasserstrom, *Philosophy and Social Issues* (Notre Dame, Ind.: University of Notre Dame Press, 1980), 26.

12. Wasserstrom, 23.

13. Wasserstrom, 26.

14. Ann Ferguson, "Androgyny as an Ideal for Human Development," in M. Vetterling-Braggin, F. Elliston, and J. English, eds., *Feminism and Philosophy* (Totowa, N.J.: Rowman & Littlefield, 1977), 45–69.

15. Carol Gould, "Private Rights and Public Virtues: Woman, the Family, and Democracy," in Carol Gould, ed., *Beyond Domination* (Totowa, N.J.: Rowman & Allanheld, 1983), 3–18.

16. Alison Jaggar, "Human Biology in Feminist Theory: Sexual Equality Reconsidered," in Gould, 41. Jaggar is serious about the possibility and desirability of what she calls the "transformation of sexuality," which is elaborated in her book *Feminist Politics and Human Nature* (Totowa, N.J.: Rowman & Allanheld, 1983), 132.

17. Alison Jaggar, "On Sex Equality," in Jane English, ed., *Sex Equality* (Englewood Cliffs, N.J.: Prentice-Hall, 1977), 102.

18. Alison Jaggar, "Prostitution," in Marilyn Pearsell, ed., *Women and Values: Reading in Recent Feminist Philosophy* (Belmont, Calif.: Wadsworth, 1986), 108–21.

19. Jaggar, "Prostitution," 117.

20. Janet Radcliffe Richards, *The Skeptical Feminist* (Middlesex, England: Penguin Books, 1980), 341–42.

21. See Sylvia Ann Hewlett, *A Lesser Life: The Myth of Woman's Liberation in America* (New York: William Morrow, 1986).

22. See, for example, Carol Gilligan, *In a Different Voice* (Cambridge: Harvard University Press, 1982); Eva Kittay and Diana Meyers, eds., *Women and Moral Theory* (Totowa, N.J.: Rowman & Littlefield, 1987); Lawrence Blum, *Friendship, Altruism, and Morality* (London: Routledge and Kegan Paul, 1980); Jean Grimshaw, *Philosophy and Feminist Thinking* (Minneapolis: University of Minnesota Press, 1986); Nel Noddings, *Caring: A Feminine Approach to Ethics and Moral Education* (Berkeley, Calif.: University of California Press, 1984).

23. See, for example, Joyce Trebilcot, ed., *Mothering: Essays in Feminist Theory* (Totowa, N.J.: Rowman and Allanheld, 1984).

24. Judith Thomson, "A Defense of Abortion," in *Philosophy and Public Affairs*, vol. 1, no. 1 (1972).

25. Thomson, 64.

26. Michael Tooley, "Abortion and Infanticide," in *Philosophy and Public Affairs*, vol. 2, no. 1 (1972).

27. Howard Cohen, *Equal Rights for Children*, chaps. 5 and 6.

28. For a defense of the special duties not assumed voluntarily, see Christina Sommers, "Filial Morality," *The Journal of Philosophy* 8 (August 1986).

29. Sir Karl Popper, *The Open Society and Its Enemies: Volumes I and II* (Princeton, N.J.: Princeton University Press, 1962).

30. Lenore Weitzman, *The Divorce Revolution: The Unexpected Social and Economic Consequences for Women and Children in America* (New York: The Free Press, 1985).

31. A. Skolnick and J. Skolnick, eds., *Family in Transition* (Boston: Little Brown, 1929), 452.

32. Weitzman, 259.

33. Bertrand Russell, *Marriage and Morals* (New York: Liveright, 1929), 236.

34. Russell, 238.

35. Rebecca West, *London Daily Express*, 1930. This is reprinted in Christina Sommers and Fred Sommers, eds., *Vice and Virtue in Everyday Life: Introductory Readings in Ethics*, 3d. ed. (Fort Worth, Tex.: Harcourt, Brace, Jovanovich, 1993), 777–78.

36. R. Nolan and F. Kirkpatrick, eds., *Living Issues in Ethics* (Belmont, Calif.: Wadsworth, 1983), 147.

37. Nolan and Kirkpatrick, 35.

38. Blustein, 230.

39. Blustein, 232.

40. William James, "The Moral Philosopher and the Moral Life," in James, *Essays in Pragmatism* (New York: Hafner, 1948), 80.

41. This paper is part of a project funded by a National Endowment for the Humanities Fellowship for College Teachers. Earlier versions were read at a conference at the University of Minnesota, "Ethics: The Personal Turn," and at the Philosopher's Forum at Long Island University. I received helpful criticism on both occasions. For the unabridged version of this paper, see Hugh LaFollette and George Graham, eds., *Person to Person* (Philadelphia: Temple University Press, 1989), 82–105.

4

Injustice in Families: Assault and Domination

Sara Ruddick

I begin *in medias res*, in this case in the middle of a conversation among feminists about justice and families. Hitherto, theorists of justice have tended to ignore families or else have contrasted explicitly the private domain of the family with the public world of justice.[1] Feminists have claimed in response that sheltering families from the demands of justice legitimates the exploitation of children by adults and women by men. At the same time, however, some feminists also argue that there are serious incongruities between moral experience in families and dominant (so-called 'liberal') theories of distributive justice.[2] This disparity has provided one motive for developing an alternative ethics of care that seems suited for—indeed, is often inspired by—central relations and moral dilemmas that arise within families.[3]

Whatever the intentions of its proponents, the presence of an ethics of care has tended to reinforce the separation between families and justice for several reasons. At least in the United States, an ethics of care has been explicitly contrasted with an ethics of justice. A long history of separate public and private spheres, as well as recent attempts to develop domain or practice sensitive ethics, makes it easy to construe care as feminine and domestic while justice remains in its traditional public domain. Finally, while certain ethicists have been creatively translating principles of care into public domains and languages,[4] few have revised dominant 'liberal' conceptions of justice in order to make them suitable to the moral experience of families.[5]

There are at least three ways to bring justice more securely into the family. One might assimilate or subordinate the concerns of care to justice and then argue that families should be subject to distributive justice as it is best conceptualized in current theories.[6] Alternatively, one could develop an ethics of care that subordinates but adequately addresses the concerns of justice,[7] or one could maintain the distinction between ethics of justice and of care, without subordinating either to the other, and reconceptualize justice in ways more suitable to the moral experience and relationships of families. It is this third way that I pursue here.[8]

Accordingly, I assume a conceptual framework that distinguishes moral orientations of justice and care. This framework is neither exhaustive nor exclusive but offers one among several ways of thinking about moral phenomena.[9] My reading of the justice/care distinction follows a suggestion of Carol Gilligan's.[10] On this reading, the whole of the moral domain can be likened to an ambiguous figure. Justice and care refer to unassimilable ways of identifying, interpreting, and responding to moral phenomena that can be seen from two perspectives, the way a single figure can be seen alternatively as a duck or rabbit, a vase or two faces. On this view, each moral orientation offers a "point of view from which alone a certain sort of understanding of human life is possible";[11] each is genuinely moral; neither can be replaced by or subsumed under the other; each covers the whole of the moral domain and therefore can check and inform the other; there is no third, mature, single integrative moral perspective within which each orientation has its place.[12]

Characteristics of justice and care, when contrasted with each other, are complex. The two moral orientations foster distinctive cognitive capacities, appeal to distinctive ideals of rationality, elicit distinctive moral emotions, presume distinctive conceptions of identity and relationships, recognize distinctive virtues, and make distinctive requirements on institutions. For the purposes of this discussion, I waive these complexities and, presuming familiarity, draw a simple contrast between requirements of just and caring relationships as a family member might see them.

From the perspective of justice, relationships require restraint of one's own aggression, intrusion, and appropriation and respect for the autonomy and bodily integrity of others. Participants attempt to devise and agree on procedures for resolving fairly inevitable conflicts. A primary temptation, according to the perspective of justice, is to flout the rules of fair play, taking whatever you can get, what you are strong or lucky enough to be able to exact. Correlatively, a person may be tempted (as well as forced) to submit to injustice without protest. She may also be tempted to watch, without protest, when injustice is inflicted on others.

From the perspective of care, relationships require attentiveness to others and response to their needs. Each participant should endeavor to give what can be received usefully and to receive what can be given usefully. A primary temptation, according to the perspective of care, is to neglect others or to project one's own needs on to them. Correlatively, a caring person may be destructively self-sacrificial, unwilling or unable to be the recipient of care, or he may be tempted to watch with indifference when others are neglected or abandoned.

I believe that justice and care, when more appropriately elaborated, usefully mark alternative moral visions, conflicts, virtues, and ways of reasoning. I also believe that the capacity to welcome irreducible differences of perspective, as much as the insight each affords, illuminates moral conflict in both personal and public contexts. If there are two irreducible orientations, individuals can learn to shift between them while discussants can acknowledge that they see the same situation, yet see so differently that they cannot at once understand each others' moral reasoning. Because there are two contrasting perspectives rather than a multiperspectival array, a disruptive and illuminating shift of moral perspective in regard to the same phenomena becomes possible.

In developmental and social psychology the contrast between justice and care has been associated, notoriously, with gender.[13] In developmental theory, it was women listening primarily to women who identified a care perspective. According to these developmental theorists, while most women and men shift appropriately between the two orientations as particular moral circumstances suggest, most also tend to focus on or consistently adopt one rather than the other perspective. While some men adopt a care orientation, most men and many women reflect a justice focus that, at least until recently, was the dominant orientation of public moral discourse in the United States; but few women adopt only a justice perspective and many (perhaps more than a third) reason primarily in the subordinated, marginal, different voice of care. These findings are controversial and continuously modified. Moreover, whatever their current associations with gender, each orientation—according to Çarol Gilligan,

the principal researcher—is rooted in childhood experiences: powerlessness and inequality in the case of justice, attachment and
fruitful interdependence in the case of care.[14] Accordingly, each orientation would normally be employed in any individual's or group's
moral thinking, although particular sociopolitical experiences of
inequality as well as disparate family forms would almost certainly
produce systematic differences among racial, ethnic, national, and
class, as well as gender, groups. Whatever the social or psychological origins of justice or care perspectives, the values of each orientation are (in my view) meant to be binding on women and men.
While care is not better than justice—any more than a duck is better than a rabbit, a face better than a vase—it is disturbing that a
humanly rooted, feminine-identified orientation of care has been
submerged both in public discussion and in the moral reasoning of
many individuals.

Partly because care is associated with femininity and partly because dominant theories of justice seem to bypass much of family
moral life, feminists have sometimes used the justice/care framework to separate the familial from the political. My reading of care
and justice as inassimilable orientations is meant to refuse this division. Justice and care each cover the entire moral domain; any
institution or relation, no matter how public or private, can be judged
from the perspective of justice or of care. This does not mean that
there are no distinctions between more public and private domains
nor some useful distinctions between personal and political, but these
distinctions do not map onto the distinction between justice and care.
Recognizing its origins within particular relationships, moral theorists have worked to extend and politicize the ethics of care. In a
similar spirit, feminists should revise theories of justice originally
devised with public institutions in mind, thus making it easier to
bring justice home.

To this end, I review a conversation among feminists, between
advocates of distributive justice in families and skeptics who believe that dominant theories of distributive justice are not respectful of family relationships and moral experience. I then consider a
particular wrongdoing, family assault, draw connections between
assault and domination, and urge that assault be considered an injustice. Finally, I offer one principle of family justice—respect for
embodied willfulness.

I bypass entirely several critical issues of family justice. I do
not consider the question of who has the right to bear and raise

children.[15] I am concerned primarily with families that already include children and, more generally, generations; the example of injustice I select for focus—family assault—is notoriously suffered by children as well as women, and the elderly are also frequently its victims. Also, I do not consider crucial issues of social or legal intervention in families to protect vulnerable members from failure of care or justice. Rather, I am concerned with justice within families, that is, with ideals of justice that family members might adopt to regulate—and inspire—their relationships with each other.

Finally, I do not take up the difficult question of defining 'families.' I have in mind moderately extended families in which—at the least—some people are identified as children, parents, grandchildren, grandparents, siblings, cousins, and so forth. (Two adults living as partners without children will typically be members of two or more families that will, together, include frail elderly and children.) Biological connections between family relatives is highly variable culturally and among families in a culture. I have no stake in an exclusive definition of 'families' and believe, along with many others, that heterosexist presumptions of family organization work against justice and care even within apparently exclusively heterosexual families.

Family Fairness

When theorists explicitly contrast the private domain of families with the public world in which justice is at stake, they usually offer three kinds of reasons for shielding families from demands of justice.[16]

Family celebrants believe that families are too good for justice. While justice negotiates between competing self-interests, family members share a single interest, the good of the family and each of its members. While outside the family just individuals restrain greed and aggression in the interests of fairness, family members, bound by ties of affection and trust, require no such restraint. There are of course bad families, but they are uncaring, not unjust.

Pessimists argue, by contrast, that families are naturally, irredeemably unjust. To support their conviction that family injustice is entrenched, they point to a disturbing record of abuse and exploitation of women by men and children by parents. The source of this allegedly omnipresent injustice is a radical, incurable inequality among family members. Very young children and the elderly

cannot contribute to the common good and therefore gain no lever-
age by withdrawing services. When they become old enough to
contribute, children remain, for many years, too weak and dependent to retaliate against abuse and therefore must accept whatever
terms of survival they are offered. Healthy women and men are not
incurably unequal. Some pessimists argue, however, that despite
notable individual exceptions, men are by nature too violent or selfish, women by nature too frightened or submissive for either to abide
by fair procedures for distributing the benefits and obligations of
family life.[17]

Finally, some argue that even if family arrangements are often
unfair and could be made fairer, efforts to impose justice are likely
to disrupt family life and harm vulnerable family members. Some
point to the importance of families in organizing resistance to racism, pooling scarce resources, and providing refuge from colonial
and autocratic governments and from heartless bureaucratic rule.
Others plead that families are more fragile than they appear and
that unjust families are better than no family at all. They worry that
the language of competing rights sets child against parent, children
against each other, women against men, generation against generation.

Feminists, and notably among them Susan Moller Okin, have
persuasively replied to each of these charges against family justice.[18]
However affectionate and trusting, individuals in families typically
have competing interests and make conflicting demands on numerous resources including food, shared space, cash, and time for non-
familial projects and pleasures. Rather than making families too
good for justice, the fact that family members are often bound by
ties of affection or depend on each other for meeting basic needs
provides some family members with especially fertile opportunities
for exploitation and domination.

Although injustice abounds in families, it is not inevitable. Families are remarkably variable social creations, some more exploitative of vulnerable members than others. Family distributions of
goods and burdens can be affected by new ways of disseminating
knowledge, contraceptive techniques, employment policies, economic
recession or prosperity, and family law. There is no a priori reason
why family organization cannot be transformed also by moral critique.

It is true that some family members are inevitably unequal to others, but even tiny children can be perceived as future contributors to a family enterprise, as well as potential aggressors against other family members. Reciprocity can be presented to older children as an ideal that governs family life. In circumstances where women can control fertility in their own interests, unfair division of family labors between women and men is clearly remediable. In particular, the fact that only females bear children does not imply that women should assume a special responsibility for childcare or any other disproportionate burden of household labor.

There are many causes of family disruption: natural catastrophe, the death of a family member, unemployment, or insufficient resources for minimally protective family life. When protests of injustice within the family threaten to disrupt family arrangements, then the suffering of disruption may be balanced by relief from the injustice. Injustices within families are painful for those directly assaulted, as well for those who watch the infliction or suffering of injustice by people they love and on whom they depend. To be sure, in families as in workplaces, ill-treated vulnerable people may fear bringing claims against aggressors because they risk losing necessary resources and connections, but the fact that protest is risky does not mean that injustice cannot be appropriately charged.

In sum, most feminists agree that families can and should be judged by strictures of justice, but many feminists also believe that traditional objections to justice within the family point to real difficulties in applying to families accounts of justice that were not devised with families in mind. It is not, these feminists argue, that families cannot or should not strive to be just. Rather, if the relationships and conflicts of family life inspire one's moral reflections, then theories that construe justice as impartial fairness seem seriously incomplete.

Four features of theories of justice figure prominently in feminist conversations. First, in theories of justice agents are individuals; families are treated as individuals when represented by heads of families. As individuals, parties of justice may care for their families. John Rawls is explicit in his assumption that just men care for future generations, but these individuals—who always sound as though they are men—are not themselves creations of relationships, but rather are rational because of their detachment from them. Seyla Benhabib's account of these agents of justice is frequently cited in feminist discussion:

This is a strange world: it is one in which individuals are grown up before they have been born; in which boys are men before they have been children; a world where neither mother, nor sister, nor wife exist.[19]

Family identities, by contrast, are constructed within and by relationships. It may be difficult even to identify a self-interest apart from self-defining relationships. In particular, the relationships of parents with children typically involve an identification through which a parent tends to assimilate her own and her child's interests and even identity.

Second, in theories of justice individuals are defined in terms of similar characteristics—usually some combination of rational self-interest and abilities to harm, contribute to joint enterprises, and abide by rules of fair play. Aside from these essential characteristics, individuals are disembodied and disembedded[20] from actual social relations and thus able to stand in for each other. To be sure, theories of justice only initially and hypothetically assume a 'generalized other' precisely in order to formulate ideals of fairness between people with different projects, living in different circumstances, but the image of a representative man of reason, a person who might be anybody, is integral to justificatory strategies.

Family relationships are often constituted in terms of the differences of their members. Children differ from each other and from adults not only in size and strength but in their reasoning, emotional responses, abilities, tastes, and interests. Fairness to each typically turns on recognizing particularities of their personalities and circumstances.[21] Family ideologies are founded on images of difference, most notably on the hitherto universal fact that only females bear children. Treating male and female parents as disembodied or similarly bodied, wishes away in advance the material, psychological, and symbolic differences between women and men that may follow on their different relations to birthgiving, and this lends itself to more general minimalization of bodily life and relationships.

Third, theorists of justice posit the fundamental equality of persons as a normative presupposition or moral ideal. To be sure, any domain that justice governs is liable to inequality. It is inequality that creates the need for justice. The aim of distributive justice, however, is (typically) to minimize inequality and to rationalize remaining instances in terms of a greater or another good or of benefit to the least well off.

By contrast, inequality is the stuff and rationale of family life. Theories of justice based on reciprocity find it difficult to account for justice to the indefinitely disabled, but the disabled are the principal subjects of family justice in that protection of the weak just because they are weak—young, old, ill, despairing, or otherwise especially vulnerable—is a principal point of family life. Fair relations between healthy adults, important as they are to family life, are not all of family relations nor are these relations separable from the unequal family relations in which women and men participate.

More Kantian theorists who assume the fundamental equality of each person also risk speaking aslant of fundamental conundrums of family moral life.[22] One can—and in certain circumstances one should—insist on the primitive equality of a healthy employed male adult and an unemployed pregnant woman who is already bearing primary responsibility for young children; of socially and academically integrated children and their sibling with Down's syndrome; and of an aphasic eighty-four-year-old person, the linguistically fluent speakers surrounding her, and a two-year-old child just beginning to talk. Such equality is, however, frankly metaphysical. In actual families stark and sometimes irreparable inequalities, like the not-atypical ones I have just mentioned, provide the primary materials of moral reflection. Someone who imagines herself ignorant of her place among unequals imagines herself outside much of family moral experience.

Finally, in theories of justice an allegedly unfair policy or relationship is tested for justice by determining whether rational self-interested individuals would consent to it. Consent is hypothetical, determined by rational reflection rather than actual negotiation. Nonetheless, the thought experiment has about it the air of real choice; it encourages individuals to imagine themselves freely undertaking or reassessing for fairness their relationships and attendant obligations.

By contrast, there is a given and yet, paradoxically, a fragile character to family obligations.[23] Although the scope of family obligation varies culturally and is subject to moral reflection, to recognize an obligation as familial is, in part, to construe it as beyond consent, a given consequence of relationship. In a daily way, children must be fed, a schizophrenic nephew housed, and the ill tended, however unfair their demands and however disproportionate the responsibilities of those who perform these tasks. To refuse these obligations freely in the name of fairness seems tantamount to freely rejecting primary moral demands that the vulnerable make on people able to respond to need. On the other hand, at least in current U.S. society, allegedly given obligations often are rejected freely. Some family members are negligent because they lack social or personal resources for effective response. Just as often, it is more independent and socially favored family members—especially men— who reassess and shun the daily work of meeting family obligations.

In sum, dominant theories of justice tend to idealize equality, transcendence of difference, and the ability to give or withhold consent. The moral dilemmas of family life tend to revolve around radical inequalities, embodied differences, and fragile obligations that seem beyond consent. The subjects of justice are rational and self-interested individuals able to cooperate with and harm each other. Family members are bound by emotional ties that foster mutual identification in contexts where some are not yet, or not now, able to cooperate or harm. Justice theorists can respond to each doubt about their understanding of family identities and relationships, but explanations, modifications, and defense often seem ex post facto and do not account for the cumulative effect of particular conceptual misfits.

In contrast to theories of justice, the ethics of care begins not with individuals, but with the relationships in which individuality is created. This ethics recognizes irremediable inequalities inherent in many relationships, highlights virtues central to family well-being such as respect for difference, and acknowledges the binding power of given obligations. It is not surprising that family moralists turn more easily to this ethics for understanding and self-governance. Yet it is exactly this turning to care in despair of justice that threatens to render care private and familial while at the same time excusing families from the demands of justice.

Family Assault

Suppose, as Aristotle would allow us to say, we make a fresh start and begin thinking about ideals of justice, as many philosophers now think about care, with the moral experience of families in mind. Suppose, too, that we begin constructing ideals of justice by identifying the typical wrongs that these ideals might right. What conceptions of *in*justice would emerge?

Consider, first, one common story of familial wrong. A healthy adult inflicts pain on someone considerably smaller or weaker—a child or a frail, disabled person. While the assaulter can cease or leave at will, the assaulted is pinned down under the blows, often by love, terror, and material dependence, as well as by force. Assault may consist primarily and perhaps entirely in abusive verbal or other nonphysical behavior in which, to invoke Simone Weil, the assaulted suffers "a humiliation" experienced as a "violent condition of the whole physical being, which wants to rise up against the outrage but is forced, by impotence or fear, to hold itself in check."[24] In speaking of assault, however, I want to underline the "whole *physical* being," the use of the body as a site of pain and fear of pain.

Scenarios of assault are particular to families and cultures. Assaulters may be enraged or deliberate; they may strike with their fists or employ familiar arms—a leather belt, for example; they may strike silently or entwine their blows with protestations of love or justifying excuses, but as I use the term, stark inequality, captivity, and the infliction of pain mark assault. There are many ills wrought by family members on each other that do not involve assault.

Assault exemplifies the features of family experience obscured by theories of justice. It typically occurs within, and is usually one expression of, a relationship. Assaultive relationships are marked by material inequalities between assaulter and assaulted. Assaultive episodes are frequently occasioned by attitudes and behavior that appear to the assaulter to express willful differences from family norms. The assaulted cannot withhold and the assaulter does not ask for consent to the relationship either generally or in its assaultive moments. If assault can be seen nonetheless as an injustice, then justice will be more firmly lodged within families.

Family assault appears to be a widespread practice that, at least in the United States, occurs in all cultural and economic groups.[25] In this paper I do not contest these practices but rather assume, against widely shared understandings, that assault is wrong. My question is: What allows us to label this putative wrong an injustice? My longer range project, however, is to chip away at the widespread practice of family assault and the beliefs that justify it. I hope that counting assault as injustice and then elaborating demands of justice will provide a particular moral understanding to assaulters and a language of redress to the assaulted.

Any family member may suffer assault and most family members can become assaulters, but women and children, and after them the elderly, are the primary victims of assault; men and parents are the primary aggressors. In this paper, I am especially concerned with assaultive relations between parents, especially mothers, and children. It is mothers with whom I identify and imagine myself trying to formulate nonassaultive ideals of family relations; it is children whom I am eager to protect.

Assault as Injustice

What, then, allows us to count assault as an injustice? First, within a framework that distinguishes two moral orientations, care and justice, family assault is more easily counted as injustice than as a failure of care. From the perspective of an ethics of care, exemplary wrongs involve indifference or neglect. Victims of sustained carelessness are abandoned—left to feed themselves, physically or psychologically. An assaulter, by contrast, lacks virtues of restraint and detachment. The victims of assault can be compared plausibly to weaker states targeted in so-called unjust wars: "they that have odds of power exact as much as they can, and the weak yield to such conditions as they can get."[26] A child cries for care: pay attention; help me; catch me if I fall—but cries out against assault: it hurts! get away; stop.

Protests against assault draw easily on languages of justice, especially of rights. "Women and children have an *absolute right* to be free from bodily harm."[27] Rights afford the assaulted a "protective distance";[28] children have rights against bodily invasion or psychological intrusion, rights to autonomy, bodily integrity, and self-assertion. More elusively, Simone Weil spoke of the "contact with injustice through pain" and heard in the cries of the assaulted a cry for justice: "Every time there arises from the depth of the human heart the childish cry . . . 'Why am I being hurt' then there is certainly injustice."[29] To her cry of hurt we might add the childlike "it's not fair," recognizing a fairness that has little to do with distribution.

The designation of assault as injustice illuminates a disturbing phenomenon. It seems that there is little correlation between tendencies to assault and to neglect. Some mothers, for example, are indifferent, inattentive, even frankly neglectful, but do not assault their children. Other mothers are protective and attentive, yet engage in assault. Caring but assaultive mothers may be exhausted or powerless before their children's will, or they may believe that assault is a useful or even necessary instrument of training, or they may act out of an identification that compels them to beat out a rebellious, shameful, or socially vulnerable self as it is expressed in the attitudes or behavior of the assaulted. Whatever the motives of assault, there is no reason, without special knowledge, to assume that assaulters care too little for the assaulted or that, in daily ways, they do not fulfill requirements of care.

None of these considerations preclude condemning assault from the perspective of care. In conventional understanding, families are caring institutions, any of whose failures are failures of care. The capacity to restrain aggression can be seen as a virtue required for caring, the ability to moderate identification as a condition of caring well. Assault is often experienced as a violation of care, a hurt levied within a particular caring relationship in which protection rather than abuse is called for. My understanding is that moral phenomena almost always can be seen alternatively from the perspective of care and justice. My point is not to exclude assault from judgments of care, but to include it as an instance of injustice.

Assault and Domination

My final strategy for revealing assault as injustice is to disclose connections between assault and domination. Domination is typically thought to be itself unjust and is sometimes thought to be constitutive of injustice.[30] Assault is both an instrument of domination and a consequence of its failure. A principle of justice, I will also argue, effectively prohibits assault only if it also prohibits domination.[31]

Roughly, and colloquially, to dominate someone is to judge and control the conditions and the outcomes of her actions. Metaphorically, a dominator treats the dominated as if she were an "object of property."[32] Some dominators may actually believe that the dominated are property, as some parents seem to regard their children, Kant regarded domestic workers,[33] and, in the worst case, slave owners regarded enslaved people. Many family dominators who would deny that they consider family members as property nonetheless reveal tacit assumptions of ownership in their actions, fears, and expressions of entitlement.

For example, because she construes the dominated as her property, a dominator believes herself entitled to instigate or halt projects
in which the dominated participate, control the conditions of their
exit from relationships and institutions, and circumscribe their pa-
rameters of choice. She may appropriate as her own her property's
labor both directly and by garnishing wages or other remuneration,
or she may insist on loyalty and love while also setting herself up
as the judge of the dominated's ambition. She may feel entitled to
intrude on friendships and sexual relations or to eavesdrop and spy
in order to uncover evidence of disturbing willfulness.

Dominators may care deeply for those they dominate; they may
believe that domination is necessary for the eventual happiness and
perhaps even the survival of the dominated. When caring dominators are benevolent and even-tempered, it is possible that neither
they nor those they dominate recognize the character of their relationship. Dominating aims become evident, however, if the dominated develops projects and ambitions, attachments and sexual desires
that are disturbing to dominators. Then the dominated appears out
of control in a double sense: he is no longer under the control of
the dominator and he appears to have lost the self-control whose
test and expression is submission or, more politely, obedience. When
confronted with incongruous willfulness, even a benign dominator
is apt to reassert ownership, to confirm the relation of owner to
object.

It is in this moment of reassertion that connections between domination and assault often become clear. In a dominator's eyes compliance is normal and disobedience is a disturbing abnormality that
must be set right. Even benign dominators who never anticipate
hurting or humiliating their property may be compelled to beat the
willfulness out of someone they are meant to own. Deliberate dominators may also decide in advance to use assault as a means of
reasserting control. Recognizing that people, especially perhaps
children, fear pain and humiliation, they exploit these fears in the
service of domination by threatening or inflicting pain and humiliation. Some dominators feel more casually entitled to visit pain and
humiliation on their property whenever he or she is displeasing. Still
other, sadistic dominators assault without provocation or else elicit
the behavior they punish. For them the willfulness of the dominated does not so much excuse assault as provide occasions for its
pleasures and excitement.

I do not want to exaggerate the connections between domination and assault. There are many indirect, nonassaultive techniques of domination—assault may be episodic, each instance sufficient unto itself and explicable in terms of the assaulted's provocative behavior and the assaulter's momentary frustration and rage—but the connections between domination and assault, though neither necessary nor even invariable, are stronger than mere association. Domination tends to lead to, explain, and justify assault; conversely, assault in the service of domination is a frequent and also often an explicitly avowed practice.

Although family assault and domination are widespread and often deliberate practices, they are neither inevitable nor unchangeable. While I have never known a parent who was not at least tempted to assault in the interests of domination or entirely free of more or less permanent desires to dominate, I have known many who disciplined themselves against assault and learned to resist their temptations to appropriate and intrude. Sadistic assaulters may profit from some combination of coercive control and therapy. More benign assaulters can learn to distinguish between domination and the training children require, query the belief that assault is an effective instrument of training, and develop alternative means of control. Since practices of assault and domination are liable to change, they are also liable to moral critique. Moral ideals of nonassaultive relationships are both instances and inspirations for change. These ideals are, on my view, for reasons I have given, appropriately construed as ideals of justice.

Respect for Embodied Willfulness

I now propose one such ideal of justice: respect for embodied willfulness. This ideal begins with the renunciation of assault as an instrument of domination but becomes a governing ideal only when it is extended to include a principled renunciation of projects of domination.

Under the concept 'willfulness' I gather, first, a cluster of capacities to move, initiate, instigate, and resist and second, capacities to choose and act. The motions of a tiny infant can be seen as reflexes but also as expressions of will and can be respected or punished accordingly. Toddlers initiate and resist. Developmentally, willfulness is transformed into capacities to act and choose, but there is no conceptual mark or developmental achievement that reliably separates desirable agency from the willfulness that appears to dominators to be out of control.

By '*embodied* willfulness' I refer to two truisms, what Wittgenstein called "very general facts of nature." First, capacities of will are expressed bodily—including, and for many adults especially, bodily speech. Second, human bodies are subject to pain, fear, and memory. These two conditions of embodied willfulness account for the familiar fact I just underlined: it is possible, often though not always, to affect a person's will by affecting her body and, more particularly, to undermine her will by inflicting bodily pain or credibly threatening to do so. People who assault with intention to dominate can be said to exploit the conditions of embodied willfulness. Conversely, a person who refuses to threaten or inflict pain, even though she is in a position to do so and understands the conditions that make exploitation possible, exhibits a minimal respect for the embodied willfulness of others.[34]

A person who refrains from assault does not thereby relinquish projects of domination. A dominator might refrain from assault because she doubts its effectiveness. Freudian theorists[35] have confirmed what many mothers have learned: although assault is often psychologically relieving to the assaulter and affects the immediate behavior of the assaulted, it is not possible to predict or to limit its consequences. Bodily pain, terror, and pleasure are embedded in fantasies about the relationships in which they are experienced and the self-identity constructed within those relationships. Children, in particular, interpret experiences of pain in ways unintended by its perpetrators. These interpretations are rarely susceptible to conscious articulation but nonetheless—or really partly for this reason—have lasting qualitative as well as quantitative consequences for capacities to will. Adult assaulters also cannot predict reliably the consequences for themselves of assaulting. However confident they may feel about the benefits of assault, the act of assaulting can excite sadistic desire, guilt, or other emotions that then undermine confidence or escalate assault.

A person who appreciates the complexities of assault may set out to develop the more effective means of domination typically available to parents, heads of households, and economic providers. Nonetheless, such a person's restraint, even though coupled with domination, can mark the beginning of respect for embodied will-fulness, because by deferring to the complexities of the experience of pain the dominator also tacitly acknowledges both the value and the unpredictable independence of the mental life of the dominat-ed. A parent may give weight primarily to the future effects of a child's experience, but she might, like self-restraining caregivers of the elderly, come to respect psychological complexities for their own sake, irrespective of any long-range consequences.

With deeper recognition of the complexities of embodied will-fulness, occasions and grounds for respect may multiply until they almost preclude domination,[36] but there is no substitute for repudi-ating domination itself, which means relinquishing the conception of a person as an object of property and renouncing the ambition to appropriate her affection or labor or to intrude upon her body or mental life. Control, and often coercion, are necessary to family life. Allegedly strong but baffled family members cannot remain kindly attentive spectators when children act cruelly or self-destructively, when disabled family members push themselves beyond their lim-its, or when failing elderly people struggle to maintain self-respect in ways that harm themselves or others. Moreover, the best inten-tioned parents occasionally assault, intrude, and appropriate in ways that, were they habitual, would become patterns of domination. Only a commitment to abjure domination, to respect embodied willful-ness on principle, affords parents and other stronger family mem-bers confidence in the character of ongoing relationships despite troubling episodes and exercises of control.

Once they are determined to create relationships as free as pos-sible of domination, and therefore to respect in advance the com-plexities of embodied willfulness, family members can more thoughtfully assess habitual techniques of family governance and compensate for unwelcome interventions as well as for occasional unplanned assaults. Justifiable coercion can be enacted in the most limited and nonassaultive ways that a particular occasion allows. Control, coercion, and even unplanned assaults can be deliberately surrounded by acts and attitudes intended to foster a sense of con-fident willfulness.

It is important not to sentimentalize. Sometimes, with aggressive senile elderly for example, or with children who are temporarily enraged or cruel without apparent compunction, compensatory en-couragement of willfulness is impossible; forceful coercion and nonassaultive punishment is, at least temporarily, the only action available. Yet even in these cases, as in happier times and relationships, a self-conscious commitment not to dominate can give family members a sense of purposive agency, self-respect, and self-control.

Concluding Remarks

It is at best premature to look for one relationship or a single wrong-doing that can reveal the essence of family justice. I do not believe that principled respect for embodied willfulness and the relinquishing of domination can provide such a reassuring essential core. I have, for example, barely alluded to retributive justice. Yet it is a requirement of justice in families, as well as in the larger polity, to name wrongs and to hold individual members responsible for their harms. Although in current practices assaulters may appeal to retributive justice to justify assault, it should be possible to articulate principles of responsibility in tandem with principles of respect for embodied willfulness.

Principles of fairness familiar from dominant theories are also integral to family justice, most evidently but not only in relations between healthy adults. Where fairness fails, women make claims against current gender arrangements within families and against men who profit from them. For children, too, fairness is no luxury. Day-care centers, playgrounds, and households ring with the cry "it's not fair!"—along with the related "my turn!" It has sometimes been argued that fairness is more superficial than principles such as respect for embodied willfulness.[37] Such ranking seems to me distracting. Unfairness is destructive of families and other institutions and often experienced by those who suffer it as a painful insult.

No matter how multifaceted the rendering of family justice, it will never constitute the whole of family morality. Within the framework I adopt, justice is always seen in tandem with care. I have described respect for embodied willfulness in terms of the restraint a just person imposes on herself, the distances she allows and keeps, and the unfair advantage and domineering appropriation she forgoes, but embodied willfulness surely, and equally, requires the responsiveness of care: feeding, comforting and holding bodies, and attending to and actively fostering the willfulness that emerges. Care also checks and informs justice when, paradoxically, it makes its claims in an intrusive or appropriative manner. Care givers who are attentive to context can recognize the fragile character of family obligations, the necessity of family connection for vulnerable people, or the restorative capacities of family connection to those assaulted by racism or other injuries for which they find no redress. If, in full consideration of these complex needs that families serve, moralists intervene in the name of justice to impose fairness or forbid assault, they will more likely "engage the moral agency" of those they seek to change or protect if they are governed by ideals of humility and mutuality associated with care.[38]

Once justice is brought into families there is no reason to divide sharply various public from relatively private moral realms. Family justice depends on the political context in which families are situated. Family assaults as well as larger patterns of family domination are often indirect reactions to public policies that legitimate bigotry and deny to some the resources that justice, as well as care, requires. All families, however impoverished, fortunate, culturally marginal, or ethnically dominant, create their moralities in an inescapably public milieu. Family values will ground and express only those public policies and commitments that already have shaped and fostered the family values they depend on.

Although family and public moralities are inextricably linked, there is no easy matching between them. As many feminists and some politicians are fond of insisting, children learn meanings of justice and care within their original families, but early childhood lessons are not as straightly read as moralists might suggest. Childhood moralities may inform adult commitment. Conversely, although less often noted, a sharper appreciation of public injustice or neglect may alter moral reasoning and action in families. Stories of childhood and adult moral development, however, are still very sketchy and outcomes are unpredictable. Children who suffer neglect and abuse may, as adults, become passionate advocates of care and justice; those who learn justice and care within their families may nonetheless be indifferent to or abusive of strangers and aliens; adults who lead just and caring public lives, out of whatever motives, may nonetheless be neglectful or abusive family members.

Whatever relationship individuals forge between their relatively early or private experiences and their public lives, family justice can inform more general theories of justice. Many public and political relations—for example, most interstate relations—are marked by radical inequality. Many forms of bigotry and violence are marked by fear of difference, especially different bodies. Political theorists might well reflect on family justice as they formulate principles that allow the stronger and the weaker to relate to each other with minimal appropriation or intrusion.

Irrespective of its public or political import, family justice is worthy of praise. Vulnerability may elicit a caring response, but also may elicit contempt or aggression. Vulnerable family members require care, yet are also often provocative and exhausting. While family relations can, theoretically, be seen alternatively under the aspect of justice or the aspect of care, in practice attempts toward attentive caring are intertwined with temptations to dominate. The complex efforts of family members simultaneously to respond and respect offer an illuminating and too little noticed example of moral endeavor.[39]

Notes

1. I refer in particular to Susan Moller Okin, *Justice, Gender, and the Family* (New York: Basic Books, 1989). I rely on Okin's work and bibliography throughout this essay.

2. By dominant theories of justice, I have in mind especially John Rawls's *A Theory of Justice* and his and others' developments of the theory. Gauthier and Darwall also have figured in recent feminist discussions of justice, for example, by Iris Young, Virginia Held, and Jurgen Habermas in discussions by Iris Young and Seyla Benhabib. I speak of 'dominant' rather than 'liberal' theories for two reasons: under certain interpretations, Rawlsian theories can be construed as radical; the failure of the dominant theories transcends politics. I recognize, however, that none of my criticisms apply directly to, for example, Marxist theories of justice. See John Rawls, *A Theory of Justice* (Cambridge: Harvard University Press, 1971); David Gauthier, *Morals by Agreement* (Oxford: Clarendon Press, 1986); Stephen Darwall, *Impartial Reason* (Ithaca, N.Y.: Cornell University Press, 1983); Iris Marion Young, *Justice and the Politics of Difference* (Princeton, N.J.: Princeton University Press, 1990); Virginia Held, *Feminist Morality: Transforming Culture, Society, and Politics* (Chicago, Ill.: University of Chicago Press, 1993); Jurgen Habermas, *The Theory of Communicative Competence* (Boston: Beacon Press, 1983); and Seyla Benhabib, *Critique, Norm, and Utopia* (New York: Columbia University Press, 1986).

3. The literature that is developing on the ethics of care is now vast. In my own thinking about care, I draw on work by Annette Baier, Seyla Benhabib, Lyn Mikel Brown, Patricia Hill Collins, Berenice Fischer, Beverly Harrison, Nancy Hirschmann, Nona Lyons, Joan Tronto, Margaret Urban Walker, Patricia Williams, the authors of *Women's Ways of Knowing*, and many

others too numerous to mention. I am especially indebted to Virginia Held's work in feminist ethics, most recently extended and recapitulated in *Feminist Morality*. I am also indebted to Carol Gilligan and Nel Noddings, the theorists most directly associated with and responsible for proposing an ethics of care. For Carol Gilligan, see especially *In a Different Voice* (Cambridge: Harvard University Press, 1982) and Carol Gilligan, Janie Ward, and Jill Taylor, *Mapping the Moral Domain* (Cambridge: Harvard University Press, 1988). For Nel Noddings, see especially *Caring: A Feminine Approach to Ethics and Moral Education* (Berkeley, Calif.: University of California Press, 1984) and *Women and Evil*, (Berkeley, Calif.: University of California Press, 1990). Mary Jeanne Larrabee, ed., *An Ethic of Care* (New York: Routledge, 1992), collects several central articles in the ethics of care and provides a useful bibliography. See also Annette C. Baier, *Moral Prejudices: Essays on Ethics* (Cambridge: Harvard University Press, 1994); Claudia Card, ed., *Feminist Ethics* (Lawrence, Kans.: University Press of Kansas, 1991); and Alison M. Jaggar, ed., *Living with Contradictions: Controversies in Feminist Social Ethics* (Boulder, Colo.: Westview Press, 1994).

4. See especially Virginia Held's *Feminist Morality*; also Nel Noddings, *Women and Evil*.

5. Occasionally, I have heard feminists come close to rejecting justice—described as abstract or masculine—in favor of care. Socialist feminists criticize dominant theories of justice, of course, but usually without explicit reference to families.

6. This is largely the tactic of Susan Okin, *Justice, Gender, and the Family*, who also offers—to my mind unconvincing—modifications of Rawls.

7. This is the tactic of Nel Noddings, particularly in "Impartiality and Care," manuscript from author.

8. Here I am closest to Iris Young and Virginia Held, on whose writings I draw.

9. There are many ways to situate moral phenomena and reasoning other than within a justice/care framework. Within the justice/care framework, other ethics or moral principles retain their salience. Principles of liberty, to take just one example, acquire distinct significance within theories and practices of care, as well as in the more familiar context of justice. Indeed, one virtue of the justice/care framework is that it gets us to think freshly about familiar principles by considering them from two shifting perspectives.

10. Gilligan has offered several versions of the relation of justice and care. Here I draw on "Gender Difference and Morality: The Empirical Base" in Eva Kittay and Diana Meyers, eds., *Women and Moral Theory* (Totowa, N.J.: Rowman & Littlefield, 1987).

11. Peter Winch, *Simone Weil: "The Just Balance"* (Oxford: Blackwell, 1989), 149. Winch is describing only Weil's account of justice, but what Winch says about Weil's view of justice I apply to both justice and care.

12. For an overview of possible relations between justice and care, see Lawrence Blum, "Gilligan and Kohlberg: Implications for Moral Theory," *Ethics* (April 1988), 472–91, and Seyla Benhabib, "The Debate over Women

86 Sara Ruddick

and Moral Theory Revisited" in *Situating the Self* (New York: Routledge, 1992).

13. For a discussion of the debate about evidence for gender difference, see Larrabee, *An Ethic of Care.*

14. See especially Carol Gilligan and Grant Wiggins, "The Origins of Morality in Early Childhood Relationships," and Carol Gilligan and Jane Attanuci, "Two Moral Orientations," both in Carol Gilligan, Janie Ward, and Jill Taylor, eds., *Mapping the Moral Domain* (Cambridge: Harvard University Press, 1988). Gilligan seems to suggest that the sense of justice develops primarily from negative experiences of powerlessness and inequality—and, I might add, humiliation and abuse—that the child experiences or, I would add, witnesses. A sense of care develops primarily from positive experiences of attachment. While a sense of justice also requires positive experiences—John Rawls's account of these still seems among the best—and a drive toward care might follow from experiencing or witnessing neglect and isolation, there is something right, I think, about Gilligan's perception. This raises one among the many complexities I resist discussing here.

15. See Will Kymlicka's "Rethinking the Family," *Philosophy and Public Affairs* (Winter 1991), 77–97, which takes Susan Okin to task for just this omission.

16. Throughout this section I am drawing heavily on Susan Okin, *Justice, Gender, and the Family,* in which she has set out the case against family justice made by, especially, Allan Bloom and Roberto Unger and, indirectly, Michael Sandel, Alasdair MacIntyre, and other theorists of justice. I draw on Okin equally in responding to the claim that families cannot provide or afford the "circumstances of justice."

17. George Gilder was an early proponent of the pessimist's view. Susan Okin attributes views like these to Allan Bloom. I have heard many times versions of the pessimist's view expressed by women and men.

18. Okin, *Justice, Gender, and the Family.*

19. Seyla Benhabib, "The Generalized and the Concrete Other," originally in Kittay and Meyers, *Women and Moral Theory,* now in the author's *Situating the Self* (New York: Routledge, 1992), 157.

20. I take these phrases from Seyla Benhabib, "Generalized and Concrete Other."

21. Especially well argued by Nel Noddings, "Impartiality and Care," unpublished manuscript.

22. See, for example, Allen Buchanan, "Justice as Reciprocity vs. Subject-Centered Justice," *Philosophy and Public Affairs,* (Summer, 1990).

23. I am indebted throughout this discussion to Nancy Hirschmann, *Rethinking Obligation* (Ithaca, N.Y.: Cornell University Press, 1992). As Hirschmann points out, what I call family obligations are often construed as duties—especially when these are assigned to women—and therefore natural and beyond consent. I am not here distinguishing between duty and obligation.

24. Simone Weil, "Love of God and Affliction," in George H. Panichas, ed., *Simone Weil Reader* (Mt. Kisco, N.Y.: Moyer Bell, 1977), 440 ff. The

entire discussion is relevant to the weighting of physical and nonphysical pain.

25. Philip Greven, *Spare the Child* (New York: Alfred Knopf, 1991), of-fers a useful and passionate account of the pervasiveness of family assault. Colleagues, coconferees, and students confirm the view that, while some fam-ilies are remarkably free of assault and domination, there is no subcultural group in the United States that does not include practices of family assault and also the view that many families consider assault a legitimate and even necessary practice. Beliefs about assault are affected by racist projections of violence onto African Americans in particular, as well as onto other minority or stigmatized groups. It is also true that parents without funds, space, and time, and who themselves are socially humiliated are more likely to assault.

26. Thucydides, quoted by Michael Walzer in *Just and Unjust Wars* (New York: Basic Books, 1977), 5.

27. Ann Jones, *The Next Time, She'll Be Dead* (Boston: Beacon Press, 1994), 4 and *passim*. Italics in original.

28. The phrase is Patricia Williams's. See Williams, *Alchemy of Race and Rights*, (Cambridge: Harvard University Press, 1991), 148.

29. Simone Weil, "Human Personality," *Simone Weil Reader*, 315. See also "The Love of God and Affliction." Weil adds: "For if, as often happens, it is only the result of a misunderstanding, then the injustice consists in the inad-equacy of the explanation." On my view there is no adequate explanation for family assault, but assaulters do explain by way of justifying or excusing themselves, tacitly acknowledging requirements of justice. Adequate explana-tion is important in countering humiliating effects of nonviolent coercion—a matter I allude to later. I am indebted to Weil's thinking about justice and also deeply at odds with her insistence on and construction of the imperson-ality of justice.

30. Young, *Justice and the Politics of Difference*.

31. When domination is identified with injustice, it, like injustice, is apt to be considered a characteristic of institutions. See, for example, Iris Young, *Justice and the Politics of Difference*, 38. On my view, domination—and jus-tice—can characterize relationships as well as institutions. To cite one exam-ple, white Americans' domination of black Americans is enacted in policies and practices that construct economic and political public life. This domina-tion is also reflected in the personal relations—sexual, procreative, family, collegial—of both races and in their daily private activities such as shopping, hailing a taxi, or ordering at a restaurant. Many social activities, which can-not be easily designated as public or private—for example, a visit to a doctor or employment office, a conversation with a potential landlord, a teacher's conference, a private journey on public transportation—are typically affected by practices of racial domination. A person's earliest experiences of domina-tion—as participant or witness—often occur within families—themselves so-cial institutions—or between family members and subordinated or dominat-ing others. Accordingly, family relationships and history offer a particularly useful vantage for exploring the phenomenology of domination.

32. I am adapting a metaphor developed by Patricia Williams with partic-

ular reference to white Americans' domination of black Americans. See *Alchemy of Race and Rights*, especially part 4. See also Maria Lugones, "Playfulness, 'World' Travelling, and Loving Perception," *Hypatia*, vol. 2, no. 2 (Summer 1987): 3–19.

33. Robin May Schott, in "The Gender of Enlightenment" (manuscript by courtesy of the author), quotes Kant as writing in a letter to C. G. Schutz, dated 10 July 1797: "The right to use a man for domestic purposes is analogous to a right to an object, for which the servant is not free to terminate his connections with the household and he may therefore be caught and returned by force."

34. An assaulter, or even a nonassaultive thorough-going dominator, often appears to her victims as unpredictably and unremittingly willful. To resist willful assaulters, it may be necessary to violate their embodied willfulness— battered women injure their batterers, armies are said to engage in just wars. As I mentioned, when I speak of assaulters I have primarily in mind mothers with whom I identify. My emphases would shift if I were thinking primarily of assaulted women.

35. What I take "Freudian" theories to reveal:

(1) The first ego is a bodily ego; the bodily ego is always already, from the start social. The ego is therefore constituted within and by physical-social relations such as holding, hurting, soothing, feeding, restraining, carrying, or beating. Because the ego is bodily/social, embodied willfulness, an ego expression, is also social. Here I draw on Freudians as diverse as D. W. Winnicott, Melanie Klein, Teresa Brennan, and, of course, Freud.

(2) The relationships within which any individual's experience of embodied willfulness is constructed turn crucially on a need, said to be as important as food, to be recognized by those on whom one depends. Here, in addition to Winnicott, I draw especially on Jessica Benjamin, *The Bonds of Love* (New York: Pantheon Books, 1988), and Nancy Chodorow, "Gender, Relation, and Difference in Psychoanalytic Perspective," *Feminism and Psychoanalytic Theory* (New Haven, Conn.: Yale University Press, 1989).

(3) These physical/social relationships do not come neat, but are created amid complex and developmentally entrenched fantasies. Hence, the bodily terror, pain, or pleasure experienced within these relationships are also embedded in fantasy. Here I draw on varieties of Freudians starting with Freud, "A Child is Being Beaten," Standard ed. (London: Hogarth Press, 1955), vol. 17.

36. A respect for embodied willfulness may lead also to a deeper appreciation of injustices that are wrought less directly through bodies. Two examples: When birthgiving is recognized as a primary expression of embodied willfulness, then attempts to appropriate birthgivers' labor or deprive women of pleasures and powers because of their capacity to give birth can be seen as an assault on embodied willfulness. Similarly, to persecute or sabotage sexual desire is to undermine the bodily ego; to alienate a person from his sexual desires is to alienate him from his own embodied willfulness.

37. This is apparently Simone Weil's view and has been discussed by Peter Winch in *Simone Weil, "The Just Balance."*

38. I borrow here from Neda Hadjikhani, "On Humility: Engaging the Moral Agency of Non-Western Women." (Manuscript courtesy of the author). Hadjikhani discusses Western women's relation to non-Western mothers who advocate female circumcision. She adapts concepts drawn from Carol Gilligan and from my *Maternal Thinking* (Boston: Beacon Press, 1989).

39. I benefited greatly from early readings of this essay by Virginia Held, William Ruddick, David Wong, and Marilyn Young. I later received very useful written comments from Nancy Hirschmann, Alison Jaggar, Diana Meyers, Elizabeth Minnich, Robin Schott, and Margaret Urban Walker. I learned—and am still learning—from numerous critiques and suggestions offered by people who heard this paper. I would like to thank especially Diemut Bubeck, Claudia Card, Ashok Gangadeen, Aryeh Kosman, Danielle MacBeth, and Lucius Outlaw.

5

On Care and Justice within the Family

David B. Wong

The family seems the appropriate domain for the ethic of care. This ethic, as characterized by Carol Gilligan, involves a concern for the well-being of particular others and for one's relationship to them.[1] It involves highly contextualized reasoning directed toward the welfare of others and toward sustaining or mending relationships with and among them. Such an ethic seems appropriate to the family because family members frequently see their relationships as important goods that may be essential to their identities. Much of what we do in the family is directed toward sustaining or mending our relationships with very particular others, and these actions cannot always be deduced straightforwardly from general moral principles.

Gilligan contrasts the care ethic with one that emphasizes fairness, justice, and rights and requires reasoning by deduction from general principles. The question arises as to whether justice applies to the family. Some have argued that justice does not fit the family well, that it conflicts with the emphasis on harmony and affection within the family. I argue that justice does apply to the family and that the relations between an ethic of care and one centering on justice are more complex than has been acknowledged. Care and justice, I argue, overlap and inform each other as applied to the family. I point out that it also is necessary to distinguish two conceptions of justice: the communitarian and the liberal. Both conceptions apply to the family, but each bears a distinct relation to care. Finally, I argue for the need to keep all these perspectives in our consideration of the family.

Michael Sandel has given a version of the argument that justice does not fit the family. In posing the question of whether Rawls's liberal theory of justice[2] should be applied to the family, Sandel asks us to:

> [c]onsider, for example, a more or less ideal family situation, where relations are governed in large part by spontaneous affection and where, in consequence, the circumstances of justice prevail to a relatively small degree. Individual rights and fair decision procedures are seldom invoked, not because injustice is rampant but because their appeal is preempted by a spirit of generosity in which I am rarely inclined to claim my fair share. . . . Now imagine that one day the harmonious family comes to be wrought with dissension. Interests grow divergent and the circumstances of justice grow more acute. The affection and spontaneity of previous days give way to demands for fairness and the observance of rights. . . . Parents and children reflectively equilibrate, and dutifully if sullenly abide by the two principles of justice. . . . Are we prepared to say that the arrival of justice, however full, restores to the situation its full moral character, and that the only difference is a psychological one?[3]

Susan Okin sees in this argument the presupposition that feelings of spontaneous affection are somehow incompatible with abiding by principles of justice. She rightly questions this presupposition.[4] I think the source of Sandel's mistake is his sentimentalized conception of family harmony. According to him, affection is spontaneous in the ideal family. Interests of family members are so united that questions of fairness and rights do not even arise. Can we seriously believe that families, even the best of them, can operate in this way? Questions of fairness and of rights arise frequently in the healthiest of families. In fact, I argue, caring about the health of a family may require thinking about justice.

To see what has gone wrong in Sandel's conception of family harmony, we need to recognize what it is to care about a relationship. Under Gilligan's characterization of the care ethic, moral action is meant to sustain and mend relationships, but relationships are dynamic processes. How we act within them determines what they are, and how we act within them is often guided by a conception of what a good relationship is. Of course, we need not always act explicitly out of such a conception, but if an ongoing relationship is significant to us, there are bound to be occasions on which it is necessary to reflect on where to take that relationship from there. Such reflection is unavoidably influenced by our ideas of what good relationships should be like, though these ideas may be revised according to our ongoing experience.[5]

It is at this point that justice informs the care perspective. As Marilyn Friedman has pointed out, personal relationships providing intimacy, support, and concern are relationships that require effort by the participants.[6] When one member of such a relationship bears a greater burden in this effort, the question of unfairness arises. It arises along gender lines if, in Marilyn Frye's words, "men do not serve women as women serve men."[7] Justice is relevant to relationships of care, furthermore, not solely as an external constraint on how such relationships are to be conducted. Justice may be necessary to the health of the relationship itself and may be in this sense internal to the care perspective. As Claudia Card has pointed out, lack of reciprocity is probably a major breakup of friendship between peers.[8] Marriage, as a friendship among peers, would be threatened by lack of reciprocity in the bearing of burdens.

In looking more closely at the relationship of justice to care, however, we need to make a distinction between two conceptions of justice. On one conception of justice, deserts and responsibilities are determined by reference to the end of achieving a common good. This common good includes the good of participation in a common life, a network of relationships conceived to be an essential part of the flourishing of all participants. The virtues of justice under this conception are those virtues required to sustain and promote the common good. In the family the common good includes an ideal set of relations between its members, which may be called a good family life. When members are not doing their parts in sustaining and promoting that life, or when they take more of the benefits of that life than they deserve in accordance with their contribution, they are being unjust. Injustice in this sense threatens the common life of the family.

The contemporary advocates of communitarian traditions fear that these traditions are disappearing or weakening.[9] They may be right, but the communitarian tradition as applied to the family still has some hold on us. Many of us still see our family life as a good essential to our flourishing and as a common good for all members. Because this common good provides a basis for deciding questions about the fairness of the distribution of benefits and burdens within the family, much depends on the ideal of family life and, in particular, on the kinds of hierarchy and subordination accepted. It is important to remember that many traditions that exemplify a communitarian conception have had conceptions of a good family life that give systematically different roles to men and to women in their contributions to the common family life and that systematically devalue women's roles—conceptions, in short, that we can no longer justify. It is equally important to note, however, that a communitarian conception of a good family life need not subordinate women or legitimate their domination. We can value a family life constituted by relations of equality between men and women, mutual support, and reciprocity.

A more recent conception of justice focuses not on the good of a common life, but on rights the individual possesses as a human being in society and on the question of fairness of distribution of important goods, where distribution ultimately is not determined by reference to the requirements for a common life and a common good, but by principles that express the moral equality of persons. This conception focuses on the conflicts between the legitimate interests of individuals and seeks a fair way to adjudicate these conflicts. This is what I want to call the liberal conception of justice.

This liberal conception also applies to the family, but in a way that is distinct from the way that the communitarian conception relates to the family. Even in the best of families, in which individuals rightly see their well-being as depending on the common life of the family, there will be conflicts of legitimate interests that cannot be resolved by reference to what best promotes that common life. In the worst families, members need enforcement of rights that they have as human beings. A parent who beats a child is being unjust not only in the sense of undermining the common life of the family, but in violating that child's rights as a human being. Furthermore, we have come to reject the idea that the only appropriate place for a woman is in the home because we have seen that restriction as an illegitimate abridgment of a woman's right to pursue a meaningful life and meaningful work, a right that any person has.

The two kinds of justice provide different moral perspectives on the family, both of which are needed. Communitarian justice focuses on the moral goods of relationship in the family. Liberal justice focuses on the moral status of family members as human beings, not as family members. Just as communitarian justice can inform the care perspective, however, so liberal justice can inform communitarian justice. Liberal justice can, for example, support those conceptions of a good family life that reject subordination and domination, and it can inform care. For example, our notions of what it is to care properly for children have come to involve the idea that we ought to raise them to know their rights, be able to assert them, and exercise them effectively. We would not care well for them if we did not.

Conversely, care informs both kinds of justice. Care requires a loving attention to the particularity of each person's traits, needs, desires, and circumstances.[10] Surely, such attention is required to know how each family member can contribute to the common family life and how each is to be accorded what is deserved in light of that contribution, and it is required to know the best ways in which each particular child must be raised to know, assert, and exercise his or her rights as a human being, as well as to respect the rights of others. The concerns of liberal justice, communitarian justice, and care can and should be interwoven in all these ways.

At the same time, these moral perspectives on the family can be in tension and sometimes outright conflict, depending on the family and the individuals in it. Caring for a family member may require intrusions that may not be justifiable from the standpoint of liberal justice. Liberal justice, when it emphasizes the rights of individuals to liberty, can conflict with demands made on the individual from other family members, and these demands may be justified from the standpoint of the common life of the family. I do not think that any one type of consideration consistently outweighs the other in cases of conflict. A lot depends on what is at stake. Intrusions for the sake of care or restrictions of liberty for the sake of communitarian justice may be justified when what is at stake is an older child's drug use, but not on other matters, even when a parent disapproves of what that child may be doing.

Even here, I think, we must allow for and accept a significant degree of cultural variability in what counts as intrusion. Traditional Chinese families, for example, allow for a sort of parental involvement in a child's affairs that would be widely considered unjustifiably intrusive in the United States. I am reminded of an incident in the movie *A Great Wall*, in which a Chinese-American family is visiting relatives in Beijing. The Chinese-American son, very assimilated, is shocked when he sees the Chinese mother opening and reading her daughter's mail without permission. The American son gives the Chinese daughter a lesson in American-style privacy. When confronted with the daughter's protests about an invasion of her privacy, the mother reacts neither defensively nor angrily but with puzzlement. "Privacy?" she asks. What she did was not an intrusion for her, nor did it need permission. I am inclined to think that such differences over the permissibility of parental involvement are to be accepted within certain limits on the grounds of the goods provided by cultural pluralism. Families are the bearers and transmitters of traditions. If we value diversity of traditions, we must allow for a certain range of variation in such matters.

The perspectives of care, of communitarian justice, and of liberal justice, then, overlap, inform each other, sometimes reinforce each other, and sometimes conflict; and, of course, I have just mentioned another moral perspective that values cultural pluralism and that can enter into these relations. Each of these perspectives is but a partial perspective on the family and needs to be informed by the others. To reinforce this point, let me consider some criticisms of liberal theories of justice as applied to the family. The proper conclusion, I argue, is not that such theories should not be applied to the family, but that such theories must be taken as incomplete perspectives on the family.

Sara Ruddick has argued that liberal theories of justice are ill suited to the family because they abstract from the particular identities of family members.[11] Consider Rawls's theory of the original position, in which the parties do not know their particular identities in deciding on principles of justice, but this kind of abstraction does not make liberal justice ill suited to the family. What it does is make liberal justice incapable of accounting for the moral requirements that flow from particular identities. Such a theory cannot explain, for example, what is required of me in virtue of my identity as a father. Some of these requirements flow from a general conception of good fatherhood and, more generally, from a general conception of a good family. Other requirements flow from my wholly particular identity as father of Liana. That is, they flow from who she is and who I am and from the way our relationship has evolved. The proper conclusion is that liberal justice is but a partial perspective on the family, a perspective that cannot account for all our moral duties and obligations.

Theories of liberal justice, however, provide a distinct and needed perspective on families precisely because they abstract from our particular identities and from communitarian conceptions of appropriate familial roles. Liberal justice provides a certain critical distance from those particular identities and conceptions, and, as I argued earlier, this perspective should move us to make the relationships between adult women and men in families truly equal and reciprocal relations that respect the (liberal) rights of both women and men. Of course, I have pointed out that liberal justice is not always compatible with the other perspectives, but that does not prevent us from attempting to make them largely compatible.

There is another way in which liberal theories cannot tell the whole moral story, but in which they must be an essential part of the story. Liberal theories are based on the paradigm of the relationship between moral equals, where the ground of moral equality is the equal possession of some trait or capacity. In Kantian theories the basis of this relationship is the possession of rationality. The question arises as to whether significant variations in the degree to which people possess such a capacity undermine the idea of moral equality. Some theorists address this problem by widening the notion of the relevant trait or quality. In Rawls's theory, the relevant basis of moral equality consists of capacities that do not need to be realized: the capacities to have a conception of one's good and to have a sense of justice, which he defines as a "normally effective desire to apply and to act upon the principles of justice, at least to a certain minimum degree."[12] Rawls counts children and infants as meeting the minimal requirements, since they have the capacities. They therefore have basic rights to receive the full protection of the principles of justice. These rights, he says, are normally exercised on their behalf by parents and guardians.[13]

With the move of defining the relevant basis of equality in a broad enough manner, Rawls is able to preserve the notion of a moral equality in virtue of which a wide range of human beings with varied capacities have the same rights. Surely, some rights are invariant over this range, such as the right against being assaulted, even if the violator is a family member, but the focus on the ways in which these human beings are the same should not mislead us into recognizing the ways in which we must treat them differently in light of their differences.[14] There might be some extended sense in which infants and children have exactly the same set of rights, but I wonder whether this sense serves as a useful guide to action. I am not sure what exactly Rawls means when he says that parents and guardians exercise rights on the behalf of children. Whatever it means, it must be consistent with the fact that children, at least up to a certain age, have a capacity for a sense of justice that to some extent is actualized but is largely a set of potentials whose development very much depends on their subsequent relations with others. They are not full moral agents, and often this means that we cannot let them exercise some rights that we would be required to let most adults exercise.

Children do, at very early ages, begin to display a sense of fairness, but it is sufficiently crude and erratically effective that much of what parents and guardians should be doing is to foster a sense of justice. To do that, children must be guided and just plain ordered at times. True, parents often assume that their children are much less capable of reason giving and of reasoned consideration than they actually are, but many parents, especially these days, I think, err on the other side of giving children options when these children are not capable of adequately considering these options, when what they need is direction instead of options. Another factor relevant to the treatment of children is their changing age. An appropriate intervention in a child's affair may become inappropriate at a later stage of maturation.

Consider also that families transmit moral and religious traditions from generation to generation. The process of transmission sometimes requires that parents not give younger children options to do or not do certain things that they would be required to give adults or mature children. For example, we would not tolerate making adults go to Sunday school, but in the case of children, I am inclined to say that within certain limits on the methods used, we should accept it. For many parents, to abstain from giving children a concrete understanding of their religion and a real sense of what it is like to live it is to fail to care for them properly. Here again, though, parents must recognize that their children's relation to a religion must change as the children mature and that their own relation with their children with respect to religion must change accordingly.

To say that children and adults have the same set of basic rights does not capture any of these complexities about the ways in which family members must act differently toward other members in light of significant inequalities—inequalities across members and inequalities across the life span of each member. The language of equal rights seems too crude an instrument to deal with these questions. Yet it seems to me that liberal justice is still relevant in bringing out ways in which family members are to be treated alike and in identifying the morally relevant respects in which a family can be a group of potential equals. The job of some family members, in fact, is to help make that equality a reality. Liberal justice provides a needed perspective on the family, but it needs to be informed by the kind of attention paid to the particularity of each individual that is at the heart of the care perspective, and it needs to be informed by a communitarian appreciation of the ways in which individuals come to form meaningful identities through institutions, such as the family, that transmit traditions.

The care and justice perspectives are abstractions from the rich and complex moral reasoning that we ought to be engaged in. These abstractions are useful to the extent that they allow us to think more clearly and more carefully about the ways in which different types of moral considerations bear on our decisions to act in contexts such as the family and on how they may sometimes interweave, reinforce each other, or conflict with each other. These abstractions are dangerous when they lead us to neglect the ways in which different types of moral considerations interweave and when we neglect a whole range of considerations in favor of one type.

There is danger in emphasizing care while tearing it away from its relations to justice, and there is danger in emphasizing one sort of justice while tearing it away from the other moral perspectives. Emphasizing liberal justice to the neglect of care and communitarian justice can lead to an impoverished family life and impoverished individual lives. This is an important truth contained in criticisms of liberal justice by care theorists and communitarians. When we are guided solely by a conception of the rights of individuals as human beings, we forget the moral considerations that help our most valued relationships to flourish. The absence of flourishing not only would make human life poorer but also would make it doubtful that there would be enough individuals who could act effectively on liberal justice itself.[15] The best way we know to foster an effective sense of justice begins with a nourishing and just life of personal relationships. We know that the first relationships a person has are especially important and that they often, if not always, affect a person's ability to be concerned about anyone.[16]

Notes

1. Carol Gilligan, *In a Different Voice: Psychological Theory and Women's Development* (Cambridge: Harvard University Press, 1982); Carol Gilligan et al., eds., *Mapping the Moral Domain: A Contribution of Women's Think-*

ing to Psychological Theory and Education (Cambridge: Center for the Study of Gender, Education, and Human Development, Harvard University Graduate School of Education, distributed by Harvard University Press, 1988); Carol Gilligan, Nona Lyons, and Trudy Hanmer, eds., *Making Connections: The Relational World of Adolescent Girls at Emma Willard School* (Cambridge: Harvard University Press, 1990). For an analysis of the distinctive features of the care perspective, see Lawrence Blum, "Gilligan and Kohlberg: Implications for Moral Theory," *Ethics* 98 (1988): 472–91.

2. John Rawls, *A Theory of Justice* (Cambridge, Mass.: Belknap Press, 1971).

3. Michael Sandel, *Liberalism and the Limits of Justice* (Cambridge, England: Cambridge University Press, 1982), 33.

4. Susan Okin, *Justice, Gender, and the Family* (New York: Basic Books, 1989), 32.

5. Recognition of these points has been impeded, I think, by an overemphasis of the idea that the care perspective is contextualized reasoning about the particular. While the care perspective does involve a focus on the particular, that focus is inevitably informed by general concepts, such as that of a good or healthy relationship.

6. Marilyn Friedman, "Beyond Caring: The De-Moralization of Gender," *Canadian Journal of Philosophy* supp. vol. 13 (1987): 100.

7. Marilyn Frye, *The Politics of Reality* (Trumansburg, N.Y.: The Crossing Press, 1983), 9.

8. Claudia Card, "Gender and Moral Luck," in Owen Flanagan and Amelie Rorty, eds., *Identity, Character, and Morality: Essays in Moral Psychology* (Cambridge: MIT Press, 1990), 205.

9. I see the following authors as representative of the communitarian movement: Alasdair MacIntyre, *After Virtue* (Notre Dame, Ind.: University of Notre Dame Press, 1984), and *Whose Justice? Which Rationality?* (Notre Dame, Ind.: University of Notre Dame Press, 1988); Charles Taylor, *Hegel* (Cambridge: Harvard University Press, 1975); "The Nature and Scope of Distributive Justice," in Frank S. Lucash, ed., *Justice and Equality Here and Now* (Ithaca, N.Y.: Cornell University Press, 1986); and *Sources of the Self* (Cambridge: Harvard University Press, 1991); Michael Walzer, *Spheres of Justice: A Defense of Pluralism and Equality* (New York: Basic Books, 1983); *Interpretation and Social Criticism* (Cambridge: Harvard University Press, 1987); and Michael Sandel, *Liberalism and the Limits of Justice*. It is ironic that Sandel, in sentimentalizing family harmony, misses the role of communitarian justice.

10. See Sara Ruddick, "Maternal Thinking," *Feminist Studies* 6 (1980); a shorter version is in *Rethinking the Family*, ed. Barrie Thorne with Marilyn Yalom (New York: Longman, 1982); *Maternal Thinking: Towards a Politics of Peace* (Boston: Beacon Press, 1989).

11. See Sara Ruddick, "Justice within Families," given at the Eastern Division Meetings of the American Philosophical Association, December 1992.

[Editor's note: Sara Ruddick makes similar points in "Injustice in Families: Assault and Domination," this volume, 71–73.]

12. Rawls, 505.

13. Rawls, 505–9.

14. Ruddick made this point in "Justice within Families." [Editor's note: See Ruddick, "Injustice in Families: Assault and Domination," this volume, 73–74.]

15. I made this argument in "On Flourishing and Finding One's Identity in Community," *Midwest Studies in Philosophy* 13 (1988): 324–41.

16. This paper emerged from a commentary on Sara Ruddick's "Justice within Families," given at the Eastern Division Meetings of the American Philosophical Association, December 1992. It was read at the conference on Community, Family, and Culture, Estes Park, Colorado, August 1993 that was sponsored by the Institute for Advanced Philosophic Research. Portions of this paper are part of a larger project supported by a fellowship from the National Endowment for the Humanities. I gratefully acknowledge this support.

Part III

Culture

6

Shaping Feminist Culture

Virginia Held

The power to shape consciousness is an overwhelming one, ruling out alternative conceptions and perceptions, crushing aspirations unacceptable to it, and leaving us devoid of the words with which to express even our skepticism and certainly our anguish and our opposition. What could be more total than the power to control the very terms with which we think, the language through which we try to grasp reality, the images with which we see or block out features of our surroundings and of ourselves, and the awareness we need to try to guide the trajectories of our lives? The culture of a society has such power.

I suggested in the first chapter of *Feminist Morality: Transforming Culture, Society, and Politics* that for the revolutionary feminist transformations of society that are occurring and will continue to occur, culture is relatively more important than for other revolutions. I included in culture a wide range of thoughts, feelings, symbols, and images. In this chapter I look more closely at the production of culture and its existing institutions, and I show how the institutions conflict with feminist values and should be transformed. I consider, too, how feminist culture attuned to feminist morality can further develop.

Culture and Consciousness

I mean by the term 'culture' something distinguishable from social structure. The social structure of a society is in possession of other forms of power than the power to shape consciousness: the state has power to coerce through law and the use of force, the economy to determine outcomes through investments, wages, profits, and contracts. Culture depends more on symbols and meanings for its influence. On some views, culture may envelop the social structure or be indistinguishable from it; on others, culture serves as reinforcement, or exists as reflection only, of the social structure. On still other views, culture may guide social structure, evaluate it, or lead it. I do not deal extensively with these issues but proceed from the view that culture ought to evaluate and guide social structure; my concern is how this can and ought to be done.

In contemporary society culture has to do with making and receiving symbolic messages, images, and ideas. It includes both the popular culture of the mass media and the high culture of art museums and literature. It includes the creation and imparting of knowledge in schools, colleges, and universities, and it includes the social and material realities in which and by which it is created and transmitted: television networks, broadcasting studios, and television sets; newspaper chains and printing presses; movie studios and theaters; university and school buildings and laboratories; and the salaries and fees of those who work in the culture industry and related activities.

Culture has receivers as well as senders, consumers as well as producers, readers as well as authors; and often what recipients make of or how they use a cultural object is different from what its senders intend. Some critics emphasize this difference, others find it easily exaggerated; most could agree that in exploring culture, especially in considering the ways we should shape it, attention needs to be focused on interactions, relationships, and communication, not on objects and their properties in isolation.

Expression and Imagination

Much of what occurs in the domain of culture requires a focus on categories relatively unfamiliar to dominant philosophical traditions and to the social sciences. I deal with the ways we express our experiences, our relations with others and our thoughts and feelings, and explore alternatives to those ways. There is thus a focus on expression and imagination of a kind that fits awkwardly with the philosophical analyses and theories that flow out of the scientific and the western liberal traditions and that can be found in Anglo-American philosophy. For my purposes, a relatively uncritical discussion of expression and imagination, especially in the experiences of women, will yield enough understanding of these concepts to be able to proceed with the inquiry and suggestions I undertake.

Much recent work in philosophy has taken the category of action as central and has tried to analyze and to understand it. This has been an improvement over focusing almost exclusively on the behavior dear to the sciences, but perhaps we need to give a much more prominent place in our inquiries than we have so far to the category of expression.[1]

What are we expressing when we raise an arm? An intention to signal someone to call on us? A desire to stretch? A plan to reach something on a shelf? To express something to someone requires a recipient of our message, but not all expression has an audience, and certainly not all expression is understood by its recipients.

When a baby smiles, she is expressing a feeling of well-being or delight. When a mother smiles back, she expresses a mutual relation of caring. Only by the artificial frameworks of science would it seem appropriate to reduce the smile of the baby and the smile of the mother to bits of behavior about which we could know only what a third person, an observer, could see or infer. Even to think in terms of action seems more artificial and less basic than to think in terms of expression. An action is by definition purposive, but it is doubtful that babies have purposes or that adults have them much of the time they do or express many things. Certainly, some of the things we do are actions, but not all and perhaps not some of the most significant.

Expression can be a shared phenomenon. The concept of action still attaches to individuals in isolation, although some of us have argued for acceptance of notions of group action and collective or corporate responsibility.[2] Expression is less limited: we can speak of the expression of trust or mutuality or conflict as something existing in a relation between persons. As we have seen, much feminist concern focuses on relations between persons rather than, as does so much traditional theory and nonfeminist inquiry, on individuals and their characteristics or actions. Perhaps we should think of such felt relationships as those expressed between mothering person and child as the fundamental fabric of society, rather than supposing that individuals acting compose society. We might think also that experience of and in such relationships should be central to our development of morality and culture and that understanding expression is essential to understanding culture.

We might think, as well, that imagination is a human faculty or capacity to which far more attention needs to be paid in philosophical thought and that what we come to mean by it will be different from traditional interpretations.[3] It has often been seen as a capacity to entertain mental pictures and images. We may find it to be more concerned with alternative feelings, and especially relationships, than with alternative pictures.

The faculty of reason and the sense of sight have been the privileged concerns of philosophy throughout most of its long history. Many feminists have questioned the suppression or exclusion of other aspects of experience, deploring the habit of disparaging emotion and ignoring moral feelings.[4] Many, too, have questioned the way male attempts to be rational divide things into opposing and hierarchically ordered categories: mind/body, reason/emotion, subject/object, man/nature, and, of course, male/female.

Such alternatives as affirmation and negation are powerful tools of logical thinking suitable for some issues, and the dualism of true and false is often needed to make sense of thoughts and actions, but such categories are unsuited to deal with much human experience, including experience of change. Reason can recognize the existing world and its negation. "The king rules" may state a fact. "The king does not rule" may express a refusal to accept the existing social reality, as well as being a logical possibility, but if we think in historical terms, a simple negation expresses an impoverished set of alternatives.

If we think, instead, in terms of human imagination, we see that the alternatives to any existing reality are multiple, yet that mere logical possibilities are not what we seek. We seek different realities, not total reversals. As Michel Foucault suggested:

> There is no binary division to be made between what one says and what one does not say; we must try to determine the different ways of not saying such things. There [are] not one but many silences, and they are an integral part of the strategies that underlie and permeate discourses.[5]

We are constituted in large part by our relations with other persons. Change for human beings is not a negation of existing reality so much as the strengthening of some relations and the weakening of others. Clean breaks are rare; even if we decide to end a relationship, historical and emotional aspects of it will linger. The tie will loosen rather than cease to exist. The language of "is" and "is not" seems clumsy rather than perceptive in describing the ever-changing relationships that connect us to others, not only in personal bonds but in the political and social ties that compose human reality as well. At the level of historical change, the strengthening and weakening of ties may be more salient than the denial of existing reality.

For very many women and for some men, changing our lives has constituted significant social change in gender relationships. Imagination plays a major role in such change and culture a primary role in nourishing imagination.

Consider a woman involved in such change. She imagines her life as other than it is, especially as she sees culturally presented alternatives,[6] but the alternatives she imagines are multiple, not the simple negation of what is, and they are not clearly distinct. The relationships in which she finds herself are transformed by other relationships, and these processes are many, rather than simple dualistic denials of those that exist. The futures she imagines for herself, for her children, and for the world are as varied as the stories she hears or tells, to herself or others, and as varied as the images she entertains or expresses.

To deal with culture and the social transformations I am exploring, the notions of expression and imagination will often be involved. Human experience should be understood to include these as centrally as it includes the reasoning and observation on which Western philosophy has been built and as centrally as the action on which moral evaluation has focused.

The Philosophical Evaluation of Culture

What arrangements concerning the culture that has such power as the power to shape consciousness would be justifiable? How should the institutions that produce culture and shape consciousness through the mass media be constituted? What would cultural practices have to be like to be legitimate? What values should be sought in the making and receiving of the works of culture? What obligations and rights do those engaged in the production of culture have? What rights and obligations do the consumers of cultural products have, and what mistakes may we be making in thinking of them as consumers of commodities? Should all or most people participate in the shaping of the culture that surrounds us and that shapes the world of our children and grandchildren, and what forms should this participation take? Ought a more participatory and less elitist culture be a goal to be sought, or should quality be the higher goal? What sort of arrangements for the creation and acceptance of culture would be agreeable from a feminist point of view, and how should they be brought about?

These are all urgent and extraordinarily important questions.[7] Philosophers have not paid even remotely adequate attention to them. The tradition of liberal political thought has laid a firm foundation for expression unhampered by certain forms of interference; for free thought and inquiry without restrictions imposed by religious authorities and for free speech not hampered or controlled by government. Support of such fundamental rights as those guaranteed in the First Amendment to the Constitution of the United States have been given eloquent philosophical formulation by John Stuart Mill, and contemporary philosophers have considered certain complex and often technical problems within the range of liberal rights to free expression.[8] Philosophers in the liberal tradition, however, have been almost blind to the problems of the control of culture by economic forces and interests and to the ways in which such control undermines free expression and restricts effective expression to those already in possession of economic power and of gender and racial advantage. Contemporary Anglo-American philosophers have been for the most part silent about the role of the mass media in affecting consciousness and thus society, about what the relation ought to be between the culture and the economy, about what arrangements for the production of such powerful cultural shapings of persons and of reality would be legitimate.

Though there have been important discussions of the media among those influenced by the Frankfurt school and by the writings of Theodor Adorno, Max Horkheimer, Herbert Marcuse, and others, these discussions have been useful mainly in dealing with questions of causality.[9] They help us understand how the media in capitalist societies reinforce capitalism's hold on the popular imagination and divert the attention of oppressed groups from an accurate perception of their actual conditions and interests. Such analyses provide the bases for significant empirical studies of the processes by which consciousness is shaped and misshaped,[10] but we still need to deal far more than contemporary philosophy has with the prescriptive questions of what roles culture and especially the media ought to play in a free, decent, and feminist society and what institutions for the production of culture would be acceptable. We need to deal with these questions from where we are here and now, considering feasible proposals that do not require the total transformation of the economic system or of society and culture all at once.

Many engaged in cultural studies dispute the view that the consumers of popular culture are stupid and passive, mere recipients of whatever the culture industry foists on them. In her summary of a representative sample of writers making this argument, Meaghan Morris says they hold that

> consumers are not "cultural dopes," but active, critical users of mass culture; consumption practices cannot be derived from or reduced to a mirror of production; consumer practice is "far more than just economic activity: it is also about dreams and consolation, communication and confrontation, image and identity."

But Morris goes on to question the critical force of most of the populism these writers study; she raises doubts about the separation of production and consumption. What their thesis amounts to, she suggests, is this: "People in modern mediatized societies are complex and contradictory, mass cultural texts are complex and contradictory, therefore people using them produce complex and contradictory culture."[11]

We can agree with those Morris describes, that some elements in popular culture encourage people to criticize society, to imagine better alternatives, and to experience genuine pleasure, but whether these elements are substantial or only minimal, we can surely argue that different arrangements for the production of culture could enhance substantially these possibilities.

A feminist morality for which the flourishing of children would be central could never agree that the enormous influence on children's development wielded by the mass media should be a mere commercial instrument, used in whichever ways will serve the economic interests of the producers of entertainment, nor could a reasonable view of how culture should shape consciousness rest content with the wholesale ceding of that capacity to those whose primary aim is economic advantage.

The Liberal Position

When we try to think of a short list of universal human rights to which all can agree that all are entitled, it seems likely that freedom of expression should be near the top of the list. The Western liberal conception of freedom of expression contains much that is valid and indispensable for an adequate view of what free expression requires and of what we should do to encourage it. It also contains serious deficiencies, especially as it has been developed and as it now prevails in the United States. This view of freedom of expression has given us a cultural marketplace in which culture other than education is produced almost entirely for the purpose of economic gain and a supposedly free market of ideas that is very largely dominated by economic power. It has given us a mass media culture that reinforces, with ever more sophisticated and insistent techniques, the corporate values of a male-dominated economic system, turning the society as a whole into one permeated to unprecedented degrees by the commercial and gendered values of the marketplace.[12] The culture of the marketplace has often reinforced sexual and racial stereotypes, presenting women's bodies as objects to be bought, sold, used, and discarded; it has made violence and domination sexually charged and appealing and in its portrayals of social realities has often distorted and obscured them in damaging ways. Liberal mass culture has failed to provide a culture capable of offering some balance to or critical evaluation of the overwhelming promotion, glorification, and enhancement of commerce.

Contemporary popular culture in the United States employs massive resources to draw persons into its orbit, and it is extraordinarily successful in achieving this result. Reports show that high school students spend three to five times as much time watching television as doing homework. American children grow up watching four to seven hours of almost completely commercial television each day. Books addressed to concerned parents counsel them on the importance of limiting their children's television viewing and promoting activities more conducive to healthy development,[13] but many parents are unable to exercise such control—parents in the television programs themselves are ridiculed for trying to—and many parents do not find the reasons to curb their children's television viewing persuasive enough to warrant the effort and conflict involved in doing so.

Program content is determined almost entirely by economic considerations. The means to economic gain for broadcasters are increased ratings and thus higher advertising revenues, and if the way to achieve these is to provide ever more violent and brutal programs and programs in which violence is increasingly sexualized, these are the programs that will be shown, however threatening to the women and men who will be victims of such violence and brutality. At the same time, economic censorship limits treatment of controversial topics.[14]

In the United States enormous sums of money are spent to fund advertising and the vast array of talent and cultural production harnessed to its demands.[15] The forces in the media that promote economic gain through advertising are controlling, and advertising, with its objectification of women, permeates public space through billboards and radio and inner perceptions through television and magazine images. The average American is subjected to five thousand advertising messages a day, and the number is growing.[16] It is hardly surprising that the consciousness of most Americans is swamped by this massive quantity of propaganda for commercialism. A culture not dominated by commercial interests has become, for most Americans, unimaginable.

Meanwhile, some popular and academic writers dismiss critics of commercial mass culture as elitist and as devoted only to a high culture in which their influence will be accorded the esteem they think it deserves. An example of this sort of argument is given by Herbert Gans in *Popular Culture and High Culture.* He ridicules the "anticommercial bias with which many scholars look at culture," suggesting that such critics esteem only culture that is "created by unpaid folk and by 'serious' artists who do not appear to think about earning a living."[17] The fact that high culture in the United States is also largely a commercial enterprise undercuts, he says, the persuasiveness of criticism of mass culture as an industry organized for profit. In characteristic ways, Gans's argument misses the point. What it shows is that there is even less of a ballast against the commercialization of everything in our society than some earlier critics of mass culture such as Dwight MacDonald and Leo Lowenthal supposed. It does not address at all the position for which contemporary critics can argue: that neither high culture nor popular culture should be dominated by commercial interests. Of course those working in the media have to earn a living, but they should be able to do so within arrangements that provide a decent level of artistic independence and intellectual integrity.

Commercialized culture presents itself as and is often accepted as the only alternative to control by such forces as those of the religious right or of government. Though we have seen a remarkable freeing of culture from governmental control in what used to be the Soviet Union and in Eastern Europe, the specter of governmental control of culture is still vivid and is intolerable to anyone who values free expression. The commercialized culture of the West often claims to be the only alternative to these forms of unacceptable control, but of course it is not the only alternative, and it is only a failure of imagination and thought that keeps us from focusing on far better arrangements for making and receiving culture than those that now prevail.

Some critics think that the shift from words to images as the currency of culture is so complete that Americans are losing their power to think coherently.[18] To these critics, the content of programs may be less significant than the overwhelming impact of the discontinuity of television and of the cultural shift from word to image as the prevailing form of representation. On the other hand, if an abstracted reason divorced from human feeling is a dubious basis for morality, and if morality should to an important extent be based on empathetic feeling for others with whom we can identify and whose stories can move us, then the images television can provide could be promising rather than deplorable. Perhaps the problem now is more the messages than the medium. On both views, however, the quantity of viewing may be a serious problem. Dialogue with actual others rather than mere passive reception of either words or images is an intrinsic aspect of satisfactory moral and intellectual development.

The shopping mall culture should not be the only alternative to limiting freedom of expression. One can imagine, for instance, a culture combining the best elements of feminist moral inquiry with the possibilities that the media can provide of enlarging communication, heightening empathetic moral understanding, and thoughtfully discussing moral and intellectual issues. The glimpses available in contemporary programming of such possibilities illustrate what popular culture might do, but the institutions that now produce what some call our televisual reality will have to be fundamentally transformed.

The Marketplace and Social Change

Can the changes needed occur within the marketplace? When enough recipients of advertising or program images or enough potential buyers of videos or movie tickets demand nonsexist or nonracist cultural messages, a shift in this direction will take place. The expression of interest on the part of the audience in exploring such topics as violence against women and the sexual abuse of children and in seeing films made by black directors has opened up possibilities for the commercial production of television programs and films with messages disturbing to viewers content with the status quo. Thus does the marketplace often respond to what audiences want. Nevertheless, the cultural influences persuading audiences to want what will support the interests of already dominant groups often overwhelm such progress as might otherwise occur.

There have been many studies of the pervasive denigration of women in advertising images, music videos, television programming, and movies.[19] There is also by now evidence of some, if sporadic, change.[20] When women, acting independently or in groups, protest a particular advertisement, advertisers sometimes do change their images if they deem it in their economic interest to do so. On the other hand, if their target audience includes enough men for whom a sexist message will be appealing, that message will be favored. The same holds for all the other cultural products—the programs, records, videos, movies, and books—tied to a system subservient to commercial domination. After two decades of complaints about sexism in television programming, almost no programs designed for and preferred by girls are offered on network television. The explanation is that girls are willing to watch programs directed at boys, but boys are not willing to watch programs directed at girls; the networks are unwilling to initiate change because the size of the audience for a program's commercials determines the content of programs.[21]

That some progress is possible even within a commercialized culture in no way indicates what might be possible in a culture liberated from commercial control. There are sound reasons for feminists to strive to free culture from the grip of commercial interests and to expect that the contribution that such a liberated culture might make to feminist goals would be much more promising than anything possible within the culture of the marketplace.

In the meantime there are fertile grounds for despair about the grip of commercialism on culture and consciousness. The role of mass media culture has a bearing on how poorly American students are doing in comparison with students in other countries in learning the basics of writing, reading, and mathematics.[22] Some social critics fear that we are being entertained to death or that we are addicted to the plug-in drug of television. Some speculate that the complete domination of the culture of the United States by the interests, techniques, and approaches of advertising are leading citizens to lose touch with reality.[23] Television determines the agenda of political debate: what it fails to attend to goes largely unnoticed.[24] Any alternatives to the corporate worldviews of fast cars, quick remedies, and magical cosmetics are, it may be thought, increasingly invisible in the media and thus absent from the minds of American viewers.

Mark Crispin Miller voices his pessimism.

By the late Seventies . . . there were virtually no more public outcries from a critical intelligentsia, but only TV's triumphal flow . . . Whereas the earlier critics could track the flagrant spread of advertising and its media through the cities and the countryside, and even into common consciousness, one could not now discern TV so clearly (if at all), because it was no longer a mere stain or imposition on some preexistent cultural environment, but had itself become the environment. Its aim was to *be everywhere* . . . and this aim had suddenly been realized. . . .

TV ceaselessly disrupts itself, not only through the sheer multiplicity of its offerings in the age of satellite and cable, but as a strategy to keep the viewer semihypnotized. Through its monotonous aesthetic of incessant change, TV may make actual change unrecognizable . . . TV preempts derision by itself evincing endless irony. . . . Thus TV coopts that smirking disbelief which so annoyed the business titans of the Thirties . . . TV protects its ads from mockery by doing all the mocking, thereby posing as an ally to the incredulous spectator. . . . Thus TV has turned the cultural atmosphere into one big ad. . . .[25]

Grounds for Hope

Those of us who have lived through and participated in the women's movements of recent decades may be encouraged to take a less despairing view of the grip of the male-dominated commercial media on consciousness. We can remember or we hear about the years when virtually everything in the culture and virtually all aspects of the society worked together to shape the consciousness of women into the forms of subservience, stunted aspirations, self-doubt, and acceptance of inequality, and yet we have lived to see very substantial change. What this suggests to us is that the more the power to shape consciousness overwhelms the views we would otherwise have, the more these subversive glimpses can open our eyes to the hidden reality. Those who have experienced periods in which an injustice was most successfully hidden from what can be thought of as public awareness may also have experienced the power of a few words or images to make visible the invisible. Once those who wish to see have seen, even if only once, they may see again and not forget, and the injustice will never again be quite invisible to them. Even when the dominant forces controlling culture successfully relegate expression to quiet or hidden avenues, the symbols and expressions of protest can circulate in furtive conversations and concealed gestures.

Angela Davis, describing the people's art that emerged from the history of militant labor struggles and the protests of African Americans, of women and peace activists, speaks of the cultural nourishment such people's art has provided for political action: "Black people were able to create with their music an aesthetic community of resistance, which in turn encouraged and nurtured a political community of active struggle for freedom."[26] Others agree that smaller scale, popular, and participatory art forms can counter the influences of mainstream or mass media culture, promoting political movements to change society. Also worth considering is the process of transforming mainstream or mass media culture from within, subverting its racism, sexism, and homophobia; many creative and responsible people have been striving to do this. Subverting the commercialism of mainstream and media culture from within may be a different and more difficult task, but it is not impossible. As talented people organize and demand cultural independence, they can make gains in attaining it, and they can find allies among their audiences.

Television viewers sometimes experience the conversion of seeing for the first time how they have been used to further the economic gains of advertisers as they boost the ratings of one show or another. Women are often startled to realize how the advertising images we may have thought of as benign or attractive have contributed to oppressive aspects of our lives: an excessive concern about appearance, a fear that only female passivity is acceptable, an assumption that male dominance is inevitable. When women understand how these damaging images are brought about by the economic interests of advertisers and corporations, anger at the culture of the media grows. As viewers come to see through the images by which they are surrounded, they find these images to be suspect rather than affecting. Learning to hold the messages of advertisements against rather than to the benefit of their senders, these viewers may never again be as naive or as receptive of the commercialized and masculinized images of media culture.

The more one has been deceived, the greater one's resentment on the discovery. When many viewers come to feel that they have been deceived by the very structure of media culture, the possibilities for a transformation of that structure are promising. Already there has been a significant decline in network viewing. There is speculation that large numbers of people seek a more participatory and nourishing culture than viewing commercial television can provide.[27]

Without denying the very great power of the media to shape consciousness and thus to wield power, we need to acknowledge that it is only a power to affect our thoughts and emotions, a power against which we are not without at least potential resources. It is not a power to kill, imprison, or deprive of sustenance, at least not directly, and of course the power of the media can be used to foster liberation rather than control.

We need theories of social change that will allow us to account for the role that elements of culture play in encouraging or impeding social progress. At present, liberal theories characteristically pay too little attention to the realities of economic power and how it is institutionalized. With respect to the media, such theories of social change show inadequate concern for such contemporary trends as the ever-increasing commercialization of the media, the increasing concentration and corporate direction of media enterprises, and the subordination of genuinely cultural values to commercial interests in capitalist cultures.[28]

On the other hand, Marxist theories of social change give an inadequate account of how such phenomena as transformed consciousness can effect social change. The salient example of the development of the women's movements in the United States suggests that economic domination and the cultural structures that sustain it are more porous than they look. A given set of realities about social situations can be given new and different interpretations, and such transformed interpretations can themselves effect social change. A consciousness-raising group can confront media dominance. Even without distinctively different economic factors bringing such changes about, changed interpretations can develop through shared expressions of changed ideas. As women come to see their situation as oppressive, they strive to alter it, and the process seems to require a theory of social change that acknowledges an independent role for such cultural factors as images, interpretations, dialogue, and conscious awareness, and even for these to develop independently of the factors that would be attended to as providing causal explanations of them and their effects.[29]

Though the power to determine what TV culture will portray may seem overwhelming, it is vulnerable to transformations in consciousness cultivated elsewhere. The revolution the women's movements are bringing about shows us how culture can be changed by nonviolent means, including such largely cultural methods of change as symbolic protests and actions, guerrilla theater, speakouts, and dialogue.[30] It also shows us how cultural change can effect change in the political and economic structure of society so often claimed by nonfeminist theory to be primary. While many feminists accept such views as that culture reflects changes elsewhere more than it causes them and that economic factors are the primary determinants of social reality, others acknowledge the capacity of consciousness and culture to shape society at least somewhat independently. The history of the women's movements seems to validate this view, as do some political events. An adequate account of the revolutions in Eastern Europe in 1989 must include attention to the part played by music and the arts. That popular music had broken down barriers that politicians could no longer maintain may have been an important factor.[31] That one of the most influential leaders in these developments was a playwright and another a conductor of an orchestra does not seem accidental.

Once we acknowledge how large a role culture can play in social change, we can consider the kind of feminist society we might aspire to build. It might be one in which culture would have a primary role in shaping both the present and future course of the society, but to be acceptable, the structure of cultural production itself would have to be very different from what it is at present anywhere in the world, but especially in the United States, where commercial domination has become the most extreme.

The Transformation of the University

When one searches in the United States for free expression that does provide critical evaluation of existing arrangements and substantive discussion of possible alternatives to them, the university is often the best place to find it, and in many regions the only place.

Universities and colleges have undergone substantial overturning of their traditional outlooks and offerings. Women's studies courses, along with courses in black studies and the studies of various minority and nonwestern cultures, are now part of the curriculum across the country. Women's studies programs have become an established part of academic life, supported by budgets and upheld by faculty lines. It is hoped that the wholesale forgetting of women's pasts and of earlier waves of feminism that occurred in previous periods can be forestalled. Historian Linda Gordon writes of the work of the first wave of women's historians in the late nineteenth and early twentieth centuries:

> I respond with a cold sweat when I remember how completely this first wave of history was suppressed. When I became a feminist and began, with a group of historians turned feminist, to find out something about women's situation in the past, I discovered these books, dusty, in the Widener library stacks, untouched for decades.[32]

This was a common experience across all fields; those of us who were students before the rise of the recent women's movements had encountered nothing whatsoever about previous feminist work.

By now nearly every academic field has felt the force of feminist criticism of its gender biases. Most fields have undergone a profound transformation, as feminist insights and theories have required fundamental rethinking of assumptions, approaches, and topics of investigation.[33] The changes I am dealing with in this book requiring rethinkings of moral and social theory are illustrative. Comparable changes in other fields are often as upsetting of established views.

Among the most significant factors in the social changes brought about by the women's movements have been the altered perceptions contributed by the academic study of women and by feminist inquiry in the various academic fields of knowledge. Courses and readings dealing with the experiences of African-American women, Latinas, lesbian women, and women in the developing countries, as

well as white North American women, have given whole generations of young women and legions of more mature women returning to college a transformed view of social reality. The gender
domination of everyday life has become visible and has by now been
investigated in almost all fields of what had been claimed to be
impartial knowledge.

The intensity of battles in the 1990s over multiculturalism and
the broadening of the curriculum attests to the stakes involved in
permitting or preventing critical views of American society from
becoming prevalent in the university.[34] Conservatives charge that
those striving for an antisexist, antiracist society are demanding
conformity and political correctness; they deny that there is anything conformist in students being taught from canons of texts composed only of the work of and presenting only the views of western
white men. The rancor expressed by those opposing changes in the
curriculum indicates how deeply conservatives and neoconservatives
feel threatened by the academic independence of colleges and universities. Many conservative foundations have been generously funded to promote antiprogressive research, and the reports and articles
produced with their support have often been made influential by the
commercial media, but many in the university have correctly seen
the output from such sources as closer to ideological public relations than to what a genuinely independent view of society would
provide. The independence that has been possible within the university often has permitted a critical view of American society to
develop; though constantly and perhaps now increasingly under attack, such independence has not been defeated by the economic and
political interests that strive to control it.

Comparatively, our institutions of higher education are less controlled by the government or by the economic sectors of the society than other institutions. Although often dependent to a very large
extent on government funding and corporate gifts, they are protected at least partially by ideals of academic freedom.[35] Educational
institutions at earlier levels are also to some extent independent.
Although they serve corporate interests in an educated work force,
and although schools are all too thoroughly influenced by the commercial values of the wider society, education is largely supported
by public funds, and the goal of creating an educated citizenry still
guides much that occurs in the classroom.

Perhaps those unaccustomed to seeing beyond the framework provided by the western liberal tradition of freedom of expression can

use the university as an example of the ways in which institutions for the production of other forms of culture, including mass media culture, could be comparably independent of, rather than subservient to, commercial interests and control, and perhaps they can learn from these observations that the alternative to government control is not necessarily commercial control but freedom from both kinds of outside pressure. There are obviously other values than commercial ones to be served by educational systems at all levels, and certainly there are other values that could be served by our cultural and media enterprises. We should proceed to delineate how these values should be understood and pursued. In the sector in which the mass media now affect the society, we could begin to offer at least possibilities of the independence and free expression that we can sometimes see in universities.

In asking for cultural independence, I have been accused by Alasdair MacIntyre and others of being ahistorical, of assuming that there could be "purely external critics" who could escape existing beliefs, conventions, and institutions.[36] On the contrary, I am comparing the possibilities for independence in existing institutions— for instance, the pursuit of knowledge in the university—with the production of culture in the television industry. Since the pursuit of knowledge has become, through protracted struggles since the seventeenth century, relatively free from outside control by church, state, and corporation, it is not unreasonable to aim at some comparable independence for other forms of culture.

The Value of Free Expression

Freedom of expression requires more than the absence of interference.[37] Although the dangers of censorship and of chilling threats of interference are not behind us, especially from religious fundamentalists and in parts of the world without First Amendment traditions or their equivalents, there are issues concerning freedom of expression that have not yet begun to be addressed adequately, even in philosophical discussions of ideal societies. Theorists should consider how concepts of free expression need to be transformed to be suitable for the realities of a mass media culture.

In a media culture, the materials of expression are not only a voice, as the still dominant legal model of the orator in the public square assumes, but television studios, airwaves, transmission facilities, and the like. Should these be available only to those already in command of large economic resources? It certainly was not the intent of the framers of our concepts of democracy and free expression that only those already powerful should be heard. And it certainly is not acceptable from a feminist point of view that those now in control of economic power should dominate the culture.

Elsewhere I have argued that we need a massive effort, comparable to that which brought about our system of public education, to publicly fund the production of noncommercial culture, including mass culture. Noncommercial culture should be as technically sophisticated, imaginative, and exciting as current commercial culture. Some such production should aim to reach large audiences, but instead of serving above all the values of commerce, it should serve the values of delight, well-being, aesthetic worth, and enhanced awareness—the values that feminists and creative people of various racial, class, ethnic, and other groups, freed from the pressures imposed by the marketplace, would choose. If a given cultural production turns out to be economically successful, that should be an incidental bonus, not the primary objective of the production, and such production should be protected from government control by standards of artistic freedom comparable to those of academic freedom.

Of course, those who create media and other culture need income and economic resources, just as those who teach in universities and schools do, but they need not be driven by the imperatives of accumulating capital and of maximizing profit. Private broadcasters and newspaper publishers can continue to turn out their products, just as private schools and colleges have continued to exist, but we need to supplement them with noncommercial alternatives, as we have supplemented private educational institutions with public ones on a truly massive scale. Public broadcasting, then, should be not a shoestring operation, as it is now, for very limited audiences, but a range of channels and stations offering highly popular programs as well as more specialized ones, all for the sake of cultural expression rather than commercial gain. Public funding, perhaps largely local but also national, for the production of documentary and other films, of drama and musical performances, of a wide range of cultural experiences, should be routine rather than exceptional. There also should be noncommercial sources of support for the tasks of the press: gathering the news and informing readers and viewers of what they need to know to be effective citizens and responsible participants in the shaping of culture. That newspapers and television news programs now often put the demands of commercial gain ahead of the goals of informing the public is a clear distortion of the work that ought to be done by the press in a democratic society.

There remains the question of whether the transition to a more independent and responsible culture should be brought about by further restraints on commercial excesses, as are now being considered with respect to the outrageous exploitation of children on commercial television programming designed explicitly to cause children to buy products, or whether it should be brought about by empowering voices that would provide alternatives to such excesses.[38]

John Stuart Mill believed that persons genuinely enabled to experience both admirable and unworthy cultural expressions—whatever we take these to be—generally will choose the admirable. If we share that belief, then of course we will advocate an empowerment of those not now able to provide noncommercial programs and productions. We will advocate empowering more expression rather than restricting the commercial production of media junk. We will choose, that is, the route of Mill, suitably repaved, rather than the route suggested by Plato's banishment of the poets, as updated by Alexander Nehamas.[39]

Even if we are highly skeptical of Mill's optimistic view, however, we still have good reasons not to choose the avenue of control until the test of empowering alternatives has been made. It certainly has not yet been made in the United States. Until the so-called consumers of the media have failed the test, there are good reasons not even to try to surmount the obstacles to the Platonic route that the First Amendment presents. The First Amendment makes restrictions on expression, even on commercial speech, difficult to uphold, but nothing in it prevents greatly increased support for noncommercial speech. As has been proposed, a tax on commercial broadcasting could well fund greatly increased offerings on noncommercial public channels. Other methods of financing would not be hard to devise.[40]

Feminists creating culture should express the values to which we give priority, not accede in the priority of commercial interests in culture. Because the struggles to free thought and expression from religious authority and from state control have often been successful, we have reason to hope that the liberation of culture from commercial domination is not an impossible goal.

Society and the Future

From the longer-range perspective of a feminist society, however, the concentration of cultural expression in the forms of the mass media, whether commercial or not, would be dubious. The sexism, racism, and elitism that still taint the university might comparably color noncommercial enterprises. A feminist objective for cultural expression might be more participatory, localized cultural expression supported by audiences no longer greatly attached to the mass media. We should try to imagine the sort of culture that women might create as we freely express ourselves and attend closely to other women. Models of smaller groups sharing in the making of cultural products, such as theater or singing groups, local bands and craft collectives, may indicate more satisfying ways to create culture than further imitation, even in less commercial forms, of the heavily promoted star whose image is manufactured to serve the interests of his backers. The importation of the star system into the university in recent decades can serve as a warning rather than a model.

Still, we will probably continue to have and to want some cultural productions that can be shared rapidly by large numbers and that will still be mass media phenomena rather than small localized ones. No doubt tension between mass media and more participatory cultural forms may continue indefinitely. We will need to design institutions for the mass media as well as encourage culture not dependent on the media. For instance, panels of peers could determine which programs are aired or which newspaper ventures funded. Some decisions, between qualified persons or groups, could be made at random, by lot.

A media culture is a culture in which the mass media are the dominant feature; the United States at present has a media culture. A media society would be a society in which the influence of the media would be the dominant influence. The United States is not yet a media society, because commercial interests are still the dominant ones, and the media are their means to uphold this dominance. If the media somehow turned against business at this stage in our social development, business would win, but this may not always be the case. Although business interests are also probably dominant in the political process, it is not clear that if government turned against the business domination of the media, business would win. It is possible that the government, or more likely the public at large, led perhaps by women's groups and by persons working in the media themselves, could gradually liberate culture from outside domination.

If widespread acceptance of either public funding at adequate levels or adequate support by readers and viewers made it possible for the media and the press to gather and honestly present the news and to create excellent popular and serious entertainment, we could have the basis for the critical evaluation of the social structure that we now often lack. Such a genuinely free culture might then exert more influence in shaping consciousness and attitudes, and thus society, than the traditional sources of power such as government or the economy. If processes for these and other kinds of cultural production were genuinely participatory and free of gender or racial or class domination, we might achieve greater gains toward the goal of a society that feminists could accept than could be achieved by striving to change economic or governmental arrangements more directly.

A society shaped by a genuinely free culture would come closer than any we now know to being a society where decisions are made as a result of competing ideas, not force; of free expression and discussion, not raw power. The faculties of imagination, reason, and feeling would shape the future through cooperative production. The word and the image rather than the sword and the dollar would rule, but it would be the word and the image freed of their role in the service of religious institutions, state power, corporate interest, or, finally, of gender or racial advantage.

A feminist program for social transformation should focus special attention on the importance of a changed culture in achieving a justifiable society.[41] A feminist view of acceptable social arrangements should advocate ones that give priority to the possibilities of a free culture shaping a society in which the traditional forms of domination have been overcome and in which the power to shape consciousness belongs not to those with military or political or economic might, or racial or gender privilege, but to people responsible for choosing our own futures.

Notes

1. See Richard Wollheim, *On Art and the Mind* (Cambridge: Harvard University Press, 1974); and John Dewey, *Art as Experience* (New York: Putnam, 1934).

2. See Virginia Held, "Corporations, Persons, and Responsibility," in Hugh Mercer Curtler, ed., *Shame, Responsibility, and the Corporation* (New York: Haven, 1987); Peter A. French, *Collective and Corporate Responsibility* (New York: Columbia University Press, 1984); Larry May, *The Morality of Groups* (Notre Dame, Ind.: University of Notre Dame Press, 1987); Larry May and Stacey Hoffman, eds., *Collective Responsibility* (Savage, Md.: Rowman & Littlefield, 1991); and Gregory Mellema, *Individuals, Groups, and Shared Moral Responsibility* (New York: Peter Lang, 1988).

3. On the topic of imagination, see Hide Ishiguro, "Imagination," in Bernard Williams and A. Montefiore, eds., *British Analytic Philosophy* (New York: Humanities Press, 1966); and Richard Wollheim, *The Thread of Life* (Cambridge: Harvard University Press, 1984).

4. For some parallel developments in aesthetics, see Carolyn Korsmeyer, "Pleasure: Reflections on Aesthetics and Feminism," *Journal of Aesthetics and Art Criticism*, in press.

5. Michel Foucault, *The History of Sexuality: An Introduction,* vol. 1 (New York: Vintage, 1990), 27.

6. For a related discussion, see Amelie Oksenberg Rorty, "Imagination and Power," in Rorty, *Mind in Action: Essays in the Philosophy of Mind* (Boston: Beacon Press, 1988).

7. For further discussion, see Virginia Held, "Culture or Commerce: On the Liberation of Expression," *Philosophic Exchange* 19 and 20 (1988–89): 73–87, and "Philosophy and the Media," *Journal of Social Philosophy* 20 (1989): 116–24.

8. John Stuart Mill, *On Liberty,* ed. Elizabeth Rapaport (Indianapolis: Hackett, 1978); see Frederick Schauer, *Free Speech: A Philosophical Inquiry* (Cambridge, England: Cambridge University Press, 1982).

9. For a brief account, see David Held, *Introduction to Critical Theory: Horkheimer to Habermas* (Berkeley: University of California Press, 1980).

10. See James Curran, Michael Gurevitch, and Janet Wollacott, eds., *Mass Communication and Society* (Beverly Hills, Calif.: Sage, 1977); Michael Gurevitch, Tony Bennett, James Curran, and Janet Wollacott, eds., *Culture, Society, and the Media* (New York: Methuen, 1982); and the journal *Media, Culture, and Society.*

11. Meaghan Morris, "Banality in Cultural Studies," *Discourse* 10 (Spring–Summer 1988): 15-19. The phrase "cultural dopes" is from Stuart Hall, "Notes on Deconstructing 'the Popular'," in Raphael Samuel, ed., *People's History and Socialist Theory* (London: Routledge & Kegan Paul, 1981): 227-39, and the quotation that follows is from Mica Nava, "Consumerism and Its Contradictions," *Cultural Studies* 1.2 (May, 1987): 204-10.

12. Susan Faludi documents the complicity of the media in promoting the backlash that grew in strength during the 1980s in the United States against feminism and the modest gains made by women. Publications from right to left blamed the women's movement, rather than its opponents, for the stresses and woes women were experiencing; films and television programs spread the message that women should "recant their independent ways." Susan Faludi, *Backlash: The Undeclared War against American Women* (New York: Crown, 1991), xi.

13. Donald Lazere, ed., *American Media and Mass Culture: Left Perspectives* (Berkeley: University of California Press, 1987), 9; Kate Moody, *Growing Up on Television: The TV Effect* (New York: New York Times Book, 1980).

14. Jeff Silverman writes, "Advertisers want a peaceful marketplace. . . . When advertisers object to the content of a show, which, by contract, they prescreen, they have the right, also by contract, to withdraw their support." Advertisers withdraw support "if they sense that a particular show, or episode, is too controversial to be associated with their products." In the same article, producer Barney Rosenzweig is quoted as saying, "It's censorship based on economics"; and Steven Bochco, producer of *Hill Street Blues* and *L.A. Law* is quoted as saying, "We're sensing a much stronger resistance to ideas than in the last half dozen years. And I would say it's getting worse." The worsening of the problem, which has been there all along, is attributed to lean economic times. Jeff Silverman, "TV's Creators Face a New Caution," *New York Times*, 8 December 1991, B1.

15. Almost $129 billion was spent in 1990. See Stuart Elliott, "A Forecast for '91 Spending Is Revised." *New York Times*, 12 December 1991, D1.

16. "Ad Clutter: Even in Restrooms Now," *New York Times*, 18 February 1988, D1.

17. Herbert J. Gans, *Popular Culture and High Culture* (New York: Basic Books, 1974), viii.

18. See Neil Postman, *Amusing Ourselves to Death: Public Discourse in the Age of Show Business* (New York: Penguin, 1985).

19. See E. Ann Kaplan, *Rocking around the Clock: Music Television, Postmodernism, and Consumer Culture* (New York: Methuen, 1987); and Faludi, *Backlash*. See also Judith Williamson, "Woman Is an Island: Femininity and Colonization," and Patricia Mellencamp, "Situation Comedy, Feminism, and Freud: Discourses of Gracie and Lucy," both in Tania Modleski, ed., *Studies in Entertainment: Critical Approaches to Mass Culture* (Bloomington, Ind.: Indiana University Press, 1986).

20. See, e.g., Judith Mayne, "L.A. Law and Prime-Time Feminism," *Discourse* 10 (Spring–Summer 1988): 30–47.

21. Bill Carter, "HBO Turns 'Baby-Sitters Club' into a Series of Specials," *New York Times*, 10 September 1991, C11. Carter writes: "It is a pattern that has become familiar to educators, feminists and parents of girls: Children's shows on network television always steer clear of properties they believe will be of special interest to girls."

22. *National Assessment of Educational Progress.* Report of U.S. Department of Education, 27 September 1990.

23. See, e.g., Raymond Williams, *Problems in Materialism and Culture* (London: Verso, 1980).

24. See Michael Parenti, *Inventing Reality: The Politics of the Mass Media* (New York: St. Martin's Press, 1986); and Michael Morgan, "Television and Democracy," in Ian Angus and Sut Jhally, eds., *Cultural Politics In Contemporary America* (New York: Routledge, 1989). See also Daniel Hallin, "Sound Bite News: Television Coverage of Elections 1968–1988," (Washington, D.C.: Woodrow Wilson International Center for Scholars, 1991).

25. Mark Crispin Miller, *Boxed In: The Culture of TV* (Evanston, Ill.: Northwestern University Press, 1988), 7, 8, 14, 17.

26. Angela Y. Davis, *Women, Culture, and Politics* (New York: Vintage, 1990), 201.

27. The networks' share of the prime-time audience fell steadily from ninety-three percent in 1976–77 to sixty-two percent in 1990–91; a slight reversal of the trend was recorded by 1991–92. "The Media Business," *New York Times*, 13 April 1992, D7. See Jon Margolis, "Are Americans Moving Away from Popular Culture?" *Chicago Tribune*, 24 November 1991.

28. On the increasing commercialization of the film industry, see Tom O'Brien, *The Screening of America: Movies and Values from "Rocky" to "Rain Man"* (New York: Ungar, 1990); and Mark Crispin Miller, ed., *Seeing through Movies* (New York: Pantheon, 1990).

29. For discussion of the role of culture in social change, see Margaret S. Archer, *Culture and Agency: The Place of Culture in Social Theory* (Cambridge, England: Cambridge University Press, 1988).

30. See F. Davis, *Moving the Mountain*; Jo Freeman, *The Politics of Women's Liberation* (New York: Longman, 1975); and Elly Bulkin, Minnie Bruce Pratt, and Barbara Smith, *Yours in Struggle: Three Perspectives on Anti-Semitism and Racism* (Brooklyn, N.Y.: Long Haul Press, 1984).

31. On how popular music can be effective in mobilizing large numbers of people for politically progressive ends, see Reebee Garofalo, ed., *Rockin' the Boat: Mass Music and Mass Movements* (Boston: South End Press, 1992), especially Peter Wicke, "The Times They Are A-Changin: Rock Music and Political Change in East Germany," and Anna Szemere, "The Politics of Marginality: A Rock Musical Subculture in Socialist Hungary in the Early 1980s."

32. Linda Gordon, "What's New in Women's History?" in Teresa de Lauretis, ed., *Feminist Studies, Critical Studies* (Bloomington, Ind.: Indiana University Press, 1986), 21.

33. See Gerda Lerner, *The Majority Finds Its Past: Placing Women in History* (New York: Oxford University Press, 1979); and Sue Rosenberg Zalk and Janice Gordon-Kelter, eds., *Revolutions in Knowledge: Feminism in the Social Sciences* (Boulder, Colo.: Westview Press, 1992).

34. See Catherine R. Stimpson, "Multiculturalism: A Big Word at the Presses," *New York Times Book Review*, 22 September 1991. See also Chandra

Talpade Mohanty, "On Race and Voice: Challenges for Liberal Education in the 1990s," *Cultural Critique* 14 (Winter 1989–90): 179–208; Joan Scott, "The New University: Beyond Political Correctness," *Boston Review*, March 1992, and "Readers Forum," same journal (May–August 1992): 30–34; Marilyn Frye, "Getting It Right," and Alice Kessler-Harris, "The View from Women's Studies," both in *Signs* 17 (Summer 1992): 781–805.

35. See Michael Parenti, *Power and the Powerless* (New York: St. Martin's Press, 1978), chap. 11.

36. See Alasdair MacIntyre, "Moral Arguments and Social Contexts," *Journal of Philosophy* 80 (October 1983): 590; and, in the same issue, Virginia Held, "The Independence of Intellectuals," 572–82.

37. On enabling access to expression and funding noncommercial culture, see Virginia Held, "Access, Enablement, and the First Amendment," in Diana T. Meyers and Kenneth Kipnis, eds., *Philosophical Foundations of the Constitution* (Boulder, Colo.: Westview, 1988).

38. On the exploitation of children by commercial television, see Stephen Kline, "Limits to the Imagination: Marketing and Children's Culture," in Angus and Jhally, eds., *Cultural Politics*; and Tom Engelhardt, "Children's Television: The Shortcake Strategy," in Todd Gitlin, ed., *Watching Television* (New York: Pantheon, 1986).

39. J. Mill, *On Liberty*, and Alexander Nehamas, "Plato and the Mass Media," *Monist* 7 (April 1988): 214–34.

40. See *A Public Trust: Report of the Carnegie Commission on the Future of Public Broadcasting* (New York: Bantam, 1979).

41. See Virginia Held, *Rights and Goods: Justifying Social Action* (New York: Free Press, 1984).

7

Of Mothers and Families, Men and Sex: The Truth about Feminism

Marilyn Friedman

Feminist women have become the females we all love to hate. They are the school marm surrogates of the nineties, at whom we defiantly aim our verbal slingshots. Nasty fictional women, such as *Fatal Attraction*'s Alex Forrest or *The Last Seduction*'s Wendy Kroy, conveniently reinforce the stereotypes that rationalize widespread feminist bashing.[1] And why not bash feminists? For more than two decades, they have been challenging deeply rooted conventions of social and cultural life. Surely it is time to strike back.

Mass media promote stereotypes that make it easy to ridicule feminists. The media caricature of a feminist hates the family, hates men, and hates sex. She has nothing but contempt for women who are full-time mothers and homemakers. She is a belligerent shrew or a whining victim (depending on what the audience most detests), yet she has clawed her way to the apex of professional power. Virtually omnipotent, she has caused every contemporary American ill from the collapse of the family to the decline of our global economic preeminence.

It seems as though many people have a perennial need to belittle some group of women or another, to make some women the targets of witch hunts and the brunt of comic routines. If we did not have feminists to hate, we would have to draft some other category of women into scapegoat service. Women in general should be grateful to feminists for shielding them from the wife and

131

mother-in-law bashing that used to be a cultural pastime. ("Family values," perhaps?)

These attacks on feminists, however, are misguided. Feminism has always sought to improve the quality of women's lives by diminishing the exploitations, abuses, and oppressions that afflict various women and by promoting diverse forms of female flourishing. Frivolous attacks on feminism can serve only to undermine the energy and motivation needed to sustain these important social projects. The cost of suppressing feminism will be the loss of real improvements in the lives of many women.

What are some of the improvements that feminism has struggled to achieve? They include ending workplace discrimination against women; increasing women's participation in government and economy; securing women's reproductive freedom; reducing violence against women; combating the multiple oppressions of minority women; fostering a female-centered eroticism; achieving equal rights for lesbians; curtailing the sexual objectification of women; eliminating cultural misogyny; correcting the scientific misunderstandings of women's health, physiology, and psychology; promoting honesty about marriage and mothering; and ending the sexual exploitation of women.

So why all the fuss? Why is feminism under attack if its goals are exemplary and its value is so great?

One of the striking features of the current campaign against feminism is its anti-intellectual slant and the fact that much of the war is being waged in mass media where a flair for glib wisecracks and an eccentric personality can score more points than thoughtful analysis. The consumers of mass media are busy with their own lives and do not have the time, energy, or inclination to plod through the complicated issues involved. Radio talk show host Rush Limbaugh is a striking example. Consider this idea from his first book: "Feminazi Trading Cards," with "all the vital statistics" on the back, including waist and hip measurements and "number of abortions."[2]

Culture critic Camille Paglia is another illustrative example. *Time* magazine recently dubbed Paglia "The Bete Noire of Feminism" and celebrated Paglia's "contempt for modern feminists," which, *Time* unabashedly admitted, has "drawn the media with magnetic force."[3] It is Paglia's personal insults against feminists that seem to attract journalists the most. (Germaine Greer is a "drone," Diana Fuss's output is "junk," the feminists concerned with date rape are "sexphobic, irrational, borderline personalities."[4]) Without the empty epithets, Paglia's actual criticisms of feminism are usually rather pedestrian—with a few bizarre exceptions, such as this: "Feminism, with its solemn Carrie Nation repressiveness, does not see what is for men the eroticism or fun element in rape, especially the wild, infectious delirium of gang rape."[5] (Is this what Harvard government professor, Harvey Mansfield, Jr., had in mind when he hailed Paglia's "fearlessness," her tendency to say "what you're not supposed to" and "tell off the boss"?[6])

Just who is this sex-phobic boss, blind to the delights of gang rape, whom the critics are so busy telling off and why is everyone so worried about her? The stereotypic feminist, you recall, hates the family, hates men, hates sex, and is contemptuous of full-time mothers and homemakers. What truth is there to this caricature? Frankly, very little.

My discussion covers these four topics: first, mothers; second, families; third, men; and fourth, sex. My goal is to demolish the distorted pictures being painted today of feminist views about these issues.[7]

Feminism and Mothers

Feminists are sometimes accused of being contemptuous of women who choose the traditional female role of full-time homemaker and mother. This view of feminists is false. Although a few feminists, mainly in the late 1960s and early 1970s, made harsh-sounding statements about the social roles of wife, mother, and homemaker, those statements cannot be understood properly out of their original contexts. In context, they were used to make certain critical points about the traditional practices in which women's social roles were embedded.

For one thing, feminists have opposed the barriers that either kept women from participating in the public world or denied us fair opportunities and rewards for doing so. No special effort is required to get women into mothering and homemaking. Numerous social norms, institutions, practices, and attitudes continue to support women who make these choices. Feminists have concentrated instead on occupations that have traditionally excluded or exploited women. To fight against those barriers, however, does not imply any value judgment whatsoever about the roles or occupations that have been traditionally open to women.

Second, feminists have challenged the socialization practices that channel girls and women toward mothering and domestic pursuits, regardless of ability or inclination. Because of this challenge, some critics accuse feminists of believing that women are brainwashed by a sexist society. Socialization is not genuinely brainwashing, of course, and no one thinks so. Between brainwashing and utter non-directedness, however, lies a wide range of possible forms of societal influence. Child rearing for gender roles clearly falls somewhere in between the extremes; it is not usually literal psychological coercion, but it is not a negligible influence either. Much child rearing is still geared toward turning girls into feminine women and boys into masculine men. Anyone who doubts, for example, that girls much more than boys are prompted toward marriage, domestic, and vanity pursuits should take a stroll through the nearest toy store.[8]

Although feminists have led the struggle for diverse opportunities for women, it is crucial to notice that many feminists also champion women's traditional roles—in new and nontraditional ways. Feminists were the ones who introduced the distinction between working inside the home and working outside the home, to correct the society-wide falsehood that only those mothers who worked at paid employment were really working mothers. Feminists have long been emphasizing that every mother is a working mother.[9] Feminists have also challenged the overly romantic view of family that obscured its material reality as a productive economic unit, but one that was based traditionally on women's unpaid domestic labor.

Feminists thus have fought consistently against the cultural devaluation of women's traditional roles and achievements and fought for women's genuine control over the realm that was supposed to be their own. Feminists, for example, have worked hard to wrest the control of women's reproductive lives away from governments and churches (both male-dominated) and place it in women's own hands. The struggle for abortion rights is well known. Less widely known are the feminist campaigns to make midwifery legal once again and to bring wonder, meaning, and maternal autonomy back into childbirth, which had long been consigned to impersonal, hi-tech clinical settings by the field of modern obstetrics (also male dominated).

In addition, major areas of feminist theory have sought to elevate cultural esteem for the special values that characterize traditional women's work. Care ethics, a widely influential, cross-disciplinary feminist development, celebrates the nurturance, caring, and general attentiveness to human relationships that characterize women's traditional work in intimate interpersonal settings. Many proponents of this view have urged that the socially underappreciated values of caring and nurturance are just as morally worthy, if not more so, than the more typically masculine values of justice and rights toward which social theorists have always gravitated.[10] Sara Ruddick's famous feminist book, *Maternal Thinking*, for example, respectfully explores and honors the intellectual dimensions of women's traditional work in nurturing and rearing children. She extracts from these patterns of thought a global peace ethic.[11]

Another widespread feminist concern about women as homemakers and mothers that has not been given its public due is the feminist concern for welfare mothers and women at the low end of the income scale, for whom full-time homemaking is simply an unaffordable luxury. Feminism set many researchers off investigating the feminization of poverty and the singular hardships facing women who struggle alone to support dependent children.[12] It was feminists who began the campaign for greater legal enforcement of the court-ordered child support that many divorced fathers still routinely evade paying.[13] In general, feminists have worked extensively with others to try to create a safety net of societal agencies and resources that can help single, divorced, and low-income mothers to care properly for their children and themselves.

Given the feminist praise for women's traditional moral concerns and interpersonal skills and the extensive feminist support for mothers who most need social support networks, it is disturbing to find that critics of feminism portray us as contemptuous of full-time homemakers and mothers. Why the distortion? Maybe the critics are just naively unfamiliar with feminist writings about mothering and care ethics. In that case, they ought to spend less time criticizing feminism and more time learning about it.

On the other hand, perhaps some critics of feminism are using this misrepresentation as a deliberate subterfuge to take attention away from the real feminist message about traditional families that makes them feel uncomfortable, even threatened. What feminist view could provoke such a response? The answer is easy: the feminist challenge to male domination—in this case, the domination of traditional family life.

Challenging male dominance is the most explosive of the feminist positions that have provoked the mistaken charge that feminists disparage traditional full-time homemakers. When the critics of fem-

inism accuse us of disparaging homemakers, those critics are simply misrepresenting feminism. The real target is men's ultimate
power over traditional family life, which feminists regard as a material peril and a moral adversity for women and their children. I
have more to say about this issue in the section on families, but a
few words will be helpful now.

The notion of the traditional family is ambiguous. Heterosexual
marriages are traditional in one respect when the husband is the
sole income provider and the wife is responsible for the domestic
work and primary parenting. A woman who participates in this sort
of relationship is not necessarily dominated by her husband. Heterosexual marriages, however, are traditional in a different, and
objectionable, manner when husbands make all the major decisions
for their family units, exercise ultimate control over the spending
of money, and generally hold topmost authority and power in their
homes.

In the mildest forms of male dominance, husbands/fathers love
and protect their wives and children with wisdom and kindness. Mild
male dominance is benevolent paternalism.[14] In the most virulent
forms of male dominance, husbands beat their wives and children
and generally tyrannize their households. Many people will concede
that tyrannical husbands are a nasty lot. Despite this concession,
however, traditional social practices and institutions often have tol-
erated such men shamefully.[15] Part of the feminist fight against male
family domination has been the uphill struggle to make social institutions more punitive toward such abuses as wife battering, marital
rape, and incest. Feminists also have argued that even seemingly
benevolent male family paternalism is a problem for women in traditional family roles.

A woman who creates a loving and supportive home life for her
family members gives them a moral as well as a material gift; such
activities can be the source of deep and justified satisfaction for
her. Child rearing, even more so, is a domain of breathtaking challenges and transcendent rewards. Child rearing is also a paramount
social necessity; when done well, it is a veritable public service.
A woman who chooses full-time homemaking and mothering is
choosing one of the various honorable vocations now available to
women.

There is nothing particularly honorable, however, about the subordination of women to men. There is no reason why a woman who
chooses full-time homemaking and mothering should therefore re-

linquish to her husband her own autonomous selfhood or an equal share of legitimate control over the home she makes or the family she is raising. The philosophical tradition is rich with praise for self-determination and the importance of being a free man. Until the recent decades of contemporary feminism, however, the ideals of liberty and autonomy were never applied by conventional (usually male) philosophers to traditional female roles.

To be sure, the concern for self-determination can devolve into a narrow moral obsession that obscures the self-enlarging values of community and relationships with others. Nevertheless, substantial self-determination is an important counterbalance to the requirements of endless service and self-sacrifice that threaten to deplete the moral resources of the traditional wife/mother role. At stake is the legitimacy of women following our own considered judgments about what is worth valuing and pursuing in the lives we make for ourselves and our families. It is no less than a question of women's moral integrity.

Male family dominance threatens more than a woman's moral integrity; it also threatens her own material well-being and that of her children. A woman who is a full-time homemaker and mother in a heterosexual marriage is economically dependent on, and therefore vulnerable to, her husband in a variety of ways.[16] For financial reasons alone, she, much more than he, needs the marriage to persist. Her financial standard of living would likely plummet after divorce while his would almost certainly rise. Because her income-earning husband can profitably leave the marriage at any time if he does not get his way, she has more need to please and defer to him than vice versa in those inevitable situations in which their desires or values conflict.[17] One overriding concern that keeps many battered women tied to their violent husbands is the fear of losing financial support, a paramount consideration when children are involved.

A woman who chooses life as a full-time homemaker and mother surely does not choose, for its own sake, the subordination and excessive vulnerability that she risks by her financial dependence on her husband. These hazards, however, inhere in the nature of financial dependence. Add to that the cultural ideals of masculinity with their incessant pressure on men to be strong, decisive, aggressive, and forceful, and the risks for women only intensify.

To be sure, there always have been some women who were strong and independent enough to stand up to their husbands for the views and values to which they were committed. Fortunately, there also have been men who did not avail themselves of the power provided by their breadwinning status and legitimized by masculine ideals. There are, in other words, genuinely good men.[18] Such men, however, run the risk of being socially stigmatized as wimps. The comic, though often sympathetic, figure of the henpecked husband makes sense only against a background presumption that men ought to prevail in their marriages. Taming the shrew is, after all, part of the Western canon. The rooster-pecked wife, by contrast, is not even a recognized category. Remember that it was his castle, not hers, where he was supposed to rule supreme.

If women are to choose their ways of life with some measure of autonomy and wisdom, then they should be informed about the risks inherent in the available options.

Feminism and Families

What about feminism's supposed hostility to the family?[19] Well, that depends on what you mean by *family*. Social commentators who praise family values usually have in mind the values of the so-called traditional family. The traditional family is a nuclear family consisting of a legally married heterosexual couple and their children, in which the man is the principal breadwinner and head of the household and the woman is responsible for all, or nearly all, the domestic work and child care. As early as 1977, however, this family form comprised only sixteen percent of all U.S. households, according to the U.S. Census Bureau.[20]

A family is, generically speaking, any group of persons who together form a household based at least partly on some sort of enduring interpersonal commitment. Legally or religiously sanctioned marriage is one example of such a commitment but it is hardly the only one. The concept of an enduring household captures the core idea of family life, and it has the credibility of having appeared in dictionary definitions of *family* even before the recent wave of the feminist movement.[21]

The notion of an enduring household does not resonate with greeting card sentimentality, however—and that is its distinct theoretical advantage. The point of the conception is to serve as an analytical category to enable understanding of the institution. To understand contemporary families in their diversity, we need a generic concept of family life that does not presuppose any norms about who is supposed to do what. Family norms should be debated as separately as possible from the relevant descriptive categories.[22]

Defining family generically as any enduring household based on interpersonal commitment allows us to acknowledge the familiness of all sorts of domestic relationships. We already know (although some of us mindlessly forget) that families by adoption are genuine families and, thus, that biological links between parents and children are not necessary for family life. It is now high time to give social recognition and support to families composed of heterosexual couples who are not married (with or without children), heterosexual couples who do not abide by traditional gender roles in domestic tasks or child rearing, lesbian and gay couples (with or without children), and single parents with children.

Any stable and nonoppressive domestic relationship will constitute a better family environment if it is, in turn, sustained by a respectful and supportive community that grants it all the privileges of family life. Feminists work to support nontraditional families, which sadly still receive substantially fewer of the privileges reserved for traditionally correct families (privileges such as inheritance rights and family health insurance) and which suffer a great deal of social stigma instead. In supporting nontraditional families, feminists promote family life more extensively and more thoroughly than our opponents who otherwise intone family values. Feminists, thus, do not oppose family life as such. Far from it. We are just as concerned as anyone else that the familial dimensions of our lives and our various enduring domestic relationships satisfy the needs and promote the flourishing of the participants in those relationships—all of the participants. It is society at large, not feminists, that, by neglecting or denying the needs of nontraditional families, is currently forsaking family life.

When feminists criticize family life, our targets are usually male family dominance and the female dependency that it promotes and enforces. It is patently obvious that to criticize this form of family life is not to oppose family life as such. It is also patently obvious that to criticize male-dominant families for the risks and oppressions that they pose for women is not to criticize the women who choose such arrangements. Rather, it is to challenge uncritical and overly romantic cultural images of those male-dominant marriage and family forms. Women, depending on their circumstances, might well derive satisfactions within male-dominated marriages and families, but at what cost? The fact that some people are content with certain social arrangements is hardly a conclusive reason to avoid questioning those arrangements.

Some critics have, nevertheless, tried to undermine feminist challenges to male-dominated family life by claiming that such families are beneficial for women and that women secretly recognize this. Philosopher and social critic Alan Bloom has argued this line.

Bloom has the candor to admit that the old family arrangements were not entirely good for women. He concedes that, because of economic changes and the recognition of injustices, "the feminist case [against the old family arrangements] is very strong indeed." The problem, in Bloom's view, is that there are no "viable substitutes." Macho men can be "softened" but they cannot be made caring, sensitive, or nurturant. Men will make positive contributions to family life only in the old-fashioned families in which they can exercise power and protectiveness over "weak," "modest," "blushing" women (Bloom's words). Women's independence, however, diminishes men's motivations for staying thus married and providing for children, and women's premarital sexual independence reduces men's motivations for getting married in the first place. "Women can say they do not care" about this loss of men's interest in them, warns Bloom, "but everyone, and they best of all, knows that they are being, at most, only half truthful with themselves."[23]

This antifeminist theme has a cunning seductiveness to it. It avoids the argument that feminism is bad because it hurts men, an argument that, we must admit, will not necessarily deter women from joining the ranks. Bloom argues instead that feminism hurts women. If the very people who might be attracted to feminism can be convinced that feminism is bad for them, then there is some chance of stopping the spread of this contagion. The argument hinges on two claims: first, by becoming feminist (too independent, too self-reliant), women will lose male love and male commitment to marriage and family; and second, women really want male love and commitment more than we want independence—regardless of what we might think.

Telling women that feminism will hurt us is not a new tactic in the public debate over women's issues. Barbara Ehrenreich found examples of it written more than two decades ago by Taylor Caldwell in John Birch Society literature.[24] Caldwell argued in 1970 that over the centuries women had entrapped and hung on to men both by avoiding opportunities to earn their own incomes and by faking dependent personalities. By encouraging female independence feminism threatens to undermine this con. In the years since 1970 certain economic realities have made it harder to persuade women to give up our incomes. Alan Bloom prudently ignores income, but the rest of the argument remains unchanged: if women act too independently, we will lose male love and the opportunity for (heterosexual) marriage and family, which, Bloom says, we really want more than anything else.

This message evokes the age-old genre of cliches that warn women not to be too sensible or too self-reliant in our habits. Not too long ago, women were routinely admonished: "Men don't make tracks for girls who wear slacks," and "Men don't make passes at girls who wear glasses."[25] (In the days before contact lenses, the latter meant giving up clear-sightedness in order to please men.) Since our cultural traditions give so little public recognition or esteem to love and friendship among women ourselves, the threat of a woman's being unloved by a man has the public meaning of being unloved, period. What women, other than lesbians, would not be made a little anxious by these sorts of messages?

Perhaps I am merely expressing a tedious feminist attitude when rejecting the Bloom line. Perhaps it is my contempt for men that leads me to do so. This brings us to a third feature of the familiar caricature of a feminist: she is a rabid man hater.

Feminism and Men

Christina Sommers has argued that feminism promotes resentment toward men. Feminism, she claims, views society as a sex/gender system that divides people into a victim class (women) and an aggressor class (men). In terms of this framework, feminism rationalizes "wholesale rancor" by women against their aggressors. Sommers rejects the concept of a sex/gender system and cannot abide resentment against men.[26] What can be said about her views?

First, feminist theory in general does not condemn individual men unless those men, as individuals, abuse, exploit, or oppress women (as misogynists, harassers, batterers, rapists, etc.). A great deal of feminist theory is devoted to analyzing institutions and practices as social wholes, along with their characteristic male biases and the individual men who rise within them to positions of power and authority. This sort of analysis is hardly identical to promoting resentment against all individual men.

Also, men differ greatly in the extent to which they benefit from or promote male privileges. Feminists recognize these differences, which are often based on race and class identities. In addition, many feminist women feel a solidarity with profeminist men who themselves challenge male-dominated social practices.[27] It is thus obvious that glib generalizations about feminism promoting resentment against men misrepresent the facts of the matter.

Second, the charge that feminists resent men ignores the focal point of feminist concern. Women, not men, occupy the center stage of feminist attention. The failure to recognize this shift in attention exemplifies the same male-centered bias of our culture that feminism challenges. Feminism seeks to promote women's support, care, love, nurturance, respect, and esteem for other women. The early feminist notion of sisterhood reveals this aim. Feminism also seeks to end the subordination of women to male-dominated social institutions and practices. The central concern, again, is women's own well-being.

In order for women to focus their energies, loves, and loyalties on other women, they must usually redirect some of their attention and support away from men.[28] As women begin to value and cherish each other more, their interest in men in general, and most men in particular, inevitably declines. Women who are intensely focused on other women might ignore men altogether. Women also sometimes get angry at men who oppose the improvements that women seek for their own lives. In addition, women who spend time challenging male-dominated social institutions often become less reverent toward, even overtly critical of, the male achievements and authority buttressed by those institutions. At what costs were they achieved? To what ends have they been put? Whose domestic service made them possible? And so on.

When women grow indifferent or angry toward men, criticize male-domination, or challenge male authority and power, it is not surprising that men feel this reaction as hostility and resentment directed at them. Those masculine feelings, however, are not the right measure for understanding women's attitudes. To think so perpetuates the very problem at issue by interpreting women's behavior and attitudes exclusively in terms of how they make men feel.[29] My point, to the contrary, is that what might appear to some people to be antimale is really profemale, a very different attitude and one that our culture at large still widely misunderstands.

Third, even if feminism does foster genuine and positive resentment against men, this attitude is a problem only if it is unjustified. Is it unjustified? Is it false that many women are significantly exploited, abused, or subordinated either by individual men or by male-dominated social practices or institutions?

My dictionary defines resentment as "anger and ill will in view of real or fancied wrong or injury."[30] Ill will is often a useless emotion, like spite or malicious envy, and may hurt most the one who feels it. No feminist wants women merely to reverberate with feelings of useless malice. Anger, however, can empower a woman to harness her energies into positive action against the constraints that harm or oppress her. It is scarcely improper for feminists to want women to harness their energies into constructive action against the wrongs that are inflicted on us.

John Stuart Mill regarded as natural the feeling we have of resentment and the desire to retaliate against those who harm us. This attitude, in Mill's view, becomes properly moral when imbued with social concern, that is, when we thereby take ourselves to be standing up for the interests of society and "asserting a rule which is for the benefit of others" and not simply ourselves. It is this complex sentiment that, in Mill's view, sanctions no less than the rule of justice.[31]

Whether resentment toward men is justified depends in part on whether the wrongs or injuries that feminists think men have inflicted on women are real or merely fancied. This issue is not settled simply by complaining that resentment is not a nice attitude. To decide whether women are justified in resenting men, we would have to consider a wide array of social practices: unwanted male sexual aggression (rape, incest, sexual harassment, and the rest), male violence against women, male power strongholds that minimize female participation, and so on.

It does not require much perceptiveness to see that women are at least sometimes wronged by men. It also does not require much historical knowledge to see that complacency has not helped women to end or to rectify those wrongs. In the United States, prior to the days of recent feminist anger, there were few places of refuge or support for battered women or rape victims, sexual harassment was not even a named problem, unwanted pregnancies could not be ended except by criminal means that threatened the lives of the pregnant women and girls, government and economy were over-whelmingly male-dominated domains, and on and on. The recent gains in women's social conditions have depended heavily on fem-inist activism. Feminist activism, in turn, has been energized by a variety of attitudes, among which anger figures prominently. Re-sentment against men would not be too high a social price to pay if it empowered some women to diminish their subordination to men and to promote their own well-being at long last.

Fourth, it might seem that feminists incorporate hostility against men into the foundations of our theories of the sex/gender system by conceiving of society as divided into male aggressors and fe-male victims locked in endless antagonism. That interpretation, how-ever, misconstrues the key concept at issue.

A sex/gender system, in general, comprises the many aspects of a social system that differentiate persons based on their sex or gen-der. The differentiations, in turn, bear significantly on the identi-ties, roles, norms, ideals, expectations, opportunities, and constraints that pertain to people.

There is no doubt that all human societies feature a sex/gender system of some sort. The institutions of sexuality, marriage, child rearing, productive activity, military defense, and governing, in most human societies, allocate roles partly according to gender. In addi-tion, most human societies sustain these wide-ranging roles with a host of child-rearing and other practices that promote in females and males the personality traits and identifications appropriate to their assigned gender roles and that discourage or forbid outright their participation in the roles of the other gender. The real issue is not whether we have a sex/gender system; obviously, we have one.[32] The real controversies have to do with its nature and origin and the extent to which it benefits or harms women.

Feminists generally believe that the sex/gender system of the United States involves widespread male dominance and female sub-ordination. This particular view is one that we can debate. To argue intelligently against this view, however, calls for careful re-consideration of a good deal of the evidence in its favor.[33] Even if the thesis of a male-dominant sex/gender system does manifest fem-inist resentment against men, the truth or falsity of that view is independent of such resentment and should be debated at least partly on empirical grounds.

Fifth, and finally, even if some women are now directing nega-tive, nasty, useless resentment toward men, that issue would be trivial in comparison to the gender-related difficulties still facing women, difficulties ranging from economic disadvantages to sexual violence. Women who express resentment toward individual and, admittedly, sometimes nonsexist men have probably suffered their share of male catcalls, gropes, put-downs, and worse and just gotten fed up with it. While two wrongs seldom make a right, a second wrong can sometimes bring the first one into clearer view.

I am far less worried about women's hostility to men than I am about the attitudes of those boys in my daughter's kindergarten class who keep telling her that girls can't be scientists, and girls can't be heroes, who bully or demean the girls on the schoolyard and, occasionally, try to pull up their skirts. (Yes, it still goes on.) Women's hostility toward men has no enforcement mechanism behind it; it will make scarcely a dent in cultural practices. Men's derogatory view of women, by contrast, has been buttressed by all forms of social power and authority. One is merely an annoyance; the other has fostered historic injustice and oppression. Most men can handle a few sneers. The so-called problem of feminist resentment against men is an issue that does not deserve our further attention.

Feminism and Sex

The fourth and last stereotypical feature of a feminist is that she hates sex. Sommers characterizes feminists as totalitarian "Big Sisters" who, like Big Brother in the novel *1984*, are out to enforce "boring . . . sexual correctness" on ordinary women.[34] Camille Paglia, as noted earlier, calls feminists sex phobic.

Feminists, however, certainly do not hate sex. Just as we challenge male-dominated family life, what we challenge in the realm of sexuality is male-dominated sex. To call this attitude sex phobic is to assume that there is no sexuality apart from male-dominated sex, so that hating male-dominated sex is equivalent to hating sex as such. That is an assumption truly worth pondering.[35] In general, to ridicule feminist cautions about sexuality seems to manifest a troubling sexual libertinism, a mindless attitude according to which, when it comes to sex, anything and anyone is fair game.

Unfortunately, sexual libertinism has yet to face the sexual crises of the 1990s. We are a culture deeply confused about sex. We live in a world so burgeoning with population that some commentators already warn of imminent brutal, militaristic, global anarchy.[36]

We live in an era when individual sexual contact can be a death-defying act. Eros has become Thanatos. We bemoan, in one breath, the problems of rampant teenage pregnancy, global overcrowding, and sexually transmitted diseases, yet, in the next breath, scold feminists for their prudery. Go figure.

Amidst all this sexual chaos, the antiseptic and well-worn notion of informed consent offers some individual and local guidance to women. Informed consent is a person's right of self-protection against the serious risks posed by sexual contact. Informed consent, however, must be genuine. Despite her raptures the next morning, Scarlett O'Hara never did consent to Rhett Butler dragging her up the stairs for some sexual brutality at his but not her instigation.[37] Even when no coercion or pressure is involved, a woman has not given informed consent unless she has both a clear understanding of the risks involved and the genuine option throughout her sexual encounters of protecting herself against those risks with contraception and prophylaxis—or refusal. If it is sex phobic to say no, then perhaps our culture needs more sex phobia.

We can no longer afford to view with tolerant amusement the glorification of male sexual aggression or the myth that women in general enjoy it. Apart from the question of women's right to protect ourselves against risky sexual contact, the idea that we enjoy sexual domination is, to say the least, perplexing. It is an odd psychology that would see no need to explain why someone enjoyed being dominated or humiliated, sexually or otherwise, and a still odder sociology that would unquestioningly attribute this phenomenon to whole groups.

The societal conditions that could promote and explain female sexual masochism are not hard to find. Typical patterns of gender socialization combine with mass media, advertising, and other cultural institutions to feed us a steady diet of messages that glorify and eroticize male sexual aggression and male sexual domination of women. Mass media and advertising compound the problem by relentlessly urging women to shape our sexuality around pleasing men—in our appearance, behavior, and sexual responses.

Critics of feminism might charge that this analysis is patronizing (matronizing?) toward women. That facile response, however, would miss the mark. For one thing, it is not only women, but men as well, whose desires are affected by socialization and cultural images. For another thing, an entire advertising industry is built on the conviction that media images and messages do impinge significantly on human desires. Are advertisers really just wasting our time and their financial millions? While the research is often inconclusive and the notion of strict determination overstates the case, nevertheless, many studies reveal complex effects of mass media on people's attitudes.[38] Why suppose that women would be immune to these influences or that it would not affect one of the most plastic of human passions, sexual desire?

Media portrayals of heterosexuality that endorse, routinize, and eroticize men's domination of women and women's deference to men are the key problem. How we solve the problem is, of course, an open question. Nothing about feminist critiques of those media entails the view that individual women—or even, with more reason, men—should be "forced to be free."[39] That is, I am not advocating that anyone be denied legally her pound of pornography or put through nonconsensual sex sensitivity training. Cultural dialogue about the issues is the approach that I and most other feminists seek. The cultural dialogue about sexuality is obstructed, however, when feminists who criticize male-dominant heterosexuality are condemned by Camille Paglia as sex phobic or by Christina Sommers as totalitarian big sisters out to enforce boring sexual correctness on innocent women.

When sex can lead to unwanted pregnancy or a fatal disease, it ought to be obvious to everyone that no one should be pressured to engage in it and no one should be denied an informed understanding of what is going on. Women should have full and genuine control over our sexuality. This has been a feminist credo from the start. Media representations of male sexual conquest, no matter how titillating to some consumers, glorify nothing less than women's loss of sexual control and consequent inability to protect ourselves in a crucial realm of our lives. Sexual correctness, or, more perspicuously, heterosexuality without male domination, may offend the sensibilities of some, but the gain in women's control is well worth the cost, and when it comes to sexual pleasure, only a sadly limited range of experience or a failure of imagination could underlie the insistence that sex minus male domination is boring.

When a woman is locked in a man's embrace, she may become aroused by the bonds of love and want the sexual contact to continue. Her compliance under those conditions, however, is hardly the sort of self-protective, informed consent that she needs these days for her own safety. The precipitous urgency of sexual arousal does not by itself provide any reason to trust a man's assurance at the time that, yes, he had a vasectomy and, of course, he is HIV negative.[40] The possibility that some women like male-dominated sex should not undercut our critical reflection on it. We, as a community, can still ask ourselves whether we want to continue supporting cultural glorifications of women being coerced, pressured, or seduced into sexual encounters over which they exercise no control.

Sex is no longer just a playful pastime and the means of reproduction; sex has become a matter of life and death. *It ain't the '60s anymore.* Sexual (as well as nonsexual) images of men dominating women and women submitting to men have always been demeaning to women. In the 1990s they represent a dangerous frivolity we cannot afford.

To conclude: Feminists are not contemptuous of full-time mothers or homemakers; instead, we esteem some of the central moral concerns of those traditional roles. Feminists do not oppose family life; instead, we support the genuine values of family life and especially of nontraditional domestic relationships. Feminists do not resent all men as individuals; what we challenge is male dominance throughout culture and society. Finally, feminists do not hate sex; instead, we encourage sexual practices by which women can truly protect ourselves. These views are not uncontroversial in American life. In order, however, to get on with the crucial debate that our society needs to have over these issues, we must bury, once and for all, the distortions that our critics circulate as a substitute for genuine public dialogue over feminist issues. I hope to have contributed to the funeral oration.

Notes

1. See Susan Faludi's discussion of the antifeminism in *Fatal Attraction* and her general survey of media caricatures of feminist women in *Backlash: The Undeclared War against American Women* (New York: Crown, 1991).

2. Rush Limbaugh, *The Way Things Ought to Be* (New York: Simon & Schuster, 1993), 204.

3. Martha Duffy, *Time* (13 January 1992): 62–63.

4. The first two of Paglia's insults are quoted by Duffy, 62; the third is quoted by Paula Chin, "Street Fighting Woman," *People* (20 April 1992): 126.

5. Camille Paglia, "It's a Jungle out There So Get Used to It!" *Utne Reader* (January/February 1993): 64.

6. Quoted by Chin, 129. Harvey Mansfield, Jr., is a current member of the advisory board for the National Endowment for the Humanities (NEH),

having been nominated for that position in 1991 by then–director of the NEH, Lynne Cheney.

7. Feminists who are widely read in feminist literature probably will find nothing new in what I have to say about feminism. This essay is addressed mainly to audiences that are hostile to, or simply uninformed about, feminism.

8. A great deal of contemporary girlhood socialization is oriented toward glamour and vanity pursuits, with Barbie shamelessly touted as the leading role model for girls. The adult hyperemphasis on the prettiness of female (but not male) children begins when babies are newborns; a stroll through the nearest infant/toddler toy store makes that social practice clear. The socialization of females toward prettiness and vanity connects indirectly with their socialization toward domestic pursuits. By fussing over their looks, women increase their chances of attracting male sexual attention and, eventually, male marital interest.

9. The early second-wave feminists who called attention to the real work carried out by women as mothers and housewives were often Marxist feminists who were especially concerned to show that women's work counted as genuine production even if it was not part of the system of wage labor and commodity exchange. See, for example, Margaret Benston, "The Political Economy of Women's Liberation," in Alison M. Jaggar and Paula S. Rothenberg, eds., *Feminist Frameworks: Alternative Theoretical Accounts of the Relations between Women and Men*, 2d. ed. (New York: McGraw-Hill, 1984), 239–47. Reprinted from *Monthly Review* (September 1969): 13–25. See also Natalie J. Sokoloff, "Motherwork and Working Mothers," *Feminist Frameworks*, 259–66. Adapted from Natalie J. Sokoloff, *Between Money and Love: The Dialectics of Women's Home and Market Work* (New York: Praeger Special Studies, 1980).

10. Feminists have debated whether different moral perspectives are genuinely correlated with gender; see, for example, the various essays in Mary Jeanne Larrabee, ed., *An Ethic of Care* (New York: Routledge, 1993). My goal here is not to take sides on this issue but rather simply to point out that many feminists applaud the moral concerns widely associated with traditionally female social roles.

11. Sara Ruddick, *Maternal Thinking: Towards a Politics of Peace* (New York: Ballantine Books, 1989).

12. For an important early study, see Diana Pearce and Harriette McAdoo, *Women and Children: Alone and in Poverty* (Washington, D.C.: Center for National Policy Review, 1981).

13. For legal developments in this area, see Carol H. Lefcourt, ed., *Women and the Law* (New York: Clark Boardman, orig. pub. 1984, loose-leaf with updates for 1987, 1988, 1989, 1990, 1991, 1992, 1993, and 1994).

14. It is curious that philosophers who, in the current lingo, go ballistic over the thought of paternalism by governments or between coequal citizens should be so unconcerned about the widespread paternalism of husbands toward wives in traditional marriages.

15. See, for example, Dorie Klein, "The Dark Side of Marriage: Battered Wives and the Domination of Women," in Nicole Hahn Rafter and Elizabeth Anne Stanko, eds., *Judge, Lawyer, Victim, Thief: Women, Gender Roles, and Criminal Justice*, (Boston: Northeastern University Press, 1982), 83–107.

16. This discussion is based on Susan Moller Okin's well-documented study, *Justice, Gender, and the Family* (New York: Basic Books, 1989), especially chap. 7, "Vulnerability by Marriage."

17. Anyone who really thinks that this is an overly adversarial view of marriage and that marriage is a blissful harmony of two concordant hearts, minds, and wills has not been married for any length of time and certainly has not raised children with a spouse.

18. Said in memory of my father, whose ways of goodness I grow to appreciate more and more with time.

19. This charge is made by, among others, Christina Sommers, "Philosophers against the Family,"in George Graham and Hugh LaFollette, eds., *Person to Person* (Philadelphia: Temple University Press, 1989), 87–88. [Editor's note: See Sommers, this volume, 44–46.]

20. Cited in Barrie Thorne with Marilyn Yalom, eds., *Rethinking the Family* (New York: Longman, 1982), 5. It is important to note that the so-called traditional family has never been traditional for all social groups in our culture. Women from low-income households often worked outside the home long before the current wave of the feminist movement.

21. I have discussed this issue of definition previously in "They Lived Happily Ever After: Sommers on Women and Marriage," *Journal of Social Philosophy* 21, nos. 2 and 3 (1990): 57. Some scholars recently have challenged the presumption that the traditional family was ever as widespread as family nostalgia buffs would have us believe. See, for example, Stephanie Coontz, *The Way We Never Were: American Families and the Nostalgia Trap* (New York: Basic Books, 1992).

22. See, for example, definition 3 of *family* in the Funk & Wagnalls *Standard Dictionary of the English Language*, internat. ed. (Chicago: Encyclopaedia Brittanica, 1965), 457. I have added "enduringness" to the dictionary definition in order to exclude transitory cohabitation arrangements.

23. Alan Bloom, *The Closing of the American Mind* (New York: Simon & Schuster, 1987), 129–32.

24. See Taylor Caldwell, "Women's Lib: They're Spoiling Eve's Great Con," *American Opinion* (September 1970): 27. Quoted in Barbara Ehrenreich, *The Hearts of Men: American Dreams and the Flight from Commitment* (New York: Doubleday, 1983), 158–61.

25. The asymmetric parlance of *men* and *girls* still has not disappeared.

26. Christina Sommers, "Feminism and Resentment," panel presentation to the American Association for the Philosophic Study of Society, Washington, D.C., 28 December 1992.

27. See, for example, Larry May and Robert Strikwerda, eds. with the assistance of Patrick D. Hopkins, *Rethinking Masculinity: Philosophical Explorations in Light of Feminism* (Lanham, Md.: Rowman & Littlefield, 1992).

28. Marilyn Frye articulates this notion well in *The Politics of Reality: Essays in Feminist Theory* (Trumansburg, N.Y.: The Crossing Press, 1983); see esp. 72–82 and 162–73.

29. Rush Limbaugh, invoking the common stereotype, brands "many" leading feminists as "manhaters" (*The Way Things Ought to Be*, 188). For him, this stance was exemplified in the controversial episode of the television series *Murphy Brown*, in which the lead character, Murphy Brown, a single woman, gives birth to a child and decides to raise it on her own. According to Limbaugh, "The real message of that *Murphy Brown* episode was that women don't need men, shouldn't desire them, and that total fulfillment and happiness can be achieved without men or husbands" (189). To equate such a message with hatred of men is an example of the error I am highlighting. Limbaugh offers no arguments against the view that he derides, but it is obvious that some women indeed do not need men (or any particular man), should not desire them, and can very well achieve fulfillment and happiness without them.

30. Funk & Wagnall's *Standard Dictionary of the English Language* (Chicago: Encyclopedia Britannica, 1965), 1071.

31. John Stuart Mill, *Utilitarianism*, ed. George Sher (Indianapolis: Hackett, 1979), 50–52.

32. More probably, we have a number of sex/gender systems, reflecting the privileges and constraints of other overlapping social groupings such as race, class, religion, and so on. Men of a socially subordinated ethnic group, for example, might be just as unlikely to hold the reins of governmental power as women of the same ethnic group. Interrelationships between those women and men might show less, or merely differently distributed patterns of, male domination than is found in white, middle–class U.S. culture.

33. Deborah Rhode has carefully documented numerous areas of male abuse or domination of women that have figured prominently in law; cf. her *Justice and Gender* (Cambridge: Harvard University Press, 1989).

34. Christina Sommers, "Argumentum Ad Feminam," *Journal of Social Philosophy* 22, no. 1 (1991): 12.

35. Some radical feminists share this view but find it lamentable and not a cause for celebration; see Catharine A. MacKinnon, *Feminism Unmodified: Discourses on Life and Law* (Cambridge: Harvard University Press, 1987).

36. See, for example, Robert D. Kaplan, "The Coming Anarchy," *Atlantic Monthly* (February 1994): 44–46, 48–49, 52, 54, 58–60, 62–63, 66, 68–70, 72–76. Kaplan believes that the contemporary U.S. emphasis on multiculturalism is weakening the ability of the United States to withstand the impending militaristic disasters (76). An alternative view, however, is equally compelling, namely, that genuine multicultural (including cross-cultural) dialogue is our only hope of forestalling mass global destruction.

37. According to Margaret Mitchell's own narrative wording, Rhett was "bullying and breaking" Scarlett in the scene in question; he "humbled her, hurt her, used her brutally" (*Gone with the Wind* [New York: Macmillan, 1936],

940). For my more extended discussion of this scene and the novel in general, see "Does Sommers Like Women?: More on Liberalism, Gender Hierarchy, and Scarlett O'Hara," *Journal of Social Philosopy* 21, nos. 2 & 3 (1990): 85–89.

Sommers rejects the word *rape* and resists even the somewhat milder notion of sexual domination ("Argumentam," 15). The producer of the movie version of *Gone with the Wind* was not so shy. David O. Selznick referred frankly to this scene as the "Row and Rape." See Helen Taylor, *Scarlett's Women: Gone with the Wind and its Female Fans* (New Brunswick, N.J.: Rutgers University Press, 1991), 130.

38. See, for example, Jennings Bryant and Dolf Zillmann, eds., *Perspectives on Media Effects* (Hillsdale, N.J.: Lawrence Erlbaum Associates, 1986); and Doris A. Graber, *Mass Media and American Politics*, 4th ed. (Washington, D.C.: CQ Press, 1993).

39. Sommers tries to convince her readers that feminists are out to impose totalitarian reconditioning on women so as to make women's sexual desires conform to feminist blueprints ("Argumentam," 11–17). To correct such distortions, it is necessary to state clearly that: (1) I criticize not the women (if any there be) who enjoy images of men dominating women, but rather the cultural endorsements and glorifications of male–dominated heterosexuality; (2) criticizing a type of cultural representation is obviously not the same as forcing one's values and ideals on other people; and most importantly, (3) I do not seek to impose my values or ideals on anyone, but rather to share my views with others through dialogue and debate. Sommers's caricatures of feminist views threaten to shut down genuine dialogue altogether. By contrast, I offer reasons to support my conviction that male-dominated heterosexuality is disrespectful to women at best, and, at worst in the 1990s, positively fatal. My hope is that we, as bearers of culture, will alter our predominant values and diminish our production and consumption of those potentially disastrous images.

40. After intravenous drug use, women's second most likely source of contracting AIDS is heterosexual contact with men who already have it. Furthermore, women are at much greater risk than men of getting AIDS through heterosexual contact alone. See Nora Kizer Bell, "Women and AIDS: Too Little, Too Late?," *Hypatia* 4, no. 3 (1989): 5. As ever, heterosexuality poses far greater risks for women than it does for men, at the same time providing insufficient intrinsic deterrents to male sexual aggression.

8

Procreative Liberty: Beyond Liberal, Radical, and Cultural Feminist Assessments

Rosemarie Tong

In *Children of Choice: Freedom and the New Reproductive Technologies*, John A. Robertson argues that because procreative liberty is one of our most deeply held moral and legal values, individuals should be free to use or not use technologies such as cloning, genetic screening, embryo freezing, in vitro fertilization, surrogate motherhood, Norplant, and RU486. Although individuals might try to change each other's minds about the value of the new reproductive technologies, the state should not seek to restrict these medical innovations unless there is strong evidence that they are truly harmful. Whichever new reproductive technology Robertson analyzes, however, he constructs a case to show that its harms are not substantial enough to outweigh its benefits. To be sure, Robertson concedes that even ardent advocates of a rights-based approach to procreative liberty sometimes worry about what would happen to society if large numbers of unreflective individuals suddenly abandoned natural for artificial means of procreation. Nevertheless, despite the social harm that such a shift might produce, there is in his estimation probably "no better alternative than leaving procreative decisions to the individuals whose procreative desires are most directly involved."[1]

Thomas Murray accuses Robertson of minimizing the harms associated with the new reproductive technologies—of underestimating how much we might lose in the way of loyalty, affection, kindness, generosity, and sympathy—if we overemphasize our pro-creative rights and overcelebrate our liberty. In contrast to some-one like Leon Kass, who worries that the new reproductive technologies might further weaken the already-threatened connec-tions between begetting, bearing, and rearing children,[2] Murray worries that the new reproductive technologies might transform re-production into just another form of production: another process to segment and specialize, another commodity to sell to the highest bidder. In particular, Murray expresses concern that the more we convert our kitchens, bedrooms, and dens into spots in the modern marketplace, the less emotional depth our family and friendship relationships will have. Eventually, concepts such as unconditional love will become obsolete. No longer will the best things in life be free. They will all have price tags and warranties inscribed with the words "caveat emptor."[3]

Robertson and Murray are both persuasive. Who doesn't value justice, rights, autonomy, choice, and liberty? Who doesn't value intimate relationships, unconditional love, affection, loyalty, gener-osity, and kindness? Certainly, feminists value all of these things. Thus, it should come as no surprise that some feminist assessments of the new reproductive technologies resonate strongly with Rob-ertson's case for them, while others resonate strongly with Murray's case against them. Does this mean that feminists are simply echo-ing Robertson's and/or Murray's thoughts? I do not think so, but since I cannot proclaim my truth ex cathedra, I must convince you through argument that feminists do have something distinctive to bring to the debate on the new reproductive technologies—some-thing that even nuanced thinkers such as Robertson and Murray either do not offer or do not offer as well.

In order to get some clarity on these matters, I focus on only three schools of feminist thought—the liberal, the radical, and the cultural—and on only one of the new reproductive technologies—namely, so-called surrogate motherhood, sometimes called contracted motherhood, or, as I prefer, gestational motherhood. (To label the child's gestational mother the surrogate mother is to suggest that she is not the real mother of the child, when it is precisely her claim to motherhood at stake.) I argue that because liberal, radical, and cultural feminists have distinct ontologies and epistemologies, they have distinct ethical and bioethical perspectives on the new repro-ductive technologies in general. I argue also that, as a result of these philosophical differences, liberal, radical, and cultural feminists

make different policy recommendations for the regulation of gestational motherhood in particular. Finally, I argue yet another, even
more complex point—namely, that no one of these feminist perspectives is, in and of itself, better equipped than any other to move us
toward the elimination of those systems, structures, and attitudes of
male domination and female subordination that, to a greater or lesser
degree, continue to work against all women's, most children's, and
some men's best interests. What we need to develop, therefore, is a
feminist lens—an epistemology as well as ontology—that is wide
enough to identify the combination of several competing feminist
solutions to a problem that is most likely to erode persisting patterns of gender inequity now.

Ontological Differences in Feminism

Given that the range of feminist perspectives is very wide, my decision to focus on liberal, radical, and cultural feminist perspectives
on gestational motherhood is largely pragmatic. These perspectives
happen to serve as excellent foils for one another. Their different
interpretations of the nature, form, and value of the self's relationship to others, and their different perspectives on reality, explain
liberal feminists' emphasis on issues of choice, radical feminists'
emphasis on issues of control, and cultural feminists' emphasis on
issues of connection. This being the case requires some explanation, however.

For quite some time, a variety of theorists have argued that lurk-
ing within the deep structure of traditional ethics (and, I would add,
traditional bioethics) is a creature known as the autonomous self,
generally pictured as a biological male, intent on maximizing his
self-interest.[4] This autonomous self has had a particularly difficult
existence, according to legal theorist Robin West. At times his separation has led him to fear annihilation by others. The interests of
separate individuals collide and, when they do so, conflict ensues.
At other times, however, the autonomous self's separateness has
caused him to feel alienation from others. He has not been able to
find friends to ease his loneliness. In sum, separation, whether it
results in annihilation or alienation, whether it is experienced as
freedom or isolation, has seemed to be *man's* tragic origin and fate.[5]

The separation thesis is not the exclusive possession of biological males, however. In their desire to secure for women the same

opportunities, occupations, rights, and privileges that men have had, many liberal feminists have adopted the male ontology of the self's separation from others.[6] Indeed, in their drive for sameness with men, these liberal feminists have sometimes denied women's sameness with women.[7] They have cautioned women against emphasizing their differences from men, viewing these biologically produced and/or culturally shaped othernesses as traps that limit women to maintaining the human species, while men strive to push it on to greater heights or lower depths.

In contrast, most radical and cultural feminists have rejected male ontology and its guiding separation thesis. In its stead, they have endorsed a female ontology, a view of reality that is oriented by a connection thesis. Thus, in West's estimation, the central insight of radical and cultural feminists seems to be

> that women are "essentially connected," not "essentially separate," from the rest of human life, both materially, through pregnancy, intercourse, and breast-feeding, and existentially, through the moral and practical life.[8]

Yet, as West also observes, cultural feminists—thinkers such as Carol Gilligan and Nel Noddings, for example—and radical feminists— thinkers such as Andrea Dworkin, Gena Corea, and Catherine Mackinnon, for example—have reacted very differently to the idea of women's connectedness.

Radical feminists have emphasized the negative side of the connection thesis. They believe connections set women up for exploitation and misery: "Invasion and intrusion, rather than intimacy, nurturance and care, is the 'unofficial' story of women's subjective experience of connections."[9] Women are connected to others, most especially through the experiences of heterosexual intercourse and pregnancy, but when the sugar coating is licked off, these connecting experiences leave an aftertaste of women's violation. This harm is unique to women; men cannot understand. Women do not fear either annihilation by others or alienation from others as much as they dread occupation by others: the uninvited penis, the unwanted fetus.[10]

Agreeing with radical feminists that connection is women's fundamental reality, cultural feminists have stressed the positive side of this state of affairs, praising women's capacities for sharing, giving, nurturing, sympathizing, and, above all, connecting. In their estimation, women value their relationships with others above everything else in life, viewing separation from others as the quintessential harm. The fact that women menstruate, gestate, and lactate gives women a unique perspective on the meaning of human connection. For women, connection is not about separate individuals signing social contracts, but about people using their blood, tears, sweat, and toil to bond with each other.[11]

Epistemological Differences in Feminism

In addition to lacking a common ontology, liberal, radical, and cultural feminists also lack a common epistemology. Apparently, liberal feminists favor so-called rational-empirical epistemology. They believe that the same objective, impartial, neutral, and universal standards of behavior govern everyone. Thus, as liberal feminists see it, when human beings let biases, prejudices, mistaken views, incorrect data, or unsound hypotheses interfere with their reasoning processes, they make false judgments. In contrast, when human beings avoid these distortions in reasoning, they make true judgments.

Because they are convinced that we live in a society that neither fully recognizes nor acts on men's and women's essential sameness as persons, liberal feminists maintain that, as they are currently practiced, medicine and science are not objective and impartial, but androcentric. Liberal feminists also maintain, however, that this situation is far from unchangeable. The facts, as opposed to myths or stereotypes, about women's as well as men's minds and bodies are available to create the kind of medicine and science that serves women's interests as well as men's interests. It is simply a matter of physicians and scientists unplugging their ears and listening to what women have to say about how their bodies and minds function and what nonmedical as well as medical remedies women think might help them. Consider, for example, that several studies have shown significant differences between the ways in which medical professionals and women of menopausal and postmenopausal age (1) rank menopausal symptoms for frequency, severity, and causality, and (2) rate their treatment preferences (counseling, hormone replacement therapy, mood-altering medication, or no treatment). On the average, medical professionals judge the various symptoms to be more frequent and severe than their patients do. Even more interestingly, medical professionals tend to use a psychogenic model, attributing symptoms to psychological causes, whereas women of menopausal or postmenopausal age tend to attribute symptoms to somatic disease.[12] In other words, when a menopausal woman complains that she is having a rough time, her physician is more likely to view these complaints as the result of mental depression rather than the result of bodily pain. Feminists who wish to interpret reality through a rational-empirical grid explain this tendency as a bias. Convinced that women's complaints about female diseases are often only in their heads, medical professionals tend to treat these complaints as signs of depression or, worse, as mere bellyaching.

Unlike liberal feminists, most other feminists believe that it will take more than accurate facts and attentive ears to make medicine and science objective. For this reason, both radical and cultural feminists adopt some version of so-called standpoint epistemology. In general, feminist standpoint epistemologists claim that the liberal feminist quest for gender neutrality, for sameness with men, and for the articulation of impartial and objective human standards is misguided. They point out that it is a major error to assume that men's and women's interests are fundamentally the same. Indeed, according to feminist standpoint epistemologists, it should be apparent already to everyone that men's and women's interests are in fact quite different: "One cannot simply be 'human,'" says Susan Bordo ". . . Our language, intellectual history, and social forms are 'gendered'; there is no escape from this fact and from its consequences in our lives."[13]

Radical feminists are inclined toward a version of standpoint epistemology that describes women's privileged status as that of the victim. They argue that because the victimizer has a vested interest in maintaining the status quo, his position functions to produce "distorted visions of the real regularities and underlying causal tendencies in social relations."[14] In contrast, because the victim has anything but a strong desire to maintain things as they are, her status as the victim enables her to see what is in fact wrong about some human beings dominating other human beings. For example, because men typically experience their power over women as normal, even beneficial to women, many (male) physicians simply assume that (female) nurses should unquestionably follow their instructions. They react angrily when a nurse dares to challenge the way in which they are managing a patient's case. According to radical feminists, however, it is not clear that the best medicine always results when a (male) physician's view prevails over that of a (female) nurse. They reason that because nurses are lower in the hospital hierarchy than physicians, they share certain vulnerabilities with the patients from which physicians are normally insulated. Thus, having had the experience of being chewed out by a physician, for example, nurses are more motivated than physicians to criticize "accepted interpretations of reality" (in this case, appropriate medical care of a patient) and to develop "new and less distorted ways of understanding the world."[15]

In contrast to radical feminists, cultural feminists are inclined toward a version of standpoint epistemology that describes women's privileged status as that of the carer. They claim that because of women's biological and/or socially constructed roles as life givers and relationship creators, they are in a better position than men to understand what is really important in life—namely, particular people as opposed to causes or principles. Thus, in cultural feminists' estimation, women's culture is one that is not likely, for example, to endorse war in the way that men's culture does.

According to cultural feminist Nel Noddings, Western men's romance with war has a very long history. It begins with Homer's *Iliad*, an epic that celebrates the warrior hero, paradoxically coupling Greek rationality and moderation on the one hand with irrationality and violence on the other. Rather than challenging the warrior hero and his deadly projects, Western ethics has tended to honor him. Indeed, even William James, who sought for a nonviolent "moral-equivalent" to war, nonetheless praised the warrior's virtues: his boldness, energy, and valor.[16] Wondering whether it is morally better to be a monk than a soldier, James initially opted for the military as opposed to the ascetic ideal. Only after he managed to reconceive the ascetic life in heroic, rather than effeminate terms, did James manage to construct an argument against war and on behalf of peace. Provided that the monk, like the soldier, strives to do his perceived duty no matter the cost to himself, his path is the one to follow, since blood is not spilled on it senselessly.[17]

As Noddings sees it, war will not be discarded once and for all in favor of peace until caring aimed at connecting replaces striving aimed at winning. Only when women's underappreciated art of relational ethics gains recognition will peace have a real chance. It is not that women do not strive. They do. It is just that, when women strive, women do so not with the intention of vanquishing their external foes and/or their internal demons once and for all, but with the realistic intention of continuing on as best they can.

> A woman knows that she can never win the battle against dust, that she will have to feed family members again and again (and that no meals are likely to go down in history), that she must tend the garden every year, and that she cannot overcome most of its enemies but must treat them with the sort of moderation that encourages harmony.[18]

She who knows that her loved ones' survival depends on her good relations even with her enemies also knows that bad relations— quintessentially, war—are not a genuine solution to the problems that beset human beings.

Liberal, Radical, and Cultural Feminist Perspectives on Gestational Motherhood

Keeping in mind the respective ontologies and epistemologies of liberal, radical, and cultural feminists, it comes as no surprise that the liberal feminist position on gestational motherhood does not differ essentially from the traditional liberal position on this social arrangement. In general, liberal feminists maintain that the benefits of the new reproductive technologies to women, especially the benefit of increased procreative liberty, are substantial. Whatever harms might accompany these benefits—including the harm of having to relinquish a child to whom one has unexpectedly bonded—they are, in liberal feminists' estimation, no worse than those harms that sometimes accompany other social arrangements that our society deems good on balance: adoption, stepparenting, foster parenting, and even nannying.[19]

Like traditional liberals, liberal feminists also claim that women (and men) should be permitted to use whatever reproduction-controlling or reproduction-aiding technologies they want, provided that they do not harm anyone in the process. Although liberal feminists concede that society is not required to enforce any and all contracts—say a contract to kill someone, a contract to sell oneself into slavery, or a contract to sell one's soul to the devil—they insist that, given widely accepted interpretations of constitutional law, two or more consenting adults have a right to contract with each other to procreate a child collaboratively. Thus, liberal feminists typically urge that contract law be used to govern the practice of gestational motherhood, provided, of course, that surrogacy contracts are drafted in ways that honor the constitutional rights of women—especially their right to bodily integrity and privacy.[20]

Largely because they espouse both a negative version of the connection thesis and a standpoint epistemology framed in terms of all women's oppression by men within patriarchy, radical feminists offer an interpretation of gestational motherhood that differs markedly from the liberal-feminist interpretation. Radical feminists do not endorse a contract approach to gestational motherhood. In fact, if they favor anything, it is either a wholesale ban on commercial gestational motherhood or a statute on the order of the 1985 United Kingdom Surrogacy Arrangements Act. Reflecting the views of Immanuel Kant, the authors of this act, which fines and/or imprisons the people who facilitate commercial surrogacy arrangements (lawyers, physicians, and social workers), claimed that gestational motherhood is always immoral.

> Even in compelling medical circumstances the dangers of exploitation of one human being by another appears to the majority of us far to outweigh the potential benefits, in almost every case. That people would treat others as a means to their own ends, however desirable the consequences, must always be liable to moral objection. Such treatment of one person by another becomes positively exploitative when financial interests are involved.[21]

Although radical feminists agree that commercial gestational motherhood is more often than not exploitative, unlike the authors of the Surrogacy Arrangements Act, they claim that they have no desire to praise *Leave it to Beaver* families and to condemn so-called blended families, for example. On the contrary, radical feminists emphasize that their paramount goal in challenging the new reproductive technologies is simply to prevent palpable harms to women (and also to children).

Radical feminists agree with Marxist feminists that, like most prostitutes, most gestational mothers are much poorer than those who pay for their services. They broaden the Marxist feminist analysis of exploitation, however, to include cases of noneconomic exploitation. They argue that the choice of a woman to serve as a gestational mother for no fee at all is not necessarily more free than the choice of a woman who agrees to work as a gestational mother for a $10,000 fee so that she can help feed, clothe, and shelter her own children. Whereas Marxist feminists emphasize that under capitalism there is always a price high enough to entice even the most resistant person to sell what is most precious to him/her, radical feminists emphasize that, frequently, not dreams of making it rich, but rather visions of helping desperately lonely infertile couples motivate women to serve as gestational mothers. Culturally constructed to believe that good women are self-sacrificial women, women often find it hard to resist even the most demanding calls to serve the needs of others. Radical feminists additionally stress that "no" is a word ominously absent from the vocabularies of those women who choose to be gestational mothers because of personal feelings of guilt. The fact that, to date, approximately one-third of all gestational mothers have previously either had an abortion or given up a child for adoption suggests that these women may be serving as gestational mothers to atone for what they regard as their past sins.[22]

Radical feminists underscore the fact that in addition to harming particular women, gestational motherhood threatens to harm women in general by creating at least two destructive divisions among them. The first of these pernicious gaps is that between economically privileged women and economically disadvantaged women. Relatively rich women hire relatively poor women to meet their reproductive needs, adding childbearing services to the child-rearing services that economically disadvantaged women have traditionally provided to economically privileged women. The second destructive division is the one that Gena Corea envisions between child begetters, childbearers, and child rearers. According to Corea, society is segmenting reproduction as if it were simply another form of assembly-line production. In the future, no one woman will beget, bear, and rear a child. Rather, genetically superior women will beget embryos in vitro; strong-bodied women will carry these test-tube babies to term; and sweet-tempered women will rear these newborns from infancy to adulthood.[23]

Finally, espousing a version of connection ontology that stresses its positive aspects and a version of standpoint epistemology that privileges the position of carers, cultural feminists aim to develop a policy on gestational motherhood that creates and/or strengthens the bonds between women and also between women, children, and men. Cultural feminists envision women engaging in gynocentric collaborative reproduction. They see one woman helping another woman secure a child who is genetically related to her and/or her partner in life. Ideally, such help should be noncommercial: a gift to be paid back on another day in another form, perhaps. After all, gift giving and receiving are some of the best ways to solidify human relationships. If, however, the woman giving the gift of life cannot do so without some financial compensation, or if the woman whom she is benefiting wants her to accept some material reward for her services, then an appropriate monetary transfer can be made. Cultural feminists believe that women engaged in collaborative reproduction can trust each other not to exploit each other. Indeed, they can trust each other even to arrange their respective parental responsibilities toward their mutual child appropriately. They can decide how large or small the respective roles of the gestational mother and the rearing mother should be in their mutual child's life. Cultural feminists claim that because women care about their human relationships more than anything else, they will be motivated to respect each other's maternal instincts and, in the event of both of them wanting to be their child's primary parent, achieve a properly Solomonic solution to their dilemma. Thus, cultural feminists urge legal and medical authorities to involve themselves minimally in gestational motherhood arrangements.

Moving Beyond Liberal, Radical, and Cultural Feminist Assessments of Gestational Motherhood

In reflecting on liberal, radical, and cultural feminist perspectives on gestational motherhood, we might wish to determine which, if any, of them is most feminist—that is, most likely to eliminate patterns of male domination and female subordination in particular and oppressive human relationships in general. Since I believe that it is a combination of liberal, radical, and cultural feminist perspectives on gestational motherhood that is most feminist, I think we need an ontological and epistemological lens wide enough to accommodate them all. In other words, we need an ontology that overcomes the self-other dichotomy and an epistemology that privileges the seer's perspective without iconizing it as inherently superior to the perspective of those who are seen.

As I see it, Sarah Lucia Hoagland provides feminists with an ontology that affirms neither the self at the expense of others nor others at the expense of the self. Hoagland replaces the concept of autonomy, which stems from the Greek words for self (*auto*) and rule (*nomos*), with the concept of autokoenomy,[24] which stems from the Greek words for self (*auto*) and community (*koinonia*). The autokoenomous woman realizes that she is a self who is related to other selves. Since she is neither inferior nor superior to these other selves, the autokoenomous woman does not feel obligated to sacrifice her interests to the interests of others. When she does something for someone, she does it because she chooses to do it—not because she has to do it. What is more, because she realizes that in choosing for herself, she chooses for others, who in turn choose for her, the autokoenomous woman understands that moral value emerges not from somewhere deep within herself or from far outside herself.[25] On the contrary, moral value emerges in the interactions between autokoenomous women as they weave connections between themselves. Thus, liberal, radical, and cultural feminists need to understand that in selecting a specific policy on gestational motherhood, they are affecting the procreative freedom and wellbeing of the women who will be harmed by their choice as well as the women who will benefit by it.

Understanding just how interactive the self-other relationship is, is a necessary condition for determining the combination of liberal, radical, and cultural feminist insights on gestational motherhood that is most likely to expand the procreative freedom and responsibility of women in general. It is not, however, a sufficient condition. What is also necessary is an epistemological lens that helps one woman see how her decisions are affecting, or might affect, other women. According to Katherine T. Bartlett and others, feminists need to proceed from a positional framework.[26] So-called positionalists claim that although there is truth, this truth is always situated and partial. Truth is situated in that it emerges from the roles and relationships that an individual has; it is partial in that no single individual or group possesses it in entirety. Knowledge comes from facts and experiences, but since our facts and experiences are inevitably limited, our truths are never total. We are never objective enough because we can never see, hear, taste, smell, or touch enough. If I wish to secure a truth greater than my own—I am a white, heterosexual, Eastern European, Catholic, well-educated, socially advantaged, able-bodied, postmenopausal, married, and so on, woman—then I must talk to as many others as possible. The truth, says Donna

Haraway, emerges through "solidarity in politics" and "shared conversations in epistemology."[27] Everyone's knowledge, including liberal, radical, and cultural feminists' knowledge, is limited.

Because truth is situated and partial and because knowledge is limited, conversing with others is more than an option for feminists. It is a moral requirement. Each feminist must be sensitive to the fact that her point of view might be offensive or hurtful to others. The fact that each feminist must be sensitive to others' partial and situated truth, however, does not mean that her partial and situated truth has no claim on her actions. Comments Bartlett:

> Although I must consider other points of view from the positional stance, I need not accept their truths as my own. Positionality is not a strategy of process and compromise that seeks to reconcile all competing interests. Rather, it imposes a twin obligation to make commitment based on the current truths and values that have emerged from methods of feminism, and to be open to previously unseen perspectives that might come to alter their commitments. As a practical matter, of course, I cannot do both simultaneously, evenly, and perpetually. Positionality, however, sets an ideal of self-critical commitment whereby I act, but consider the truths upon which I act subject to further refinement, amendment, and correction.[28]

Using an autokoenomous ontology and a positional epistemology, liberal, radical, and cultural feminists would, I believe, come to the conclusion that none of their respective positions on gestational motherhood, in and of itself, serves women as well as might be hoped for. In affirming the so-called contract approach, liberal feminists fail to consider, first, that contracts do not typically serve vulnerable people as well as they serve powerful people. Women's relationships to their helpless infants, aging parents, and ailing siblings—relationships between persons who are not equally rational and powerful—do not fit the contract model. The way in which two bankers negotiate a business deal is not to be compared to the way in which a mother negotiates a bedtime for her child. Life is about more than conflict, competition, and controversy, about making sure that one's interests are protected. It is, as mothering persons know, also about cooperation, community, and consensus, about meeting other people's needs. Thus, feminist Virginia Held speculates that were the relationship between a mothering person and a child, rather than the relationship between two rational contractors, the paradigm for good human relationships, society might look very different.[29]

Certainly, there would be little temptation to view children as commodities and gestational mothers as incubators.

Second, and probably more to the point, the liberal feminist position privileges the position of the women (and men) who contract for gestational mothers. Neither thorough information nor adequate psychological screening will prevent a percentage of gestational mothers from bonding intensely with the infants whom they have carried to term. On the liberal feminist view, it is the gestational mother who must bear the full burden of this unanticipated event. Were it not for the fact that in the past increases in the procreative freedom of relatively privileged women have been bought at the price of decreases in the procreative freedom of relatively unprivileged women, this might not be such a great cause for alarm. As it stands, however, history shows, for example, that the permissive sterilization laws that white, well-to-do women sponsored enabled some less than beneficent health care professionals to push many indigent women, especially African-American and Hispanic indigent women, into the operating room for tubal ligations.[30] Thus, the fact that gestational mothers generally are not as socially and economically advantaged as the women (and men) who contract for their services should serve as a danger sign.

If liberal feminists tend to overemphasize women's ability to make free choices, radical feminists probably overemphasize the status of women as victims. In their desire to protect women from abuse, radical feminists generally advocate restrictive legislation of practices over which women can gain little control. Thus, for example, radical feminists have far fewer objections to the practice of sperm donation than to the practice of egg donation. Women can inseminate themselves easily with donor sperm, but they cannot transfer eggs between their bodies without the assistance of physicians. Noting not only this fact, but the fact that the provision of infertility services is an increasingly lucrative business in a society that traditionally has identified motherhood with being a fulfilled woman, radical feminists are correct to ask just whose interests gestational motherhood serves.[31] After all, no matter which one of women's sexual or reproductive services we consider, there is a case to be made that, in providing the service specified, more women have probably been harmed than benefited. Nevertheless, banning gestational motherhood (at least, its commercial variety) would not necessarily benefit women—not unless one also thinks, for example, that the continuing criminalization of prostitution, for example, is necessarily serving women's best interests.[32] A ban on even commercial gestational motherhood would tend to drive the practice underground, where women's best interests would be served even more poorly than they are aboveground, so to speak. Rather than resorting to a remedy that, by the way, gives law—a patriarchal institution if there ever was one—more control over women, one would think that radical feminists would prefer to control the practice of gestational motherhood through the feminist process of consciousness raising. If women became convinced that gestational motherhood arrangements were, on the average, something women should avoid, then patriarchy in the form of law and/or medicine would lose a measure of control over women.

Perhaps one of the reasons that radical feminists are not convinced that consciousness raising is a viable alternative to a legal ban on at least commercial gestational motherhood is that not only liberal feminists but also cultural feminists favor the practice. To be sure, as was noted above, cultural feminists are more favorably disposed to noncommercial gestational motherhood than to commercial gestational motherhood. Nevertheless, they remain convinced that women can reproduce collaboratively even when money passes between their hands. Unfortunately, what cultural feminists tend to ignore is that not all women are carers, any more than all women are victims or contractors. Moreover, even women who enter a gestational motherhood arrangement caring about each other might soon discover that their care has its limits. Two friends, two sisters, or a mother and daughter might agree to an arrangement that will permit both of them to play a relatively equal role in rearing their mutual child, only to discover after the child is born that both of them want to be the primary mommy. Should this happen, there will be no court of any clear resort to help them mediate their disagreement as their mutual child lives in a limbo of love that rapidly transmutes into a hell of unspecified magnitude.

Working toward a Feminist Solution to a Practical Policy Problem

Hopefully, there is something that I can say over and beyond the fact that, from the perspective of an autokoenomous ontology and a positional epistemology, neither the liberal, radical, nor cultural feminist position on gestational motherhood unproblematically serves the best interests of all women. Ideally, it should be possible for me to use this perspective to point to a mediated position on gestational motherhood that most, if not all, feminists could recognize as the one most likely to serve most women's interests now, though not in a society that is either more or less patriarchal than ours. Challenged in this way, I recommend an adoption approach to gestational motherhood. Assimilating gestational motherhood into properly modified adoption law—for instance, by creating nonprofit state surrogacy boards—would eliminate profit-making middlemen without necessarily requiring gestational mothers to perform their demanding tasks for free. Being paid for one's gestational service does not necessarily demean those services nor does it necessarily reduce one to what Kant termed a "mere means."[33] On the contrary, provided that gestational mothers are permitted to control the course of their pregnancies and, as in adoption law, to change their mind about relinquishing their birth child, they are being treated as so-called ends in themselves: that is, persons worthy of as much respect and consideration as the persons who contracted for their services.

To be sure, neither liberal, radical, nor cultural feminists will object to a woman controlling the course of her pregnancy, but liberal feminists probably will object to giving the parental edge to the gestational mother as opposed to the woman who contracts for her services. Thus, it is incumbent on me to persuade liberal feminists that in the patriarchal society in which we now live, less harm is done to more women by stacking the cards in favor of the gestational mother. The fact that the gestational relationship (a relationship that only women can have to their children) traditionally has been downplayed as being not nearly as important as either the genetic relationship (the only relationship that men initially can have to their children) or the rearing relationship (a relationship that men and women both can have to their children) is quite disturbing given that at the moment of birth, the gestational mother, more than anyone else, is the one who has made the largest "biological and psychological" investment in the child.[34] What makes a parent a parent would seem to be more than wanting to have or intending to have a child. Rather, it would seem to be showing an actual commitment to the child and, certainly, sustaining a nine-month pregnancy is more than a matter of a mere intention. Indeed, it is quite a bit more than a matter of readying a nursery for a child or setting up a savings account for him or her.

I admit that in my desire to correct for the ways in which our society has undervalued the gestational connection—so much so that in one contested custody case California Superior Court Justice R. N. Parslow equated gestating an embryo with providing day care or nanny services for it—[35] there is a danger of overvaluing this bond. In the first place, however primary the gestational relationship is, it is a relationship that is supplemented readily and replaced gradually by other caring acts of parental commitment—the kind of acts a father or grandparents, for example, can perform: feeding, rocking, diapering, and washing the baby. Second, although the genetic connection has been overemphasized in patriarchal society because it is the only kind of connection that a father can have to his child at its birth, most parents—female as well as male—hope to see some physical and psychological aspects of themselves reflected in their children. Rather than automatically condemning this desire as an egoistic one, feminists might wish to affirm it, within limits, as a typically human one. After all, most people take comfort in the fact that our bodies as well as our minds can survive us in and through our children. Third, stressing the importance of the gestational connection can work just as easily against as for women's interests. Increasingly, the general public regards pregnant women who smoke, drink alcohol, or shoot drugs as child abusers or neglecters. Given a worrisome social tendency to control these women's pregnancies—even to punish these women for giving birth to less than perfect infants—it might be politically inadvisable for women to overemphasize the degree to which mothering begins in the womb.[36]

Nevertheless, despite these dangers, I remain convinced that it serves women's best interests to shape a policy on gestational motherhood that gives the gestational mother the parental edge not only because pregnancy is a testimony to a woman's commitment to a child, but also because in this day and age women are more free than ever not to get pregnant—to do what Jeffner Allen has urged: namely, to "evacuate motherhood," even if by doing so women threaten to end the human race.[37] In a patriarchal society the power to give birth does remain women's trump card. Medical expertise is such that we still cannot grow babies ex utero, and men do not seem all that interested in readying their abdomens for pregnancy. Society needs women for its very survival. Without the gestational connection there can be no genetic or rearing connection.

To be sure, it is sad to think about the women (and men) whose hopes to rear a child who is genetically related to them will be dashed by those gestational mothers who decide to claim their birth children as their own. Fortunately, though, such sadnesses are likely to be few since most gestational mothers really do not want to rear the children they bear, which, of course, does not necessarily make it any easier for the children born to them to understand why their gestational mothers gave them up.

It is this last consideration that inclines me to think that ultimately the most feminist solution for gestational motherhood is to obviate the need for it by developing (1) the kind of sexually sensitive health care and environmentally safe workplaces that prevent the conditions that often contribute to infertility, (2) the type of medical research policy and practice that puts more dollars into preventing infertility than in finding cures for it, and (3) the kind of social milieu that assures women in particular that their worth is independent of their ability to have children (because as long as women continue to see their essential function as reproductive, they will fall prey to those who want to treat them as baby machines and their children as commodities). For now, however, feminist women have to help each other as well as nonfeminist women to realize the collective consequences of women's separate choices, because, as I understand the term *feminism*, a woman cannot be a feminist unless she is as conscious as she can be of how her choices affect other women—all kinds of other women. Thus, for me, feminist ethics is a collective process, an ongoing conversation. Even as I struggle to achieve a reflective equilibrium between feminist principles, rules, ideals, values, and virtues on the one hand and particular cases involving actual women on the other, other feminists (and nonfeminists) who focus on the same particular cases, but from different perspectives, engage in a similar struggle. Ethics requires communication, corroboration, collaboration, and, yes, conflict. It requires feminists to accept our limited ability to explain and justify our decisions and actions to each other as well as to nonfeminists, even as it insists that we try harder to find the words that will make us not only partners in virtue, but friends in action; individuals who, proceeding from different perspectives, find ways to forge collective policies that weaken rather than strengthen patterns of human dominance and subordination.[38]

Notes

1. John A. Robertson, *Children of Choice: Freedom and the New Reproductive Technologies* (Princeton, N.J.: Princeton University Press, 1994), 235.
2. Leon Kass, *Toward a More Natural Science* (New York: The Free Press, 1985).
3. See Thomas H. Murray, "Communities Need More Than Autonomy," *Hastings Center Report* (May-June 1994), 32–33.
4. See, for example, Caroline Whitbeck, "A Different Reality, Feminist Ontology," in Ann Garry and Marilyn Pearsall, eds., *Women, Knowledge, and Reality: Explorations in Feminist Philosophy* (Boston: Unwin Hyman, 1989), 51–76.
5. Robin C. West, "Jurisprudence and Gender," *The University of Chicago Law Review* 55, no. 1 (Winter 1988): 5–12.
6. See, for example, Alison M. Jaggar's critique of liberal feminist theory in Jaggar, *Feminist Politics and Human Nature* (Totowa, N.J.: Rowman and Allanheld, 1983), 39–47.
7. It is important to note that not all liberal feminists stress women's sameness with men. Some liberal feminists who specialize in legal theory, for example, have raised concerns about so-called sameness feminism. See Mary Joe Frug, *Postmodern Legal Feminism* (New York: Routledge, 1991), ix–xxxv; 3–52.
8. West, 3.
9. West, 29.
10. West, 29–36.
11. See, for example, Virginia Held, "Non-Contractual Society: A Feminist View," in Marsha Hanen and Kai Nielsen, eds., *Science, Morality, and Feminist Theory* (Calgary: University of Calgary Press, 1987), 127.
12. Gloria Cowan, L. W. Warren, and J. L. Young, "Medical Perceptions of Menopausal Symptoms," *Psychology of Women Quarterly* 9 (1985): 3–14.
13. Susan Bordo, "Feminism, Postmodernism, and Gender Scepticism," in Linda J. Nicholson, ed., *Feminism/Postmodernism* (New York: Routledge, 1990), 152.
14. Sandra Harding, *The Science Question in Feminism* (Ithaca: Cornell University Press, 1986), 191–96.
15. Jaggar, 370.
16. Nel Noddings, *Women and Evil* (Berkeley, Calif.: University of California Press, 1984), 179.
17. Noddings, 181.
18. Noddings, 182.
19. Lori B. Andrews, "Alternative Modes of Reproduction," in Richard T.

Hull, ed., *Ethical Issues in the New Reproductive Technologies* (Belmont, Calif.: Wadsworth, 1990), 365.

20. Andrews, "The Aftermath of Baby M: Proposed State Laws on Surrogate Motherhood," in Hull, 365.

21. Surrogacy Arrangements Act, 1985, United Kingdom, Chapter 49, 2(1)(a)(b)(c).

22. Patricia A. Avery, "'Surrogate Mothers': Center of a New Storm," *U.S. News and World Report* (6 June 1983): 76.

23. Gena Corea, *The Mother Machine* (New York: Harper & Row, 1985), 276.

24. Sarah Lucia Hoagland, *Lesbian Ethics* (Palo Alto, Calif.: Institute of Lesbian Studies, 1989), 12.

25. Hoagland, 241.

26. Katharine T. Bartlett, "Feminist Legal Methods (1990)," in D. Kelly Weisberg, ed., *Feminist Legal Theory: Foundations* (Philadelphia: Temple University Press, 1993), 384.

27. Donna Haraway, "Situated Knowledges: The Science Question in Feminism and the Privilege of Partial Perspective," in *Simians, Cyborgs, and Women* (New York: Routledge, 1991), 191.

28. Bartlett, "Feminist Legal Methods (1990)," 390.

29. Held, 127–28.

30. Adele Clarke, "Subtle Forms of Sterilization Abuse: A Reproductive Rights Analysis," in Rita Arditti, Renate Duelli Hein, and Shelley Minden, eds., *Test Tube Women* (London: Pandora Press, 1984), 193–94.

31. Susan Sherwin, *No Longer Patient: Feminist Ethics and Health Care* (Philadelphia: Temple University Press, 1992), 54–55.

32. Alison M. Jaggar, "Prostitution," in Alison M. Jaggar, ed., *Living with Contradictions: Controversies in Feminist Social Ethics* (Boulder, Colo.: Westview Press, 1994), 102–12.

33. Immanuel Kant, *Foundations of the Metaphysics of Morals*, trans. L. W. Beck (Indianapolis, Ind.: Bobbs-Merrill, 1959).

34. Sherman Elias and George J. Annas, "Noncoital Reproduction," *Journal of the American Medical Association* 225 (3 January 1986), 67.

35. Ellen Goodman, "Whose Child?" *Charlotte Observer* (Sunday, 28 October 1990), 30.

36. Lawrence J. Nelson and Nancy Millchen, "Compelled Medical Treatment of Pregnant Women: Life, Liberty, and Law in Conflict," in Hull, 224–40.

37. Jeffner Allen, "Motherhood: The Annihilation of Women," in Joyce Trebilcot, ed., *Mothering* (Totowa, N.J.: Rowman and Allanheld Publishers, 1983), 315–16.

38. Parts of this discussion have been adapted from my "Feminist Perspectives and Gestational Motherhood: The Search for a Unified Legal Focus," in Joan C. Callahan, ed., *Reproduction, Ethics, and the Law: Feminist Perspectives* (Bloomington, Ind.: Indiana University Press, 1995).

9

Longing for Home: An Ecofeminist Philosophical Perspective

Karen J. Warren

Introduction

When I was just fourteen years old, my mother, sister, and I took a trip around much of the world. Many of my memories of that trip have faded; others are sharp and telling. They provide an autobiographical backdrop for what I want to say in this essay about an ecofeminist philosophical perspective on the longing for home.

I vividly remember being in both Old and New Delhi. I can still feel the sense of shame that I felt as I walked through the marketplace and children my age tugged on my clothes, sometimes five or six at a time, begging for money from this foreigner, this "rich American." That sense of shame turned to bewilderment as we later visited one of India's most famous sights, the majestic Taj Mahal: such wealth and beauty all in one place, home to millions of Asian Indians. Around the edge of the grounds of the Taj were peasant laborers, working in pairs to cut the heavy slabs of marble that would be used to replace broken or missing marble from the Taj Mahal. I remember asking our guide how long it took them to cut one slab of marble and what they got paid. His answer shocked me: "It takes about eleven days and they get paid about seven cents a day." I was aghast and, again, ashamed. These people's homes, I surmised, could not be at all like mine.

In Hong Kong I remember the bustling, commercial, touristy downtown, in sharp contrast with the vast hillside smothered with deteriorating shacks housing millions of people. There were as many as four or five families living together in one very small dwelling, without running water or toilets or beds. Women were climbing the treacherous and winding roadside up to their homes, carrying water on their heads from pumps located intermittently by the roadside. Never before had I seen such a concentration of people in such dilapidated, overcrowded conditions. I felt confused about who I was and why some people lived this way and others didn't.

In Burma, now Myanmar, I was horrified by the sight of dead, homeless, and indigent people lying along the roadside. One man would urinate in the same stream that a woman would draw her drinking water from and in which yet another woman would do her laundry. I felt wretched about the affluence I took for granted at home.

As an adult and mother, I later took my own fourteen-year-old daughter, Cortney, to the Ecofeminism Seminar in Rio de Janeiro, part of Global Forum held in conjunction with the United Nations' Earth Summit in 1992. I hoped that this experience for Cortney, then the same age as I was when I took the trip that forever changed how I felt about home, would have an impact on her in similar ways. With intense curiosity and anticipation I witnessed Cortney become fascinated by the *favella* on the hillside overlooking the beautiful beaches of Ipanema and Copacabana and stare in deep bewilderment at the thousands of children roaming the streets of Rio, begging foreigners like herself for money or stealing what they could from our human consumptive waste. Their homes were what Westerners would call slums or urban shantytowns. Cortney was both aghast and mesmerized by the experience. Just as I had years earlier, Cortney began to have a new understanding of the previously only vague concepts of classism, racism, imperialism, and ethnocentrism.

The following year, Cortney and I attended the World Congress of Philosophy in Moscow, where once again she was confronted with the confusion I remember having felt at her age by the abject poverty and destitute living conditions of so many people, in this case the average Russian. The family with whom we stayed worried that their sister-in-law's farm would not provide enough potatoes to get them all through a cold Russian winter. Their homes and homelife were being threatened by food shortages and high prices. Cortney and I were helping by paying them to let us stay with them in their home.

Although I have never revisited any of these places, I am still haunted and challenged by what I saw and felt, especially about what constituted home for millions of people. At times I have felt the bioregionalist sense of being foreign—not native—to place, of feeling not at home and even of not having a home. As an environmental philosopher I have become intensely interested in what home is and how gender, race, class, and natural environment affect cross-cultural meanings of homes. Since the word *ecology* itself comes from the Greek *oikos*, "for home—an indication that home is much broader than simply the nuclear family,"[1] as an ecofeminist philosopher I have become interested in the concept of home and the work that has been done there in the context of societies that traditionally have devalued both women and home.

In preparing this essay I have pondered the expression "longing for home." I have come to see how an ecofeminist philosophical perspective on home contains important insights about what a home is or should be and why. Within the prefeminist socioeconomic realities of contemporary patriarchy, colonialism, classism, and racism, it simply may not be possible to consistently feel or be at home. Sometimes, the best we can do is long for home. At least, this is what I shall try to show.

What Is a Home?

The homesick miss their homes. The homeless are said to have no homes or to have streets as their homes. Refugees are uprooted from their homes, immigrants are looking for new homes, and weary travelers yearn to go or come home. Death is sometimes referred to as coming or going home. We say that a house is not a home, that a home is where the heart is, or, to quote Byron, "Without hearts there is no home." Something or someone can be homeborn, homebound, homebred, homeless, homelike, homemade, or attending a homecoming. Movie character Forrest Gump runs nobly for three years across the United States until he simply stops one day, presumably his grieving and searching over, and announces, "It's time to go home." The lovable but lonely extraterrestrial E.T. just wants to phone home, and Dorothy in the *Wizard of Oz* finally learns from the Good Witch of the East that what she has been searching for "has been inside you all along." Dorothy simply has to click her heels together three times and say, "There's no place like home. There's no place like home. There's no place like home" to return to her native farm

in Kansas. "Home, sweet home" is a familiar expression that reflects a deeply held sentiment among North Americans that, in print,
often adorns the entrances to many houses and announces the alleged specialness of what is to be found inside. Musician Ann Reed's
song, that "Love's a Long Road Home," just as so many other popular songs (e.g., "Home on the Range," "Sweet Home, Alabama"),
makes frequent references to the importance of homes in their lyr-
ics. For some, a man's home is his castle.

So what is a home? What, if anything, do these different references to home have in common? As I use the term, there are at
least three distinct senses of 'home' and a fourth, unified, generic
sense of 'home' that are variously at play in the expressions and
commentaries given above. In the first sense, which I call the house
sense, a home is a house, a domicile or residence, a dwelling place.
In this sense, homes can be human or nonhuman, as in a home for
orphans or veterans and the home of the seal or eucalyptus. Since
ecology typically signifies the relationships among living organisms
and their natural habitats, ecosystems are indeed homes, that is,
habitations or dwellings for nonhuman natural beings in the house
sense of 'home'.

In the second sense, what I call the intentional community sense
of 'home', a home is a self-consciously, deliberately chosen, familiar or accepted, abiding place of one's affections, as in "home is
where the heart is." These homes may or may not be nurturing,
functional, good places to be, but they are where one's affections
lie. Presumably, it is here that E.T. wants to go, that makes Alabama sweet home for some, and that makes her native farm in
Kansas more than just a dwelling place for Dorothy.

In a third sense of 'home', what I call the bioregional sense,
home is a bioregion or natural place (for example, a watershed)
laced with local natural history and human lore. A home in the bioregional sense may, but does not necessarily, include either a house
(the first sense of 'home') or an intentional community (the second
sense of 'home'). It is the sense of 'home' in "this land is my home"
or "The great plains of Minnesota are my home" (or, "are where I
make my home").

What does it mean, then, to long for home? Longing for home
is at least wanting or desiring something one presently lacks or
misses but holds valuable or worthwhile. E.T. longs for home, as
do so many soldiers during wartime. In the movie "Gone with the
Wind," Scarlett O'Hara longs to see Tara again; stated more collo-

quially, she longs to see the old homestead again ('home' in at least the house sense). It also may be a longing to be with one's friends (to be in a chosen community) or to be "home on the range, where the deer and the antelope play" (in one's familiar bioregion). One can long for home in any of the three senses of 'home'.

Can one meaningfully be said to long for home when one already is at home? I think the answer is "yes," and "yes" for an important reason: One can be at home, that is, in one's house, intentional community, or bioregion (all three senses of 'home') without being in sustaining, nurturing, life-affirming surroundings or relationships. So, one can be at home while being quite lonely and unfulfilled. Longing for home, then, is, minimally, both an internal and external yearning or desire for what is (or is perceived to be) a safe, comfortable, satisfying, life-affirming, loving self- and other-respectful place; one find's home or is truly peacefully at home when one is in such a place, so one can be in a house, intentional community, or bioregion and not be at home.

One reason that this "yes" answer is important is that it suggests a fourth, inclusive, generic sense of 'home', what I call the ecofeminist sense of 'home': a house, intentional community, and bioregion where one's individually and mutually satisfying basic needs and life-affirming and sustaining values are met. These are needs and values that take into account both human and nonhuman environmental concerns and are satisfied in respectful and ecologically sustainable ways. This is the sense of 'home' in which one can say, with deepest respect and veracity, that the earth is our penultimate home: it is where we dwell, form intentional communities, and live in relationship with nonhuman nature. When we commune with nature in a personally and ecologically respectful way, we are treating the earth as our home ('home' in the ecofeminist sense).

As an aside, some have even claimed that "the [human] body is an ecosystem."[2] If this is correct, then our embodied selves are our ecological selves, and our human homes must include our bioregions. As a philosophical position, this means that at the most basic level, the human body—where we live—ought to be our home (in the fourth, ecofeminist sense). This notion of body is not the Cartesian body fractured from all that is mental and spiritual, but the whole embodied, interactive, social, relational self. I assume, then, that part of what is involved in longing for home is the yearning to be where one's relational, embodied self is genuinely safe, comfortable, and respected; as such, home in an ecofeminist sense is free from such familiar but unacceptable phenomena as sexual assault, verbal abuse, and air and water pollution. This is to be or to long to be at home in the fourth, ecofeminist sense. Where the homes and institutions that house them (e.g., patriarchy, colonialism, racism, classism) are dysfunctional,[3] the homes are, ultimately, unhealthy, neither life-affirming nor nurturing, and disrespectful, that is, literally not good for you. These are homes (senses one, two, and three) in which millions of people presently find themselves, homes characterized by such social realities as domestic abuse, emotional neglect, sexual assault, and disrespectful gender-role expectations and divisions of labor. In contrast, functional homes and institutions are ones that are genuinely safe, where roles and expectations are clearly negotiated, and the basic needs and life-affirming values of its members are met—ecofeminist homes.

Why call this fourth sense of 'home' ecofeminist? After a brief discussion of ecofeminism, in what follows I show that there are at least eight important insights into the nature of women and homes that ecofeminism can contribute to a cross-cultural, historically accurate understanding of homes and a longing for home. It is because of these contributions that I have chosen to identify homes that are functional and worth yearning or longing for as ecofeminist homes (or, homes in an ecofeminist sense).

Ecofeminism

Just as there is not one feminism, there is not one ecofeminism.[4] Despite differences among ecofeminists, all ecofeminists agree that there are important connections—historical, empirical, conceptual, literary, linguistic, and theoretical—between how one treats women (and other subdominant groups) and how one treats the non-human natural environment (or, simply, nature). As an ecojustice theory, ecofeminism uses sex-gender analysis to make visible the connections among all "isms of domination." All ecofeminists claim that a failure to see these connections results in an inadequate feminism, environmentalism, and analysis of environmental problems. An ecofeminist analysis of 'home' and 'longing for home', then, is one that sees women (and other subdominant human groups) and nature as integral to any adequate analysis of what a home is or ought to be.

Crucial to understanding why any ecofeminist philosophical perspective must be a social justice perspective is an understanding of the importance of oppressive, including patriarchal, conceptual frameworks. As I have argued elsewhere,[5] a conceptual framework is a set of basic beliefs, values, attitudes, and assumptions about oneself and one's world, including one's home. Oppressive conceptual frameworks are characterized by five features: (1) value-hierarchical (up-down thinking), which ranks as most valuable, prestigious, or of high status that which is associated with whatever is "up"; (2) value dualisms (either-or thinking), which use a spatial metaphor to describe things in oppositional (not complementary), exclusive (not inclusive) pairs in which one member of the pair is more highly valued than the other; (3) power-over conceptions and relationships of power, which are exercised by the "ups" over the "downs"; (4) conceptions of privilege, which systematically advantage or give higher status to what is "up"; and (5) a logic of domination, a moral premise that justifies the subordination of what is "down" by what is "up." The logic of domination functions in an argumentative structure that presumes that superiority justifies subordination ("upness" justifies "downness").

In patriarchal, racist, classist, colonial oppressive frameworks, all five features are present, justifying behaviors that subordinate the "downs" by the "ups." The subordination of women, people of color, the poor, and colonized peoples is justified by the same logic of domination. Since all feminists must oppose this logic of domination, all feminists (including ecofeminists) must oppose oppressive conceptual frameworks and the behaviors they sanction. What an ecofeminist adds to the analysis is that in a naturist conceptual framework, the exploitation and degradation of nonhuman nature is justified by the same logic of domination: environmental degradation—degradation of *oikos* or home—involves a logic of domination that functions to explain, maintain, and justify systems of domination.

Eight Ecofeminist Insights

According to Charlotte Bunch, there are four important features of a theory: to describe reality, to analyze that reality, to provide a vision for change, and to hypothesize strategies for change.[6] I think there are at least eight ways that ecofeminist theory can do all this for our understanding of the concepts of 'home' and 'longing for home'. These eight insights provide eight sorts of reasons why one should revision or reconceive homes in an ecofeminist sense.

First, ecofeminism can describe and analyze why the alleged private, domestic sphere of the home and the nonhuman, noncultural natural environment are devalued vis-á-vis the male-gender identified public sphere or culture, at least in those cultures that are part of historical civilization, typically associated with the rise of intensive agriculture about ten thousand years ago. How? Remember that ecofeminism is opposed to oppressive, especially patriarchal, conceptual frameworks and the sorts of behaviors they sanction, maintain, and justify. Women and things that historically (e.g., in Western peasant, agricultural, and industrial cultures) have been identified with the female gender have included commonplace references to both the home and nature. Both homes (in at least the first and third senses of 'house' and 'bioregion') and nature historically have been feminized. Homes (during the last ten thousand years, anyway) belong to the care and work of women. This is especially true of Western, industrialized society, where the so-called private or domestic sphere typically is contrasted sharply with the so-called public, male-gender identified sphere of culture, business, and government. In such cultures at least, mother nature or mother earth is raped, mastered, conquered, mined, penetrated; her womb is put into the service of "the man of science." Virgin (not stud) timber is felled, cut down. Fertile (not impotent) soil is tilled and land that lies fallow is barren, useless, like a childless woman (not man).

Just as homes and nature have been feminized, both historically have been naturalized. In the case of nature, whatever is instinctive or animal-like is deemed inferior to whatever is rational, consciously chosen, or willed (actions). Behaviors of mere brutes, in contrast to rational animals, are devalued behaviors of automata. In the case of women, language once again both evidences and reinforces the naturalization of women and, as such, our inferiority: we are pets, cows, sows, foxes, chicks, serpents, beavers, bitches, bats, old hens, mother hens, pussycats, pussies, cats, cheetahs, birdbrains, harebrains, and flea brains. In a patriarchal culture, when women (and whatever is feminized) and nature (and whatever is naturalized or animalized) are already deemed inferior or "downs," relative to superior male-gender identified reason and culture (as a language that both animalizes and naturalizes women and nature does), one simply reinforces and authorizes the domination of both women and what women do (e.g., work in homes, take care of homes) and nature. One way the exploitation of women, especially women's domestic or house work, and the exploitation of nature are justified is by naturalizing and feminizing both.

By appeal to both the reality of such descriptions and the analysis of oppressive conceptual frameworks and the behaviors they sanction, ecofeminism thereby can show, in both theory and practice, that the five sorts of characteristics that typify patriarchal oppressive conceptual frameworks exist linguistically and behaviorally in social reality; they affect how one perceives nature and women-identified homes—namely, as inferior or important in a less valued sense than that in which the polis or culture is important. Ecofeminism thereby can show what is wrong both with such patriarchal conceptual frameworks and the language and behaviors they sanction and perpetuate.

Second, ecofeminism can show, in theory and practice, that homes in all three senses—houses, intentional communities, and bioregions—must be recognized as historically either the special province of women or places where women's role is of supreme importance. It can thereby show why one ought to long for ecofeminist homes. This is because, although what counts as home historically reflects the different practices and values of people located in diverse material circumstances, nonetheless, what homes as house, intentional communities, and bioregions have in common is that historically their human dimension has been associated predominantly with women and so-called women's work.[7] This fact poses a special challenge to theorists attempting to explain the subordination of women. For example, according to Karl Marx and Friedrich Engels, the subordination of the female sex is viewed as a kind of class subordination brought about by the development of private property and women's exclusion from the public realm of production. Their solution was to bring women out of the home and into the public sphere of production and industry. As Engels states in a much quoted sentence, "The first condition of the liberation of the wife is to bring the whole female sex into public industry."[8]

Two questions that Mark and Engels could not answer, however, with this class analysis of the female sex are, first, why women do women's work, that is, why cross-culturally women rather than men, or men and women together, tend to do the domestic chores, and second, why men own the property. Their inability to explain these phenomena are at least partly because Marx and Engels had no concept of gender (e.g., woman, man), only sex (e.g., female, male). Ecofeminism can make the interconnecting gendered and natured conception of homes visible and also show why the Marxist concept of production must include the domestic production, including reproductive, work of women, both in their homes and in nature (shown below at points three and four).

Third, ecofeminism can show that what counts as a home must be understood contextually, and, especially in the Southern hemisphere ("the South"), as intimately connected to women's relationship to the biroegion or land.[9] Houses that are homes (ecofeminist sense) emerge out of respectful intentional practices and relationships, including clan, tribe, kinship, and community relationships that people have with each other and with nature. For instance, in the South women have gendered role responsibilities to collect firewood and water. In places where trees and water are scarce, this means that it is women who must walk farther for firewood and water (e.g., one to fifteen kilometers daily through rough terrain in Uttarakhand, India) and often must carry the firewood and water back themselves (e.g., without the help of men, oxen, tractors, or carts). As the primary users of forest commodities in most of the South, women's day-to-day, hands-on involvement with forestry provides them with epistemic privilege (or indigenous technical knowledge) that many men and outside professional foresters lack. For example, in a Sierra Leone village, local women were able to identify thirty-one products from nearby trees and bushes while local men could identify only eight.[10] This means that local women know more about uses of trees than local men. This knowledge—women's local, hands-on, epistemic privilege about the concrete realities of their daily lives—grows out of and reflects their lived experiences as household, community, and bioregional managers of trees, tree products, and water collection and distribution, that is, as managers of homes in all three specific senses.

As a fourth and related point, ecofeminism can show why women and their homes—in all three senses of 'home'—are disproportionately harmed by environmental destruction, especially in the South. Consider trees again. In the South women are more dependent than men on tree and forest products.[11] Trees provide five essential elements in household economies: food, fuel, fodder, products for the home (including building materials, household utensils, gardens, dyes, and medicines), and often the only income-generating activities (tree products) available to women. Where there are tree shortages, women are the primary sufferers of resource depletion. According to one estimate, women in New Delhi walk an average of ten kilometers every three or four days for an average of seven hours each day just to obtain firewood.[12] As men increasingly seek employment in towns and cities, women must carry out men's former jobs plus the laborious tasks of collecting and processing forest products on degraded soils.

Consider water. Since women and children perform most of the water collection work, it is they who experience disproportionately higher health risks in the presence of unsanitary water. Only about fifty percent of the South has a source of potable water or facilities for sewage treatment. Drinking water often is drawn from public bathing and laundering places, and the same water frequently is used as a public toilet. Such contaminated water is touched first by women and children and, hence, it is they who are harmed disproportionately by its existence.

In the United States Harriet Rosenberg claims in her essay "The Home Is the Workplace: Hazards, Stress, and Pollutants in the Household"[13] that a rigid sexual division of labor in the home (i.e., house) contributes to significant health and safety hazards for women who work in the home. There are health hazards in cleaning products and appliances, and the average household in the United States has about 250 chemicals that, if ingested, could cause serious illness, especially in children.

Consider farming. Women farmers grow at least fifty-nine percent of the world's food and perhaps as much as eighty percent, and in places in Africa they grow ninety percent of the food. Yet the gender-division of labor puts men in charge of cash crops while the women manage food crops, that is, crops for the home (senses one, two, and three). The invisibility of what women do, for example, in Africa, is clear in agricultural work, where women do most of the ploughing, planting, caring for livestock, harvesting, weeding, processing, and the storing of crops.[14]

Last, consider poverty. Worldwide the largest poverty group is that of households headed by women.[15] The three worst environmental problems in the Third World—soil erosion, deforestation, and desertification—disproportionately affect the poor and, among them, women and children.

What the examples given above (at points two, three, and four) show is that how one treats and talks about women and the home (in all three senses) is intimately connected to, and has consequences for, how one treats and talks about nature. Ecofeminism can show why this is so.

Fifth, ecofeminism can show why environmental racism is a major factor in the exploitation of the homes (in all three senses) of communities of both color and nature. In 1987 the United Church of Christ Commission for Racial Justice published a study entitled *Toxic Waste and Race in the United States.* The study concluded that race is a, and sometimes *the,* major factor in the location of hazardous waste in the United States. Three out of every five African and Hispanic Americans and more than half of all Asian Pacific Islanders and American Indians live in communities—homes—with one or more uncontrolled toxic waste sites. Seventy-five percent of residents in the rural Southwest United States, mostly Hispanic Americans, drink pesticide-contaminated water. Native American women face noteworthy health risks because of the presence of uranium mining on or near reservations. Reproductive organ cancer among Navajo teenagers is seventeen times the national average.

Such environmental racism, that is, the inferior, unjust, and disproportionate destruction of the natural environment and homes (in all three senses) of communities of color, is a reality that ecofeminism can describe and analyze by reference to the oppressive conceptual frameworks and emanating behaviors that characterize patriarchy and racism: "ups" with power and privilege over "downs" exercise that power and privilege in ways that sanction and justify such racist behavior. As a related, sixth point (discussed directly below), it is sexist and classist behavior as well.

Sixth, whatever else it is, ecofeminism is quintessentially a grassroots organizing movement that grows out of women's concerns for nature and for their homes (in all three senses). As Cynthia Hamilton claims,

> Women often play a primary role in community action because it is about things they know best. They also tend to use organizing strategies and methods that are the antithesis of those of the traditional environmental movement. Minority women . . . have found themselves part of a new radical core of environmental activists. . . . These individuals are responding not to "nature" in the abstract but to their *homes* [emphasis mine] and the health of their children. . . . Women are more likely to take on these issues than men precisely because the *home* [emphasis mine] has been defined as a woman's domain.[16]

The Chipko movement, Mothers of East Los Angeles, and the

Ecofeminist Greens are just a few of the hundreds of grass-roots organizations begun by women and low-income minorities throughout the world to stop the destruction of their homes—the houses, intentional communities, and bioregions in which these homes find place.

Seventh, ecofeminism shows why earth-based spiritualities can and often do play an important role in healing the wounds of environmental degradation and the deterioration of bioregional homes. How does ecofeminism do this? Ecofeminism is opposed to patriarchy and naturism (i.e., the unjust exploitation of the earth). Patriarchy is a social system of unequal distribution of power, benefits, and burdens between women and men. It can be understood only in its diverse socioeconomic, historical circumstances. (For example, in the United States this inequitable distribution is pronounced between white men and women of color, among women of color, and between African-American women, Hispanic women, and Native American women.) Furthermore, as I have argued elsewhere,[17] there may be no such thing as a totally healthy or functional home (in all three senses) within patriarchy. This is where earth-based ecofeminist spiritualities fit in.

Earth-based ecofeminist spiritualities upset a patriarchal conceptual framework and the behaviors and institutions it supports by challenging it at is core: its basic beliefs, values, attitudes, and assumptions. In terms of Charlotte Bunch's four-stage model of theory,[18] they thereby provide both a vision for what can be changed and a strategy for changing it. Ecofeminist spiritualities can be powerful survival, resistance, and empowerment strategies that people in the prefeminist patriarchal present can exercise by consciously, deliberately, and fundamentally challenging the basic conceptual framework that fuels patriarchy and related naturist thinking, behavior, and institutions.

What makes these earth-based ecofeminist spiritualities spiritual is that they are conceived and practiced as life-affirming, loving, caring, nurturing, respectful responses to life under patriarchy that posit or assume some creative power (energy, force, deity, deities, being, presence) greater than any one ego-self. Often they are part of coalition-building between, for instance, the women's, peace, and environmental movements in the creation of healthy intentional communities—homes in the ecofeminist sense. They presume that there is liberating power (e.g., power with power or coalitionary power) between intentional and bioregional communities that are both individually and community strengthening. Ecofeminist spiritualities build kinship ties with nature that challenge basic patriarchal and naturist attitudes, values, beliefs, assumptions, behaviors, and institutions of anthropocentric and androcentric domination.

What makes these earth-based spiritualities feminist is that they are opposed to patriarchy and patriarchal ways of thinking. According to ecofeminists, the dysfunctionalities or unhealthiness of patriarchy is viewed as socially constructed, historically molded, economically fashioned, politically nurtured, and socially engineered phenomena. So understood, earth-based feminist spiritualities constitute a diversity of proactive, corrective responses to patriarchy within patriarchy. In effect, they serve as antidotes, however momentary or fleeting, to the felt, lived experience and social reality of the twin dominations of women and nature.

What makes these spiritualities ecofeminist is that they recognize that, under patriarchy, the domination of women and whatever is women-gender identified (e.g., homes, in all three senses) is intimately connected to the domination of nature. They are or could become practices that honor, cherish, respect, or otherwise affirm the value of the earth as our home (in all three senses) and our responsibility to preserve and protect it.

Ecofeminist spiritualities are philosophically significant because, for those who practice them, they do or can represent important recovering challenges—visions and strategies—of change to patriarchy, racism, and colonialism and the effect each has had on the destruction of the planet. They permit one to become a recovering naturist, racist, sexist, or classist in the immediate patriarchal present. Ideally, they represent intentional personal and communal practices that individuals and groups may exercise at any particular time and place to challenge the "isms of domination" while, at the same time, replacing them with liberating, nondominating beliefs, values, attitudes, assumptions, behaviors, and institutions. In short, they are or can be offered as disruptive challenges to present forms of oppression that replace oppressive practices with ones that are not oppressive in the nonutopian, prefeminist present.

Eighth, as all of the above suggests, ecofeminism shows why a change in our most cherished beliefs, values, attitudes, and assumptions—our conceptual frameworks—about women, homes, and nature is needed for any adequate feminism, environmental philosophy, or practice. In agreement with Charlotte Bunch, an adequate theory not only provides an appropriate description of reality and analysis of the problems under consideration; it also provides a vision of what is possible and alternative strategies for long-term change. Ecofeminism is beginning to do all that, not only through empowering personal transformations, but through coalition and community building supported by a theoretical basis for explaining the lived social realities of women in homes connected to nature.

Conclusion

In this essay I have distinguished three senses of 'home': home as house, intentional community, and bioregion. I have argued that longing for home is a yearning, a searching, a remembering, a desiring for a place and set of practices that is life-affirming, and where one's basic needs (physical, emotional, and spiritual) are met. For ecofeminists it is a yearning for healthy homes, in all three interconnected senses of 'home'—for ecofeminist homes (i.e., 'home' in the fourth, inclusive sense).

In dysfunctional patriarchal systems it is extremely difficult, if not impossible, for homes (in any of the three senses of 'home') to be fully life sustaining, healthy, and respectful, no matter what the intentions are of individuals who attempt to make them so. That is because the basic conceptual and institutional structures that constitute the theoretical core and practice of contemporary patriarchy interfere with making them so. For ecofeminists, unless and until patriarchy is dismantled and healthy, functioning homes and systems, including ecosystems, are put in their place, we will continue to long for home ('home' in the ecofeminist, fourth sense).

I suppose I have been becoming an ecofeminist since I first took that trip around much of the world when I was fourteen. For it was then that I first began truly to see systems of domination in practice and the role that nature played in determining whether humans and nonhumans survived. I now know that what I began to see then was the interconnected systems ("isms") of domination among women, people of color, the underclass, children, indigenous peoples, and the earth, and I am still in the process of trying to see more clearly those connections in order to help eliminate systems of domination that keep them intact. In this sense, I, too, am still longing for home.

Sometimes this longing for home is a troubling, nagging, uncomfortable feeling with what I have. Sometimes it is a hopeful, empowering sense of what I can do to make my own home, community, and ultimate dwelling place—earth—a better place. I know because of the sense of shame and bewilderment I felt as a child traveling around the world that this longing rejects the conception of the earth as a lifeboat, and any lifeboat ethics that hold that we in the First World are morally obligated to help only those people and countries who or that help themselves control population growth. It rejects conceptions of the earth as a spaceship manned by scientists who do not see the organismic nature of human-nonhuman relationships. It also rejects notions of the earth as a frontier to be conquered and controlled or as a pristine wilderness to be preserved with no attention to urban ecological issues. I know I reject all these because they are too simplistic: they fail to see the complex and interconnected roles that "isms of domination" play in the creation and maintenance of population growth, wilderness destruction, and urban decay.

In this context it is worth noting that many ecofeminists have objected to the very popular poster of the earth as seen from outer space: it is the photo of a blue ball accompanied by the caption "Love Your Mother." Presumably, the popular power of that slogan is its challenge to patriarchal devaluing of mothers' work and roles and its elevating of the earth to some level of sanctity of idealized motherhood. Nonetheless, I share many of these ecofeminists' concerns. It is an unsettling poster for me because, for many of the earth's inhabitants, mothers and what they do have not had a very positive or valued status in historical, socioeconomic reality. Furthermore, many of us often have had very ambiguous, if not outright destructive, relationships to our own mothers. If the best we can do to preserve the planet in present patriarchy is to love it as we do our mothers, I think we are in deep trouble!

What the image of the earth as seen from outer space does suggest is that we are all in this together—humans and nonhumans alike. It does suggest a sense of the earth as home to all of us, in all three senses of 'home', humans and nonhuman natural objects alike. It is a home that must be clean and well kept, nurtured and respected, and protected from unwarranted exploitation and destruction.

I suggest that we recaption the poster featuring the earth as seen from outer space to read, simply, "Love the Planet—Your Home," in the ecofeminist sense of 'home'. Perhaps then one would really see what I think ecofeminism is attempting to show about the interconnections between how one conceives and treats women and other human subdominants and how one conceives and treats our ultimate home, the planet Earth. It is here—on planet Earth—that we build our houses and establish intentional communities and do so within specific, cross-culturally varied bioregions. Stated differently, it is on the planet Earth that we build our earthly 'homes' (in all three senses). The earth truly is our home.

To end, I am reminded of an age-old wisdom: "If we don't take care of our bodies, where will we live?" To paraphrase that wisdom, if we don't take care of the planet Earth—our ultimate home (in all three senses of 'home')—where will any of us, human and nonhuman natural objects, live? We need, and ought to long for, the planet as our home, in the ecofeminist sense of 'home'.[19]

Notes

1. Judith Plant, "Revaluing Home: Feminism and Bioregionalism," in *Home! A Bioregional Reader*, ed. Van Andruss, Christopher Plant, Judith Plant, and Eleanor Wright (Philadelphia.: New Society Publishers, 1990), 21.

2. Graydon Royce, "The Body is an Ecosystem," in *Minneapolis Star Tribune* (12 September 1994), 8A.

3. For a discussion of the notion of a dysfunctional system and, in particular, patriarchy as a dysfunctional social system, see my essay "A Philosophical Perspective on Ecofeminist Spiritualities," in *Ecofeminism and the Sacred*, ed. Carol Adams (New York: Continuum/Crossroads Books, 1993), 119–32.

4. See Karen J. Warren, "Feminism and Ecology: Making Connections," *Environmental Ethics*, vol. 9, no. 3 (1987): 3–20, and "The Power and the Promise of Ecological Feminism," *Environmental Ethics*, vol. 12, no. 2 (1990): 125–46.

5. See my essay, "Towards an Ecofeminist Peace Politics," in *Ecological Feminism*, ed. Karen J. Warren (London: Routledge Press, 1994), 179–99.

6. Charlotte Bunch, "Four Stage Model of Theory," oral presentation in "Ecofeminism and the Greens," a video produced by Greta Gaard, University of Minnesota, 1994.

7. More will be said on the third, bioregional sense of 'home' in the text, point three. For a more elaborate discussion of women-bioregion connections see my essay, "Taking Empirical Data Seriously: An Ecofeminist Philosophical Perspective," *Ecofeminism: Multidisciplinary Perspectives*, ed. Karen J. Warren (Bloomington, Ind.: Indiana University Press, forthcoming).

8. Frederick Engels, *The Origin of the Family, Private Property, and the State* (New York: International Publishers, 1972), 137–38.

9. Engels, 137-38

10. *Restoring the Balance: Women and Forest Resources*, (Rome: Food and

Culture Organization (FAO) of the United Nations, with assistance from the Swedish International Development Authority (SIDA), 1987), 4.

11. For a more complete discussion of the ways in which women are disproportionately harmed by environmental destruction, see my "Taking Empirical Data Seriously."

12. Marilyn Waring, *If Women Counted: A New Feminist Economics* (New York: Harper and Row, 1988), 263.

13. Harriet Rosenberg, in *Double Exposure*, ed. Wendy Chavkin (New York: Monthly Review Press, 1984), 210–24.

14. See the United Nations *Handbook on Women in Africa* (Economic Commission for Africa, 1975).

15. Jonie Seager and Ann Olson, *Women in the World: An International Atlas* (New York: Simon and Schuster, 1987), 114.

16. Cynthia Hamilton, "Women, Home, and Community," in *woman of power: a magazine of feminism, spirituality, and politics*, 20 (Spring 1991): 43.

17. See Warren, "A Philosophical Perspective on Ecofeminist Spiritualities," in Adams.

18. See Bunch.

19. I gave an earlier version of this paper as a speech at the Boston University School of Theology Colloquia Series, 8 October 1994. My thanks to that audience; Bruce Nordstrom; Janet Folina; Henry West; my daughter, Cortney Warren; and my friends at Costello's Espresso Bar in Eagan, Minnesota, for their support and feedback as I tried to work through what I wanted to say in this paper.

10

Cross-Cultural Ecologies: The Expatriate Experience, the Multiculturalism Issue, and Philosophy

A. Pablo Iannone

An Ambiguous Paradise

The expatriate experience, with its unstable mixture of melancholy and exhilaration, permeates the end of the twentieth century. The experience itself is not new. Indeed, it has been recorded or orally passed down in the stories of people of Jewish or Gypsy descent through the centuries. Yet, the scope and magnitude of this experience in the twentieth century is quite unprecedented, at times not only exceeding all expectations, but moving cross-cultural realities beyond the wildest speculations of fantasy and fiction.

The experience results partly from massive migrations occurring over decades, such as the influx of European and, later, other immigrants who, in the 1880s, began migrating to such countries as Argentina and the United States. It also results from sudden exile brought about by a variety of events. Religious, ethnic, or cultural persecution, for example, led Bosnians who were able to escape Serbian ethnic cleansing into exile in the United States and Western Europe in the 1990s. Throughout the century, coups d'etat, civil wars, and political repression, sometimes coupled with rapidly deteriorating national economies, have significantly contributed to the growing influx of immigrants from Eastern Europe and

North Africa into Germany; from the Caribbean into the United States; from some Spanish-speaking countries into other Spanish-speaking countries; and from every Spanish-speaking country into a range of other countries, from Australia to France and, significantly, the United States, where this influx has led to the rapid growth of the Hispanic diaspora.

Migrations such as these need not occur between countries alone. As in the case of Peruvian peasants migrating to Lima, Argentine peasants migrating to Buenos Aires, and Puerto Ricans migrating to the United States mainland, they can occur within countries. In the introduction to *Paradise Lost or Gained? The Literature of Hispanic Exile*, Fernando Alegría poignantly characterizes the scope of the resulting expatriate experience: "Exile no longer has borders."[1]

This experience is part and parcel of the multiculturalism issue: a cluster of sharp differences of opinions or conflicts of demands concerning cultural diversity and self-assertion, together with what people do to uphold their opinions or satisfy their demands.[2] In the heated discussions that constitute it, there are those who hail cross-cultural experiences and interactions as ways out of ethnocentric parochialism and see in them a new freedom for long-oppressed ethnic groups. Others argue that such intermingling of cultures and the position that supports it, pluralism, are merely forms of confusion and that this confusion is undermining national economies—say, those of Germany and the United States and, indeed, the very foundations of Western culture.

In this essay, I discuss some salient characteristics of the expatriate experience and ask: Can they help us to understand and deal with the cultural fragmentation and cross-cultural conflicts involved in the multiculturalism issue? How? Can they help to delineate philosophy's role in dealing with the fragmentation and conflicts? I argue for two theses.

First, some salient characteristics of the expatriate experience are: (1) ambiguity about one's evoked or hoped-for homeland; (2) a fluid transculturational balance, that is, a changing equilibrium in the expatriate's interactions with and adaptations to his or her foreign environment; (3) a heightened awareness of local conventions; and (4) an increased reliance on convention-settling processes, that is, on social decision processes—from argument and negotiation to quiet resistance and outright confrontation—whose aim is to settle new conventions in the expatriates' encounters with their foreign environments.

The second thesis is that, given their analogy with some salient features of philosophy, the characteristics of the expatriate experience can also help to delineate philosophy's role in dealing with the fragmentation and conflicts involved in the multiculturalism issue.

In the process of arguing for these theses, I will, to the extent that space permits, formulate and provide some reasons for adopting two hypotheses. One hypothesis is that the features characteristic of the expatriate experience can help us to understand and deal with the cultural fragmentation and cross-cultural conflicts involved in the multiculturalism issue. The other hypothesis is that these characteristics can help by indicating the concerns characteristically involved in the multiculturalism issue—for example, the concern with retaining one's sense of personal identity while attaining one's aims in a foreign environment—as well as the convention-settling processes—for example, as previously mentioned, argumentation, negotiation, quiet resistance, and various forms of outright confrontation—that are used in seeking settled resolutions of the issue.

Constructing Others

The use of words has consequences and, sometimes, the use of one and the same word in different linguistic contexts has quite disparate consequences. Take the Spanish word *gringo*, which is said to derive from the Spanish word *griego*, whose English translation is "Greek." In the United States, Mexico, and some areas of the Caribbean, *gringo* is exclusively a disparaging term, typically used among Hispanics to refer to foreigners, especially to United States nationals of British and northern and eastern European descent. In Argentina, however, the word *gringo* can be used in either an endearing, disparaging, or mixed way to refer to foreigners or descendants of foreigners, especially those whose paternal last name is not Spanish.

A friend can say endearingly during a soccer game: "That was a great pass, *gringo!*" An example of its disparaging use can be found in the following story: A mestizo guide from Cerro Colorado, a small town in the mountains of the Argentine province of Cordoba, once was telling me that the Italian farmers in the area, on buying their land and without any consultation with the locals, had enforced their newly acquired property rights by setting up fences around their farms to prevent free-ranging goats, including the guide's own goats, from destroying their crops. He stopped for a second and commented: "What would you expect from them? They are *gringos*." The implication was that *gringos* characteristically pursued their own interest without paying attention to the way in which their actions upset local traditions concerning land use.

As for mixed uses, one of the attendants at a party in Lobos, a town in the pampas of the Argentine province of Buenos Aires, once said on hearing me play a gaucho drum: "Look at this *gringo*! He can play as well as or better than us!" The implication of such surprised praise was that I had played well, but also that it was surprising because *gringos* were inept when it came to playing Argentine folk music.

This latter case is instructive concerning the manner in which Argentines tend to identify *gringos*. A lower- or middle-class Argentine descendant of Italians and Spaniards whose father's last name is Italian and whose mother's last name is Spanish—say, as in my case, Iannone Díaz, typically grows up believing that he or she is a Caucasian of Italian and Spanish descent who happened to be born in Argentina. The same will happen if the father's last name is Spanish while the mother's last name is Italian—say, Díaz Iannone. Yet, since, except for some upper-class families and some families of purely Spanish descent, Argentines tend to use only their paternal last names, people will typically apply the term *gringo* only to the first case above.

Whatever the identification criteria, few, if any, social groups fail to use some of them. In using them, they engage in an ethnification process that affects the sense of identity of children growing up and, indeed, of foreigners living in, or in contact with, these groups, because foreigners, not unlike children, have to learn many things from scratch. Suppose, for example, that the previously described Argentine moves to the United States. Hispanics in the United States, as well as non-Hispanics, would be quite unlikely to apply the term *gringo* to this person. Nonetheless, as soon as he or she enters the country, the ethnification process begins. Given the history and the role of the legal system in the United States, the ethnification process is based on racial classifications reflected in legal classifications. The alien is required to fill out a form indicating his or her ethnicity in a manner that mixes race and culture. One of the choices is Caucasian. Another is Hispanic. The form explains that the box for Hispanic includes all those individuals from

countries where the predominant language is (as in Argentina) Spanish. Caucasians are something else.

This is a construction and one the Argentine previously described
may have difficulty understanding. Though racially a Caucasian, he
or she is legally characterized as a Hispanic, not a Caucasian. The
initial response may amount to the unintended or, sometimes, intended failure to fill out the form as required. It may also involve
a range of emotions: from bafflement, through amusement, to in-
dignation, and these may be enhanced, often in mutually conflictive ways, with an additional realization. In the United States, though
an alien, this person is not perceived as a *gringo* or *gringa*, but as
a member of a varied group that includes, among many others, precisely the individuals who would use these terms to disparage him
or her in an Argentine context.

This may not simply prompt conflicting emotions but also un-
settle the person's sense of identity. After all, as an Argentine *gringo* or *gringa*, this person belonged to a group that, however
disparaged, had acquired significant economic and political power
in society. By contrast, as a Hispanic in the United States, the person belongs to a disadvantaged minority. The variety of intellectual
and practical responses to this change in cultural constructs surrounding the newcomer centrally constitutes the expatriate experience that I examine next.

Modeling the Expatriate Experience

Varieties of Numbness, Pain, and Nostalgia

The expatriate experience is as varied as the number of expatriates times the number of their circumstances, yet some stages and
salient features can be found in this variety. At least among exiles
and immigrants, the expatriate experience begins with numbness,
pain, and nostalgia.[3] Numbness and pain can, though need not be,
relatively unreflective reactions to cultural shock brought about by
relatively sudden changes in one's cultural environment. For example, numbness, pain, and nostalgia can be reactions to changes in
the language predominantly used—say, from Spanish to English; the
customary ways in which people relate to each other in public places—say, how seriously they take the question "How are you?" or what
noise level they consider to be loud; the attention generally paid to

the legal system; or the compound effect of all these and other similar changes. By contrast with numbness and pain, nostalgia, which can begin with unreflective mistakes such as expecting a type of food to be ready for dinner or a dear place to be just around the corner, develops along somewhat more reflective lines. Often, though by no means always, nostalgia is felt for the remembered homeland to which expatriates want to return.

By contrast with foreign expatriates, internal expatriates, depending on the degree of adaptation reached by the ethnic group in which they are born, may initially grow up accustomed to being treated like cultural foreigners, say, like *gringos* in Argentina or Puerto Ricans in the United States.[4] This may contribute to the absence of numbness and pain at least during the first years of life, before the individuals develop the ability to reflect. Later, however, numbness and pain may appear in response to their realization that they have been allotted undesirable social places through various constructs that they find alien to their conceptions of themselves.[5]

A further, more reflective development may appear with the natural desire to leave an environment where the expatriates are treated in such manner, which, also quite naturally, may lead to reflection about one's origins in the search for finding a place where one belongs. Thus, one may, and people do, imagine homelands. This notion may concern, as is the case among some African Americans, a homeland they never visited, or, as is the case among some members of the United States or Argentine Jewish communities, it may concern Israel, a place they now have and that, before 1945 and for many centuries, they always identified as home in their collective memories.[6]

The Experience of Going Back Home

Many expatriates can, and some do, go back to the place they call home. The effects are often disquieting and, indeed, can be self-shattering. This can readily happen to internal exiles who have fantasized their homeland for many years. For example, an Italian descendant born in Argentina, whose grandfather was from the Italian eastern-central province of Abruzzi-Molise and whose grandmother was from the Italian southern province of Potenza, may, on "returning home" to Italy, have great difficulty coming to terms with the deep animosities he finds between a number of people from the provinces he had grown up to imagine as a harmonious and welcoming whole. The same thing may happen to an African American who goes home to an imagined Africa, only to experience great alienation on being asked to what tribe he or she belongs and being scorned because he or she does not know what to answer. Whoopi Goldberg pointed to these disparities quite clearly and humorously when, during an award ceremony televised in 1994, she said: "I've been in Africa and there is one thing I can assure you: I'm an American!"[7]

Going back home, however, need not be dramatic in order for it to affect one's sense of identity. Small, ordinary things may have the same effect. A Spanish speaker may go back home and find that, though still able to speak his or her native Spanish—say, an Argentine dialect—like a native, he or she cannot understand it as readily as before because of having spent much time talking with speakers of some other, say, Mexican or Venezuelan, Spanish dialect. This person may have developed a foreign accent and be told so by friends or family members. In any case, realizing that this has happened and that one's native language may not be as natural and as constitutive of one's own identity as one had assumed sometimes has a destabilizing effect.

Such destabilization is compounded by the fact that the longer the time one spends abroad, the less verifiable one's memories of one's homeland become. One's bed is not where it used to be any longer. One's cherished places have changed. Perhaps they have disappeared under the bulldozers and cranes of development. People have changed, perhaps becoming less trusting as a result of long years of oppression and civil wars. The list is long and it shows that it is impossible to return to much of the homeland of one's memory. This realization tends to have a significant effect on many expatriates' sense of identity, because this sense is highly dependent on memory, and the expatriate experience of going back home tends to collapse memories and fantasies together in the never-never land of the unconfirmable. In this way, expatriates begin to find themselves living in a cultural and personal limbo.

Rejecting One's Homeland

The experience of living in a cultural and personal limbo leads some expatriates to engage in desperate adaptation efforts. They may turn their back on their countries of origin, perhaps even on their families. Their attempts may lead to a variety of personality developments. Some may experience a buildup of internal conflicts with different degrees of tension and a variety of effects on their ability to live full lives. Others may pragmatically live with rejection until forgetfulness and time allow them to get used to the idea that home, as they had imagined it, does not exist. Still others may reject their homeland or dreamt homeland without any upsetting consequences.

In any case, a significant number of expatriates—my impression is many, but by no means all—may eventually need to develop further adaptations so as to overcome the undesirable state in which rejecting their homeland puts them. For example, they may need to accept the fact that, no matter how hard they try, they are still Argentines, or Norwegians, while recognizing that they do not any longer fit in their homelands as well as they used to fit in the past. Second, they may need to acknowledge that they will not ever fit perfectly in their foreign environment. Third, they may need to identify areas of social life, say, marriage or business, in which they can function reasonably well in their foreign environment. At any rate, this process of seeking further adaptations is double edged and varied and involves much that is positive and much that is negative about the expatriate experience. Furthermore, it is not a one-shot or simple deal, but typically takes place through a variety of transformations or cultural adaptations between individuals, between individuals and groups, and between the groups themselves.

Imagining Home, Transforming Oneself

The transformations characteristic of the expatriate experience concern the expatriates' past, present, and future and often manifest themselves in expatriate attitudes about their homeland, evidencing various forms of ambiguity. In "Women Poets of the Cuban Diaspora," for example, María A. Salgado has substantially documented the fact that women poets of the Cuban diaspora "are aware that they have ceased to be part of Cuban history and that their poems, written in a foreign culture, are no longer part of Cuban literature."[8] Their ambiguity about Cuba is torn: their portrayals of their past are idyllic, but they treat this past as destroyed and express deep alienation from the present and from themselves.[9]

By contrast, the Argentine writer Julio Cortázar, responding to the fact that his books were banned in his own country, displays a pragmatic ambiguity about the experience and about his homeland.

He describes the experience as "not for me an altogether negative trauma" and talks of turning "the negative value of exile into a positive value."[10]

In both cases the expatriates have significantly adapted to the realities of the foreign culture, thus achieving a somewhat fluid transculturational balance that includes their ambiguity about their homeland. This ambiguity, however, is not peculiar to cases in which expatriates accept the realities of expatriation, including the fact that it changes them. For example, the Puerto Rican writer Alfredo Villanueva Collado observes: "If one does, like I have, refuse to metamorphose, one must nevertheless choose some kind of official identity."[11]

Such an identity, however, is proposed by the reluctant expatriate as a way of settling conventions for presenting oneself in everyday life in the foreign culture; and the success of this proposal is not a one-way street. It involves give-and-take and mutual adaptations. Indeed, it cannot succeed without significant cross-cultural interpretation and interaction—a process that, like being married, changes people in many respects and not always in a manner that they can easily articulate. What used to bother them—from people answering their questions with an "aha" instead of "yes" to people talking to them loudly as soon as they heard their foreign accent— may not bother them any longer. What once did not bother them— from an inefficient phone system to ethnic jokes—may bother them now. Even if they have not changed much or even in these ways, however, at the very least the process makes them better performers, and this is a disposition one cannot develop without a heightened awareness of local conventions or, at least, an increased ability to rely on the convention-settling processes involved in establishing new relations between people such as new roommates, new neighbors, or new coworkers.[12]

This is not to deny that rejection of the foreign culture can occur. Expatriates can have difficulty with, resist, or openly refuse to go along with a variety of cross-cultural adaptations. Some may refuse to adapt to new driving practices. Others may have difficulty adapting to personal relations entered with different assumptions about love and loyalty. Still others may resist adapting to the foreign culture's decor patterns whereby their homeland's ordinary talk is considered loud talk. There are those—among whom I have found a number of writers whose intellectual life was closely tied with their native language—who simply will refuse to learn the foreign culture's language.

Whatever the rejections, however, individuals must get on with their lives while in the foreign culture. As a result, a variety of adaptations need to, and do, occur. Indeed, they often serve as correctives for non-negotiable cultural rejections, and they involve many personal changes, not the least of which is a heightened awareness of local conventions and an increased ability to rely on the convention-settling processes likely to help in the absence or ignorance of established conventions.

This completes this essay's reasons in support of its first thesis. Some salient characteristics of the expatriate experience are (1) ambiguity about one's evoked or hoped-for homeland; (2) a fluid transculturational balance—that is, a changing equilibrium in the expatriate's interactions with and adaptations to his or her foreign environment; (3) a heightened awareness of local conventions; and (4) an increased reliance on convention-settling processes—that is, social decision processes, from argument and negotiation to quiet resistance and outright confrontation, whose aim is to settle new conventions in the expatriates' encounters with their foreign environments.

These characteristics of the expatriate experience invariably have an epistemological aspect—cross-cultural interpretations—and a practical aspect—interactions aimed at resolving conflicts or bridging communication gaps with others. The same epistemological and practical aspects, or aspects of these same types, are, however, at the center of the differences of opinion or conflicts of demands that, as indicated at the outset, are at the center of the multiculturalism issue. They are part and parcel of the sharp divergences of opinion central to this issue because these differences often involve interpretations of members of ethnic groups other than one's own with whom one disagrees or interpretations of the groups themselves. They are also part and parcel of the conflicts of demands concerning cultural diversity and self-assertion, because they often involve interactions ranging from shouting matches and demonstrations to going about one's own business side by side with members of other ethnic groups whose demands conflict with one's own.

The identities and similarities just mentioned provide reasons that, because of space limitations cannot be further detailed here, for formulating two hypotheses. One is that the features characteristic of the expatriate experience can help us to understand and deal with the cultural fragmentation and cross-cultural conflicts involved in the multiculturalism issue. The other hypothesis is that these characteristics can help by focusing on the concerns characteristically involved in the multiculturalism issue—for example, the concern with retaining one's sense of personal identity while attaining one's aims in a foreign environment—as well as the convention-settling processes—for example, as previously mentioned, argumentation, negotiation, quiet resistance, and various forms of outright confrontation—that are used in seeking settled resolutions of the issue. With these hypotheses in mind, I next turn to the role that philosophy can have in dealing with the issue.

Philosophy as a Form of Intellectual Expatriation

What is philosophy's role in dealing with the multiculturalism issue? When addressing this question, the ambiguities of the term "philosophy" are likely to create confusion. There are at least four senses of this term: (1) personal philosophy, or a person's outlook on things, as in "My philosophy is not yet significantly formulated"; (2) group philosophy, or a group's predominant outlook on things, as in "Aymara philosophy includes the belief that time is circular"; (3) a philosophical theory, or a generalized device for formulating, clarifying, and dealing with problems about reality, knowledge, reasoning, norms, and values, as in "Aristotle's and Confucius's philosophies are worth comparing with each other"; and (4) a branch of inquiry, or a critical activity about philosophies in the personal, group, and theory senses, as in "philosophy is not an exact science." In addressing the above question, I focus on philosophy in the sense of a branch of inquiry and draw on some features of those who pursue it in a sustained manner.[13]

I have argued elsewhere that, if philosophy is to have any significant role in resolving problems of human life such as those posed by the multiculturalism issue, it needs to interlock fully with the human sciences and the nonacademic world. Otherwise, philosophy will be unable to address problems thoroughly and realistically. Some concerns will likely fall through the conceptual and methodological cracks of the languages of philosophy, academic disciplines, politics, technology, and so on. The general public will be unrepresented and their concerns might well be missed.[14]

A significant problem here, however, is how to interlock with the human sciences and the general public, which, in effect, is a public fragmented along cultural lines. The expatriate experience can help to clarify the place and role of philosophers and philosophy in this process. Let us see why.

Traditionally, philosophers, from Heraclitus, Socrates, and Mo Tzu to Ibn Khaldun, Karl Marx, and Mohandas Ghandi, have approached their times and cultures with a critical, distant eye. This is no accident and it holds true even of philosophers who (as it is sometimes said of Aristotle, Thomas Aquinas, and Georg Friedrich Wilhelm Hegel) had the purpose of providing, or whose positions amounted to, a justification of their times, cultures, faiths, churches, or states. It is no accident, because a critical, hence detached, approach is crucial to philosophy and the wonder with which it is supposed to begin. As Arthur E. Murphy put it:

> The philosophic mind is, in the first place, an inquiring mind. It is right and illuminating to say, with Aristotle, that philosophy begins in wonder. But not just any kind of wonder. The marvelous, the occult, the merely freakish and "colossal," are objects of wonder for the popular mind and arouse an interest that illustrated weeklies, motion pictures, sideshows and various forms of commercialized superstition exist to satisfy. The wonder that generates a philosophical inquiry is of a different sort—it is elicited not by the marvelous but by the familiar, by the things that everybody "knows" and takes for granted.[15]

This wonder about the familiar that everyone takes for granted turns philosophers into strangers in their times and cultures. They are a bit marginal, partly because they critically approach what these times and cultures assume to be known by everybody.

As evidenced by this essay's discussion of the expatriate experience, this marginal place and critical role of philosophers is quite analogous to the place and many a role of expatriates, because expatriates characteristically wonder at what everyone takes for granted. It is, for example, a common experience for recent expatriates who have come to the United States from Europe, Latin America, or Asia to wonder why, on running into United States acquaintances on the street or at a mall or campus, being asked "How are you?" and, accordingly, beginning to answer the question, the acquaintances often show a sort of restlessness, as if they had not meant to learn how the expatriate was after all. Of course, in the United States, casually asking, "How are you?" in the said circumstances is largely equivalent to saying, "Hi." Everybody knows this, takes it for granted, and, accordingly, gives a short answer: "Fine. And you?" For recent expatriates, however, this is a source of wonder and, often, of criticism. They get the initial feeling that their acquaintances—perhaps all United States persons—simply do not care about others and they cannot understand why their acquaintances take the trouble to pretend to care by saying, "How are you?"

Granted, this is an example of a superficial misunderstanding that a little bit of time and listening can easily resolve. In the case of philosophers, the situation is different, but the example does exemplify the type of critical wonder that gets the inquiry started and begins to create feelings of estrangement. Further, the analogy goes deeper. For, just as with expatriates, philosophers often experience a mixture of melancholy and exhilaration in doing philosophy; they develop adaptations to worlds they find, at least in some respects, foreign or unfamiliar enough to deserve examination. Given their concern with the unfamiliar, they rely significantly on convention-settling processes—from proposing new social arrangements and ways of thinking about the world to suggesting and practicing ways of changing it. That is, just as individual expatriates, as well as entire cultures, make use of these processes in building a place for themselves in a foreign world, so too philosophy involves the use of the same kind of processes insofar as it aims at bringing about conceptual and practical changes in the world in which we live.

These features provide a certain commonality with those involved in cross-cultural conflicts caused by cross-cultural fragmentation and interactions. Hence, they provide a way in which philosophy can find a common ground that can help it to interlock with nonphilosophical activities. It also can help philosophers to communicate and engage in meaningful dialogue and convention-settling interactions with nonphilosophers involved in the multiculturalism issue. These are reasons for this essay's fourth and last thesis: in the same manner in which the salient characteristics of the expatriate experience can help us to deal with the multiculturalism issue and, by analogy, with some salient features of philosophy, the characteristics of the expatriate experience also can help to delineate philosophy's role in dealing with the fragmentation and conflicts by helping to bring out the analogies between the said concerns and processes and the concerns and processes significantly involved in the philosophical enterprise.

The role here envisioned for philosophy cannot be discussed in detail within the constraints of this essay. Suffice it to say that it should proceed in accordance with the conception of philosophy as diplomacy that I have developed elsewhere.[16] By *diplomacy* I do not simply mean, as cynics would have it, the activity of doing and saying the nastiest things in the nicest ways. I mean, quite broadly, the activity of dealing with states, nations, other social groups such as the business sector, the financial community, the U.S. urban and rural communities, and the various ethnic groups in the United States, and even individuals, so that ill does not prevail.[17] As for philosophy as diplomacy, I mean a branch of inquiry aimed at dealing with a variety of problems, for example, cross-cultural problems, in ways that are feasible, effective, and crucially sensitive both to the often unsettled and conflictive nature of the concerns that contribute to pose the problems and to the variety of open-ended social decision procedures that may help settle these concerns and often deal with the problems through policies and decisions and on the basis of reasons worked out in the policy-making process.[18] Among these decisions and reasons are those involved in the convention-settling processes previously discussed.

To say that philosophy as diplomacy aims at avoiding ill might lead one to think that philosophy as diplomacy is primarily a consequentialist notion—that is, that it takes the justifiability of policies and decisions to depend only on the value of their consequences—but it does not because ill may consist in the violation of a right or failure to act in accordance with a duty or with principles of justice. These are deontological considerations. They take the justifiability of policies and decisions to depend only on their accordance with rights, duties, or principles of justice.[19]

The conception of philosophy as diplomacy is also not primarily deontological. It does not rule out the possibility that in certain cases, arguably in cases of widespread community deterioration, the social consequences are so catastrophic as to take precedence. This need not be so because other deontological considerations take precedence, because the situations envisioned approach state-of-nature situations. In any such situation, it is at least questionable whether deontological considerations such as rights or the obligations correlated with them carry much, if any, weight.[20] At any rate, the relative weight of these various considerations is at issue in such situations and its determination needs to be worked out in the policy-making process. It is in this regard that social decision procedures such as convention-settling processes take center stage.

Accordingly, philosophy's general role would proceed in accordance with a method introduced by Edith Cobb in her seminal *The Ecology of Imagination in Childhood.*[21] Cobb used this method, which is based on the ecological model of interchanges and mutual adaptations and interconnections between organisms and their environment, to analyze children's development of cosmic sense. As Margaret Mead commented, however, the method has a wide scope of applicability and "makes it possible to compare the most diverse cultural developments."[22] Indeed, it may help us to understand not only, at the level of individuals, the mutual adaptations that the expatriate experience involves between individual expatriates and the foreign cultures where they live, but also, at the societal level, the adaptations developed between groups whose respective cultures differ. It also may help us to delineate and seek to develop additional sound adaptations.

Along the lines of this method, philosophy's general role would be that of proceeding in a manner sensitive to the dynamics and constraints of cross-cultural ecologies and help us to mold them in ways that make room for mutually supportive developments of the cultures and persons interacting in the multiculturalism issue. This is crucial given the curiosity of humans and their urge to reshape their environment, because if cultural purposes and social aims are not expanded to make room for the general satisfaction of this urge among those involved in the issue, only conflict will remain. Indeed, as Edith Cobb puts it, the urge "will be displaced onto the ingenuity of delinquency and crime."[23] The cooperative, convention-settling focus of the approach here suggested should help to avoid these consequences and enable us to deal more intelligently and less parochially with the multiculturalism issue.[24] It also offers us humans hope of forging a home or, at the very least, a more welcoming social environment out of our conflictive times.[25]

Notes

1. Fernando Alegría, "Introduction," in Fernando Alegría and Jorge Ruffinelli, *Paradise Lost or Gained? The Literature of Hispanic Exile* (Houston: Arte Público Press, 1990), 15. For an indication of the extent to which migrations are turning societies in every continent into multicultural societies where significant numbers of individuals acquire transcultural self-images, see Scott Heller, "Worldwide 'Diaspora' of Peoples Poses New Challenges for Scholars," *The Chronicle of Higher Education* (3 June 1992): A7–A9. Some significant recent studies concerning particular regions are: Yossi Shain, *The*

Frontier of Loyalty: Political Exiles in the Age of the Nation-State (Middletown, Conn.: Wesleyan University Press, 1989); Yossi Shain, *Governments in Exile in Contemporary World Politics* (New York: Routledge, 1991); Richard G. Fox, *Recapturing Anthropology: Working in the Present* (Santa Fe, New Mexico: School of American Research, 1991); Gay Wiletz, *Binding Cultures: Black Women Writers in Africa and the Diaspora* (Bloomington, Ind.: Indiana University Press, 1992); Constance R. Sutton and Elsa M. Chaney *Caribbean Life in New York City: Sociocultural Dimensions* (New York: Center for Migration Studies, 1992); Karla F. C. Holloway, *Moorings and Metaphors: Figures of Culture and Gender in Black Women's Literature* (New Brunswick, N.J.: Rutgers University Press, 1992); Nina Glick Schiller, Linda Basch, and Cristina Szanton, *Towards a Transnational Perspective on Migration: Race, Class, Ethnicity, and Nationalism Reconsidered* (New York: New York Academy of Sciences, 1992); Hamid Naficy, *The Making of Exile Cultures: Iranian Television in Los Angeles* (Minneapolis: University of Minnesota Press, 1993); Ron Kelley and Jonathan Friedlander, *Irangeles: Iranians in Los Angeles* (Berkeley, Calif.: University of California Press, 1993). For previous general migration studies, see Kenneth C. W. Kammeyer, *Population Studies* (Chicago: Rand McNally, 1975), especially section 3, 169–237.

2. For a more detailed characterization of issues, see my *Philosophy as Diplomacy: Essays in Ethics and Policy Making* (Atlantic Highlands, N.J.: Humanities Press, 1994), Essay 1: "Issues and Issue-Overload: A Challenge to Moral Philosophy," 1–12.

3. See, for example, Fernando Alegría, "Introduction," in Alegría and Ruffinelli, 11. This is an excerpt from "Literature in Exile," *Review* 30 (September 1981): 10-23.

4. I talk about the expatriate experience in the wider sense that also covers the experience of members of groups—say, members of the Jewish community in the United States or Argentina, African Americans or Puerto Ricans in the United States, and peasant mestizos in Argentina and other American countries—who, even when born in a given country, are treated as foreign or marginal to the predominant culture. That is, I talk about the expatriate experience in the wider sense that also covers what sometimes is called "internal exile." For the notion of internal exiles, see, for example, Lucas Lackner, *Internal Exile: Poems & Illustrations* (Santa Barbara, Calif.: Santa Barbara Press, 1983), and Association of American Publishers, *Soviet Writers and Journalists in Labor Camp or Internal Exile* (New York: The Association, 1983).

5. The expatriate experience can be studied by reference to cross-cultural approaches to personality development. See, for example, Margaret Mead, "The Cross-Cultural Approach to the Study of Personality," in J. L. McCary, ed., *Psychology of Personality* (New York and London: Grove Press and Evergreen Books, 1959), 223–24, 233; and Edith Cobb, *The Ecology of Imagination in Childhood* (New York: Columbia University Press, 1977). In this regard, symbiotic relations between different species may serve as a submodel for this purpose.

6. The existence of a homeland is not a requirement. Among some Gyp-

sies, for example, a homeland may concern a place that does not exist and, arguably, is not supposed to have existed, at least in any sedentary sense, because Gypsies were originally a nomadic, Caucasoid people who migrated from India and, throughout the centuries, settled for extended periods of time in Asia, Europe, and, more recently, also in the American continent. That at least some Gypsies look—but do not look back—for a homeland is confirmed by the fact that, in the late 1960s, Gypsy representatives approached the Argentine government asking that Argentina allow them to establish a Gypsy homeland in the largely empty Atlantic shores of Patagonia. Their homeland is supposed to be, if anywhere, in the future. I saw the news of this request announced in Buenos Aires newspapers around 1966.

7. I witnessed Whoopi Goldberg making these remarks on one of the television networks.

8. María A. Salgado, "Women Poets of the Cuban Diaspora: Exile and the Self," in Alegría and Ruffinelli, 232.

9. Salgado, in Alegría and Ruffinelli, 230.

10. Alegría and Ruffinelli, 9–10.

11. Silvio Torres-Saillant, ed., *Hispanic Immigrant Writers* (New York: Ollantay Press, 1989), 40, quoted in Teresa Justicia, "Exile as 'Permanent Pain,' Alfredo Villanueva Collado's 'En el Imperio de la Papa Frita,'" in Alegría and Ruffinelli, 183.

12. See, for example, Erving Goffman, *The Presentation of Self in Every Day Life* (Anchor, N.Y.: Doubleday: 1959), 251.

13. I have discussed various senses of the term 'philosophy' and how they relate to philosophy's aims, philosophers' motives, and philosophy's schools and traditions in my *Through Time and Culture: Introductory Readings in Philosophy* (Englewood Cliffs, N.J.: Prentice Hall, 1974), 452–61.

14. A. Pablo Iannone, "Dealing with Diversity: Cultural Fragmentation, Intercultural Conflicts, and Philosophy," essay presented at the Philosophy and Cultural Diversity Conference of the Society for Philosophy in the Contemporary World, Estes Park, Colorado, 15–21 August 1994. In this regard, the conception of philosophy as diplomacy, which I have characterized and substantially discussed in my *Philosophy as Diplomacy*, Essay 6: "Philosophy as Diplomacy," 70-84, should be of help. In a nutshell, philosophy as diplomacy addresses the policy and decision problems posed by issues

> in ways that are feasible, effective, and crucially sensitive both to the often unsettled and conflictive nature of the concerns that contribute to pose the problems and to the variety of open-ended social decision procedures that may help settle these concerns and deal with the problems through policies and decisions, and on the basis of reasons worked out in the process. (75–76)

Applications of this conception and discussions of how it contrasts with other philosophical approaches can be found throughout the book.

15. Arthur E. Murphy, "The Philosophic Mind and the Contemporary

World," *Reason and the Common Good* (Englewood Cliffs, N.J.: Prentice Hall, 1963), 368.

16. Iannone, *Philosophy as Diplomacy*, see note 14.

17. See Iannone, *Philosophy as Diplomacy*, 71–73.

18. See Iannone, *Philosophy as Diplomacy*, 73.

19. See Iannone, *Philosophy as Diplomacy*, 74.

20. Iannone, *Philosophy as Diplomacy*, 73–84.

21. Edith Cobb, *The Ecology of Imagination in Childhood* (New York: Columbia University Press, 1977).

22. Margaret Mead, "The Cross-Cultural Approach to the Study of Personality," in J. L. McCary, ed., *Psychology of Personality* (New York and London: Grove Press and Evergreen Books, 1959), 233. Mead had seen Cobb's unpublished manuscript for this book and cited it as such in her 1959 article.

23. Cobb, 211.

24. Anthropologists have expressed the concern that the multiculturalism issue should be addressed in an anthropologically informed manner. See, for example, Richard J. Perry, "Why Do Multiculturalists Ignore Anthropologists?" *The Chronicle of Higher Education* 4 March 1992: A52. For interdisciplinary discussions of culture, see Richard A. Shweder and Robert A. LeVine, *Culture Theory: Essays on Mind, Self, and Emotion* (Cambridge, England, and New York: Cambridge University Press, 1994).

25. This essay has greatly benefited from discussions with the participants at the Philosophy and Cultural Diversity Conference of the Society for Philosophy in the Contemporary World, Estes Park, Colorado, 15–21 August 1994. My thanks go to all of them. My very special thanks go also to Professor Nancy Snow for her detailed and very helpful comments on earlier drafts of this essay.

Selected
Bibliography

Allen, Jeffner. 1983. "Motherhood: The Annihilation of Women." In *Mothering*, ed. Joyce Trebilcot, 315–30. Totowa, N.J.: Rowman & Allanheld Publishers.

Anyanwu, K. C. 1987. "Cultural Philosophy as a Philosophy of Integration and Tolerance." *International Philosophical Quarterly* 25 (September): 271–87.

Baier, Annette C. 1994. *Moral Prejudices: Essays on Ethics*. Cambridge: Harvard University Press.

Benhabib, Seyla. 1986. *Critique, Norm and Utopia*. New York: Columbia University Press.

———. *Situating the Self*. 1992. New York: Routledge.

Buchanan, Allen. 1990. "Justice as Reciprocity vs. Subject-Centered Justice." *Philosophy and Public Affairs*, vol. 19, no. 3 (Summer): 227–52.

Card, Claudia. 1990. "Gender and Moral Luck." In *Identity, Character, and Morality: Essays in Moral Psychology*, ed. Owen Flanagan and Amelie Rorty, 199–218. Cambridge: MIT Press.

———, ed. 1991. *Feminist Ethics*. Lawrence, Kans.: University Press of Kansas, 1991.

Chodorow, Nancy. 1989. *Feminism and Psychoanalytic Theory*. New Haven, Conn.: Yale University Press.

Cobb, Edith. 1977. *The Ecology of Imagination in Childhood*. New York: Columbia University Press.

Coontz, Stephanie. 1992. *The Way We Never Were: American Families and the Nostalgia Trap*. New York: Basic Books.

Corea, Gena. 1985. *The Mother Machine*. New York: Harper & Row.

Davis, Angela Y. 1990. *Women, Culture, and Politics*. New York: Vintage.

De Bary, William. 1991. *The Trouble with Confucianism*. Cambridge: Harvard University Press.

de Lauretis, Teresa, ed. 1986. *Feminist Studies, Critical Studies*. Bloomington, Ind.: Indiana University Press.

Ehrenreich, Barbara. 1983. *The Hearts of Men: American Dreams and the Flight from Commitment*. New York: Doubleday.

Faludi, Susan. 1991. *Backlash: The Undeclared War against American Women*. New York: Crown.

Fingarette, Herbert. 1972. *Confucius—the Secular as Sacred*. New York: Harper & Row.

Friedman, Marilyn. 1987. "Beyond Caring: The De-Moralization of Gender." *Canadian Journal of Philosophy,* supplementary vol. 13: 87–110.

———. 1989. "Feminism and Modern Friendship: Dislocating the Community." *Ethics* 99: 275–90.

———. 1990. "Does Sommers Like Women?: More on Liberalism, Gender Hierarchy, and Scarlett O'Hara." *Journal of Social Philosophy*, vol. 21, nos. 2 and 3 (Fall/Winter): 75–90.

———. 1990. "'They Lived Happily Ever After': Sommers on Women and Marriage." *Journal of Social Philosophy*, vol. 21, nos. 2 and 3 (Fall/Winter): 57–65.

Frug, Mary Joe. 1991. *Postmodern Legal Feminism*. New York: Routledge.

Frye, Marilyn. 1983. *The Politics of Reality.* Trumansburg, N.Y.: The Crossing Press.

Geertz, Clifford. 1973. *The Interpretation of Cultures*. New York: Basic Books.

Gilligan, Carol. 1979. "Woman's Place in Man's Life Cycle." *Harvard Educational Review* 49: 431–46.

———. 1982. *In a Different Voice: Psychological Theory and Women's Development*. Cambridge: Harvard University Press.

———. 1987. "Moral Orientation and Moral Development." In *Women and Moral Theory*, ed. Eva Kittay and Diana Meyers. Totowa, N.J.: Rowman & Littlefield.

Gilligan, Carol, Janie Ward, and Jill Taylor, eds. 1988. *Mapping the Moral Domain: A Contribution of Women's Thinking to Psychological Theory and Education*. Cambridge: Center for the Study of Gender, Education, and Human Development, Harvard University Graduate School of Education, distributed by Harvard University Press.

Gilligan, Carol, Nona Lyons, and Trudy Hanmer, eds. 1990. *Making Connections: The Relational World of Adolescent Girls at Emma Willard School*. Cambridge: Harvard University Press.

Habermas, Jurgen. 1983. *The Theory of Communicative Competence*. Boston: Beacon Press.

Hall, David, and Roger Ames. 1987. *Thinking through Confucius*. Albany, N.Y.: State University of New York Press.

Harding, Sandra. 1986. *The Science Question in Feminism*. Ithaca: N.Y.: Cornell University Press.

———. 1991. *Whose Science? Whose Knowledge?* Ithaca, N.Y.: Cornell University Press.

Held, David. 1980. *Introduction to Critical Theory: Horkheimer to Habermas*. Berkeley: University of California Press.

Held, Virginia. 1983. "The Independence of Intellectuals." *The Journal of Philosophy* 80 (October): 572–82.

———. 1984. *Rights and Goods: Justifying Social Action*. New York: Free Press.

———. 1987. "Non-Contractual Society: A Feminist View." In *Science, Morality and Feminist Theory*, ed. Marsha Hanen and Kai Nielsen, 111–38. Calgary: University of Calgary Press.

————. 1988. "Access, Enablement, and the First Amendment." In *Philosophical Foundations of the Constitution*, ed. Diana T. Meyers and Kenneth Kipnis, 158–79. Boulder, Colo.: Westview Press.

————. 1988–89. "Culture or Commerce: On the Liberation of Expression." *Philosophic Exchange* 19 and 20: 73–87.

————. 1989. "Philosophy and the Media." *Journal of Social Philosophy* 20: 116–24.

————. 1993. *Feminist Morality: Transforming Culture, Society, and Politics*. Chicago: University of Chicago Press.

————, ed. 1995. *Justice and Care: Essential Readings in Feminist Ethics*. Boulder, Colo.: Westview Press.

Hirschmann, Nancy. 1992. *Rethinking Obligation*. Ithaca, N.Y.: Cornell University Press.

Hoagland, Sarah Lucia. 1989. *Lesbian Ethics*. Palo Alto, Calif.: Institute of Lesbian Studies.

Hull, Richard T., ed. 1990. *Ethical Issues in the New Reproductive Technologies*. Belmont, Calif.: Wadsworth.

Iannone, A. Pablo. 1974. *Through Time and Culture: Introductory Readings in Philosophy*. Englewood Cliffs, N.J.: Prentice Hall.

————. 1994. *Philosophy as Diplomacy: Essays in Ethics and Policy Making*. Atlantic Highlands, N.J.: Humanities Press.

Jaggar, Alison. 1983. *Feminist Politics and Human Nature*. Totowa, N.J.: Rowman and Allanheld.

————. 1994. "Prostitution." In *Living with Contradictions: Controversies in Feminist Social Ethics*, ed. Alison M. Jaggar. Boulder, Colo.: Westview Press.

Jones, Ann. 1994. *The Next Time, She'll Be Dead*. Boston: Beacon Press.

Kingston, Maxine Hong. 1976. *The Woman Warrior: Memoirs of a Girlhood among Ghosts*. New York: Alfred A. Knopf.

Klein, Dorie. 1982. "The Dark Side of Marriage: Battered Wives and the Domination of Women." In *Judge, Lawyer, Victim, Thief:*

Women, Gender Roles, and Criminal Justice, ed. Nicole Hahn Rafter and Elizabeth Anne Stanko, 83–107. Boston: Northeastern University Press.

Kohlberg, Lawrence. 1977. *The Psychology of Moral Development: The Nature and Validity of Moral Stages*. New York: Harper and Row.

———. 1981. *The Philosophy of Moral Development*. San Francisco: Harper and Row.

Kymlicka, Will. 1991. *Liberalism, Community, and Culture*. Oxford: Oxford University Press.

———. 1991. "Rethinking the Family." *Philosophy and Public Affairs* vol. 20, no. 1 (Winter): 77–97.

Larrabee, Mary Jeanne, ed. 1993. *An Ethic of Care*. New York: Routledge.

Lerner, Gerda. 1979. *The Majority Finds Its Past: Placing Women in History*. New York: Oxford University Press.

Lugones, Maria. 1987. "Playfulness, 'World' Travelling, and Loving Perception." *Hypatia*, vol. 2, no. 2 (Summer): 3–19.

MacIntyre, Alasdair. 1984. *After Virtue*. Notre Dame, Ind.: University of Notre Dame Press.

———. 1988. *Whose Justice? Which Rationality?*. Notre Dame, Ind.: University of Notre Dame Press.

Mason, Andrew. 1993. *Explaining Political Disagreement*. Cambridge: Cambridge University Press.

May, Larry, and Robert Strikwerda, eds., with Patrick D. Hopkins. 1992. *Rethinking Masculinity: Philosophical Explorations in Light of Feminism*. Lanham, Md.: Rowman & Littlefield.

Meyers, Diana T., Kenneth Kipnis, and Cornelius F. Murphy, Jr., eds. 1993. *Kindred Matters: Rethinking the Philosophy of the Family*. Ithaca, N.Y.: Cornell University Press.

Noddings, Nel. 1984. *Caring: A Feminine Approach to Ethics and Moral Education*. Berkeley: University of California Press.

————. 1990. *Women and Evil*. Berkeley: University of California Press.

Okin, Susan. 1989. *Justice, Gender, and the Family*. New York: Basic Books.

Parenti, Michael. 1978. *Power and the Powerless*. New York: St. Martin's Press.

Pateman, Carole. 1988. *The Sexual Contract*. Oxford: Polity Press.

Purdy, Laura. 1992. *In Their Best Interest? The Case against Children's Rights*. Ithaca, N.Y.: Cornell University Press.

Rawls, John. 1971. *A Theory of Justice*. Cambridge: Harvard University Press.

————. 1993. *Political Liberalism*. New York: Columbia University Press.

Rhode, Deborah. 1989. *Justice and Gender*. Cambridge: Harvard University Press.

Rorty, Amelie Oksenberg. 1988. *Mind in Action: Essays in the Philosophy of Mind*. Boston: Beacon Press.

Ruddick, Sara. 1989. *Maternal Thinking: Towards a Politics of Peace*. Boston: Beacon Press.

Shils, Edward. 1951. "The Study of the Primary Group." In *The Policy Sciences: Recent Developments in Scope and Method*, ed. Daniel Lerner and Harold D. Lasswell, 44–69. Stanford: Stanford University Press.

Sommers, Christina. 1990. "The Feminist Revelation." *Social Philosophy and Policy*, vol. 8, no. 1 (Autumn): 141–58.

————. 1991. "Argumentum Ad Feminam." *Journal of Social Philosophy*, vol. 22, no. 1 (Spring): 5–19.

Thorne, Barrie, with Marilyn Yalom, eds. 1982. *Rethinking the Family*. New York: Longman.

Warren, Karen J. 1987. "Feminism and Ecology: Making Connections." *Environmental Ethics* 9 (Spring): 3–20.

————. 1990. "The Power and the Promise of Ecological Feminism." *Environmental Ethics* 12 (Summer): 125–46.

————. 1993. "A Philosophical Perspective on Ecofeminist Spiritualities." In *Ecofeminism and the Sacred*, ed. Carol Adams, 119–32. New York: Continuum/Crossroads Books.

————. 1994. "Towards an Ecofeminist Peace Politics." In *Ecological Feminism*, ed. Karen J. Warren, 179–99. London: Routledge Press.

————. 1995. "Taking Empirical Data Seriously: An Ecofeminist Philosophical Perspective." In *Ecofeminism: Multidisciplinary Perspectives*, ed. Karen J. Warren. Bloomington, Ind.: Indiana University Press.

Wei-ming, Tu. 1979. *Humanity and Self-Cultivation: Essays in Confucian Thought*. Berkeley: Asian Humanities Press.

West, Robin C. 1988. "Jurisprudence and Gender." *The University of Chicago Law Review* vol. 55, no. 1 (Winter): 5–12.

Wong, David. 1988. "On Flourishing and Finding One's Identity in Community." *Midwest Studies in Philosophy* 13: 324–41.

————. 1989. "Universalism versus Love with Distinctions: An Ancient Debate Revived." *Journal of Chinese Philosophy* 16 (December): 252–72.

————. 1992. "Coping with Moral Conflict and Ambiguity," *Ethics* vol. 102, no. 4 (July): 763–84.

Young, Iris Marion. 1990. *Justice and the Politics of Difference*. Princeton, N.J.: Princeton University Press.

Index

abortion, 52–53, 57, 134, 162. *See also* gestational motherhood; pregnancy; procreation; procreative liberty; reproduction; reproductive rights; reproductive technologies

abuse, 69, 70, 77, 83, 86n14, 115, 141, 151n33, 166, 178. *See also* aggression; assault; assault, and domination; assault, as injustice

academic study of women. *See* women, academic study of

advertising, 113, 115–17, 146

agency. *See* moral agency

aggression, 66, 69, 77, 84, 143, 146, 152n40. *See also* abuse; assault; assault, and domination; assault, as injustice

alienation, 11, 155, 156, 197, 198

Allen, Jeffner, 169, 172n37

Analects, of Confucius, 19, 20, 23, 37n34

androgyny, 46, 51

arbitration, 32, 36n31

Aristotle, 42, 74, 201, 202

assault, xv, 51, 65, 68, 69, 74–83, 87n25, 87n29, 88n34, 178; and domination, xv, 68, 77, 79, 87n25; as injustice, 75–77. *See also* abuse; aggression

assimilationist ideal, xiv, 47, 49, 51. *See also* radical feminism

autokoenomy, xviii, 164, 165, 167. *See also* Hoagland, Sarah Lucia

autonomous self, 137, 155; as a biological male, 137. *See also* autonomy

autonomy, xii, xviii, 23, 43–45, 58, 66, 76, 134, 137, 138, 154, 164

Bartlett, Katherine T., 164, 172n26, 172n28

Benhabib, Seyla, 71, 84n2, 85n12, 86n19

bioregion, 176, 177, 180, 187, 189n7

Bloom, Allan, 86n16, 140, 141, 150n23

Blum, Lawrence, 51, 63n22, 85n12, 100n1

Blustein, Jeffrey, 60, 62n6

Bunch, Charlotte, 179, 185, 186, 189n6. *See also* four stage model of theory

capitalism, 12, 13, 110, 162

Card, Claudia, 85n3, 89n39, 93, 100n8

care, 9, 10, 44, 46, 50–53, 56, 59, 61, 65–69, 71, 74, 76–78; and ethics, 134, 135; and perspective, xv, 51, 67, 93, 94, 99, 100n1, 100n5. *See also* Gilligan, Carol; justice, and care

child rearing, 46, 51, 134, 136, 139

childbearing, 44, 45, 162

About the
Contributors

Marilyn Friedman teaches philosophy at Washington University in St. Louis. Her published articles fall in the areas of feminist theory, ethics, and social philosophy. In addition, she is the author of *What Are Friends For?: Feminist Perspectives on Personal Relationships and Moral Theory*; the co-author of *Political Correctness: For and Against*; and the coeditor of two anthologies: *Mind and Morals: Essays on Ethics and Cognitive Science* and *Feminism and Community*.

Virginia Held is a professor of philosophy and a professor of women's studies at Hunter College and the Graduate School of the City University of New York. Among her books are *Feminist Morality: Transforming Culture, Society, and Politics* (1993); *Rights and Goods: Justifying Social Action* (1984); and *The Public Interest and Individual Interests* (1970). She has been a fellow at the Center for Advanced Studies in the Behavioral Sciences, has had Fulbright and Rockefeller fellowships, and is on the editorial boards of five journals in the areas of philosophy and political theory.

A. Pablo Iannone is professor of philosophy at Central Connecticut State University. His philosophical publications include various articles and reviews, as well as four books: *Contemporary Moral Controversies in Technology* (Oxford, 1987); *Contemporary Controversies in Business* (Oxford, 1989); *Philosophy as Diplomacy* (Humanities, 1994); and *Through Time and Culture* (Prentice Hall, 1994). He has published a book of poetry in Spanish, *Asterida* (Gog y Magog, 1973); his story "South" has been included in *Paradise Lost or Gained? The Literature of Hispanic Exile* (Arte Publico, 1990);

and his poem "Second Awakening," has been included in *Songs in the Wind* and *The Sound of Poetry* (The National Library of Poetry, 1955).

Andrew Mason is a lecturer in philosophy at the University of Reading. He is the author of *Explaining Political Disagreement* (Cambridge University Press, 1993) and currently is working on a study of community and the different levels at which it might be realized.

Sara Ruddick teaches philosophy and women's studies at the New School for Social Research. She is the author of *Maternal Thinking: Toward a Politics of Peace* and is currently working on a book that is tentatively titled: *Ordinary Mother's Work: Moral Struggles in Bearing and Raising Children.* She is also the coeditor of two collections of women's reflections on their chosen work: *Working It Out: Twenty-three Women Writers, Artists, Scientists, and Scholars Talk about Their Lives and Work* and *Between Women: Biographers, Novelists, Critics, Teachers, and Artists Write about their Work on Women.* Her recent articles include "Procreative Choice for Adolescent Women," published in *The Politics of Pregnancy,* edited by Annette Lawson and Deborah Rhode, Yale University Press; "Notes toward a Feminist Politics of Peace" in *Gendering War Talk,* edited by Miriam Cooke and Angela Woolacott, Princeton University Press; "Thinking Mothers, Conceiving Birth" in *Representations of Motherhood,* edited by Donna Bassin, Margaret Honey, and Meryle Maher Kaplan, Yale University Press.

Christina Hoff Sommers is an associate professor of philosophy at Clark University and the author of *Who Stole Feminism? How Women Have Betrayed Women* (New York: Simon and Schuster, 1994). She has written extensively on the subject of feminism and American culture. Her articles include "Filial Morality," *The Journal of Philosophy* (1986); "Feminist Philosophy," *The Chronicle of Higher Education* (1989); "The Feminist Revelation," *Ethics, Politics, and Human Nature* (1990); "Do These Feminists Like Women?" and "Argumentum ad Feminam," *The Journal of Social Philosophy* (1991); "Sister Soldiers," *The New Republic* (1992); and "Camille Paglia's *Sex, Art, and American Culture,*" review for the *Times Lit-*

erary Supplement (1992). She is coeditor of *Vice and Virtue in Everyday Life: Introductory Readings in Ethics* (1984) and editor of *Right and Wrong: Basic Readings in Ethics* (1985).

Rosemarie Tong is Thatcher Professor in Medical Ethics and Philosophy at Davidson College. Her professional interests are focused on bioethics, clinical ethics, feminist philosophy, and the philosophy of law. Her major publications include *Women, Sex, and the Law* (Rowman and Allenheld, 1984); *Feminist Thought: A Comprehensive Introduction* (Westview Press, 1989); *Feminine and Feminist Ethics* (Wadsworth, 1993); and *Controlling Our Reproductive Destiny* (MIT Press, 1994). Currently, she is working on two books: *Feminist Bioethics* (Westview Press) and *Feminist Philosophy* (Prentice Hall).

Karen J. Warren, associate professor of philosophy and chair of the philosophy department at Macalester College, has published more than forty articles and edited two journals and five books in the areas of environmental ethics, ecofeminism, feminism, ethics, critical thinking, and philosophy for children. She also is co-author with Jim Cheney of the forthcoming book *Ecological Feminism* (Westview Press). She has taught courses and conducted workshops in these scholarly areas in kindergarten through twelfth grades, adult education, business, a prison, colleges, and universities. The video "Thinking Out Loud," in which she teaches critical thinking about raptors to first and fourth graders, won the First Place Gold Hugo Award in 1994 at the Chicago International Film and Video Competition, and during the Spring, 1995, she was the Ecofeminist-Scholar-in-Residence at Murdoch University in Perth, Western Australia.

David B. Wong is Harry Austryn Wolfson Professor of Philosopohy at Brandeis University. His published work includes *Moral Relativity* (University of California Press, 1984); "Coping with Moral Conflict and Ambiguity" (*Ethics*, 1992); "Universalism versus Love with Distinctions: An Ancient Debate Revived" (*Journal of Chinese Philosophy*, 1989); and other articles in ethical theory, comparative ethics, Chinese philosophy, and continental rationalism.